T0301607

Monetary Policy Challenges in Latin America

NEW DIRECTIONS IN POST-KEYNESIAN ECONOMICS

Series Editors: Louis-Philippe Rochon, Laurentian University, Sudbury, Canada and Sergio Rossi, University of Fribourg, Switzerland

Post-Keynesian economics is a school of thought inspired by the work of John Maynard Keynes, but also by Michal Kalecki, Joan Robinson, Nicholas Kaldor and other Cambridge economists, for whom money and effective demand are essential to explain economic activity. The aim of this series is to present original research work (single or co-authored volumes as well as edited books) that advances Post-Keynesian economics at both theoretical and policy-oriented levels.

Areas of research include, but are not limited to, monetary and financial economics, macro and microeconomics, international economics, development economics, economic policy, political economy, analyses of income distribution and financial crises, and the history of economic thought.

For a full list of Edward Elgar published titles, including the titles in this series, visit our website at www.e-elgar.com.

Monetary Policy Challenges in Latin America

Edited by

Fernando Toledo

Professor of International Monetary Economics, Faculty of Economic Sciences, University of La Plata, Argentina

Louis-Philippe Rochon

Full Professor, Laurentian University, Canada, Editor-in-Chief, Review of Political Economy, *and Founding Editor Emeritus,* Review of Keynesian Economics

NEW DIRECTIONS IN POST-KEYNESIAN ECONOMICS

Edward Elgar
PUBLISHING

Cheltenham, UK • Northampton, MA, USA

Cover image: "Blue Ice" by Jacques Pilon. jacquespilon.ca; painting is from the personal collection of Louis-Philippe Rochon.

Published by
Edward Elgar Publishing Limited
The Lypiatts
15 Lansdown Road
Cheltenham
Glos GL50 2JA
UK

Edward Elgar Publishing, Inc.
William Pratt House
9 Dewey Court
Northampton
Massachusetts 01060
USA

A catalogue record for this book
is available from the British Library

Library of Congress Control Number: 2023943166

This book is available electronically in the **Elgar**online
Economics subject collection
http://dx.doi.org/10.4337/9781802200706

ISBN 978 1 80220 069 0 (cased)
ISBN 978 1 80220 070 6 (eBook)

Printed and bound in Great Britain by
TJ Books Limited, Padstow, Cornwall

Contents

Figures

Tables

About the editors

Louis-Philippe Rochon is Full Professor of Economics at Laurentian University, Canada, where he has been teaching since 2004. Before that, he taught at Kalamazoo College in Michigan, USA. He obtained his doctorate from the New School for Social Research in 1998 where he earned the Frieda Wunderlich Award for Outstanding Dissertation for his dissertation on endogenous money and post-Keynesian economics.

In January 2019, he became co-Editor of the *Review of Political Economy*, and its Editor-in-Chief in 2021. Before that, he created the *Review of Keynesian Economics*, was its editor from 2012 to 2018, and is now Founding Editor Emeritus. He has been Guest Editor for the *Journal of Post Keynesian Economics*, the *International Journal of Pluralism and Economics Education*, the *European Journal of Economic and Social Systems*, the *International Journal of Political Economy*, and the *Journal of Banking Finance and Sustainable Development*. He has published on monetary theory and policy, post-Keynesian economics, and fiscal policy.

He is on the editorial board of *Ola Financiera*, the *International Journal of Political Economy*, the *European Journal of Economics and Economic Policies: Intervention*, *Problemas del Desarrollo*, *Cuestiones Económicas* (Central Bank of Ecuador), *Bank & Credit* (Central Bank of Poland), *Bulletin of Political Economy*, *Advances in Economics Education*, *Il Pensiero Economico Moderno*, the *Journal of Banking, Finance and Sustainable Development*, and *Research Papers in Economics and Finance*.

Rochon is also Editor of the following series: *Elgar Series of Central Banking and Monetary Policy*, *New Directions in Post-Keynesian Economics*. He has been a Visiting Professor or Visiting Scholar in Australia, Brazil, France, Italy, Mexico, Poland, South Africa, and the United States, and has further lectured in China, Colombia, Ecuador, Italy, Japan, Kyrgyzstan, and Peru. He is the author of some 150 articles in peer-reviewed journals and books, and has written or edited close to 35 books. Rochon has received grants from the Social Sciences and Humanities Research Council in Canada, the Ford Foundation, and the Mott Foundation, among other places.

Fernando Toledo is Professor of International Monetary Economics at the Faculty of Economic Sciences at the University of La Plata, Argentina. He is currently Associate Researcher in the International Monetary Project, led by Louis-Philippe Rochon (https://lprochon2003.wixsite.com/rochon/the-monetary-policy-project). He obtained his MA in Economics at the Universidad Nacional de La Plata, Argentina. His research fields include international macroeconomics, monetary economics, economic development, and Latin American economic thought.

Toledo is a reviewer for the *Journal of Applied Economics*, *Structural Change and Economic Dynamics*, and *Bulletin of Economic Research*. He has received grants from the Central Bank of the Argentine Republic and Red de Diálogo Regional sobre Sociedad de la Información. He has published in the *Review of Political Economy*, the *International Journal of Political Economy*, the *Journal of Post Keynesian Economics*, the *Journal of Globalization and Development*, *El Trimestre Económico*, and *Económica*.

Contributors

Nelson H. Barbosa-Filho holds a PhD in economics from the New School for Social Research and is currently Professor at Fundação Getulio Vargas and the University of Brasilia, Brazil. Barbosa Filho has also worked as an economic analyst at the Brazilian Central Bank and, from 2006 through 2013, he was part of the senior economic staff at the Brazilian Ministry of Finance, first as Secretary of Economic Monitoring (2007–08), and later as Secretary of Economic Policy (2009–10) and Deputy Finance Minister (2011–13). Barbosa Filho's main fields of research are economic growth, income distribution, and applied macroeconomic models.

Nicolás Bertholet is Assistant Professor of Macroeconomics at the University of Buenos Aires, Argentina, and Doctoral Fellow at IIEP (UBA-CONICET). He is a PhD candidate in economics and holds a master's degree in economics from the University of Buenos Aires. His topics of research are international macroeconomics and time series and panel data.

Pablo G. Bortz is co-director of the MA in Development Economics at the National University of San Martín, Professor at the National University of the West, and Tenured Researcher at the National Council of Sciences and Technology, all in Argentina. He previously worked at the United Nations Conference on Trade and Development, and in the Ministry of Finance, the Ministry of Foreign Affairs, and the Central Bank in Argentina. He obtained his PhD at the Delft University of Technology. He has published in journals such as *Development and Change, Review of Keynesian Economics, International Journal of Economic Policies, European Journal of Economics,* and *Economic Policies.* He is the author of *Inequality, Growth and "Hot Money"* (2016, Edward Elgar Publishing).

Esteban Pérez Caldentey is currently Coordinator of the Financing for Development Unit within the Economic Development Division at the Comisión Económica para América Latina y el Caribe (Santiago, Chile). He holds a PhD in economics from the New School for Social Research and does research in development economics, macroeconomics and monetary economics, and history of economic thought. He has published extensively on finance and macroeconomics on Latin American Issues. He is Co-editor of the *Review of*

Keynesian Economics and Co-editor of the *Palgrave Dictionary of Economics*. He is a member of IDEAS Development Associates.

Jorge Carrera holds degrees in economics and in accounting from Universidad Nacional de La Plata, Argentina, and a PhD in economics awarded by the Italian Republic in 1994 (Università di Pavia). He is Full Professor of International Finance at Universidad Nacional de La Plata, and Full Professor of International Monetary Economics at Universidad de Buenos Aires, Argentina. Carrera has written more than 50 papers, eight chapters, and three books. He was Editor of Ensayos Económicos (*Economic Essays*) and of the series titled Estudios del BCRA (BCRA Research, 2006–16), and is part of the editorial committee of national and international journals. His recent research focuses on the theoretical and empirical implications of international financial integration for emerging economies. He has also focused on the relationships among inequality, financial deregulation, and macroeconomic dynamics.

Alfredo Schclarek Curutchet is Associate Researcher at the National Scientific and Technical Research Council (CONICET), Argentina, and Associate Professor at the National University of Córdoba, Argentina, where he teaches macroeconomics for undergraduate and PhD students. He has published in, among others, the *Journal of Banking and Finance*, *Journal of International Financial Markets, Institutions & Money*, *World Development*, and the *Journal of Financial Stability*. Since 2018, he has been a Ford Foundation Visiting Research Fellow at the Institute of New Structural Economics at Peking University, China. Alfredo holds a PhD, MA, and BA in economics from Lund University, Sweden. He worked at the European Central Bank, Germany; the United Nations, Denmark; and the National Agency for Investment Development, Argentina. He has won several awards, including the prize "Ten Outstanding Young Persons of the Year 2007" and the Córdoba Stock Exchange and Economic Research Annual Award 2007, Category: Young Professionals, Central Bank of Argentina.

Simone Deos is Professor of Economics in the Department of Economics, University of Campinas, Brazil. She is also a researcher at the Center for the Study of International Economic Relations (CERI) and at the China Brazil Study Group at the same university, and she is Senior Researcher at the Brazilian Center of International Relations (CEBRI). Deos serves as Chairman of the Board of the Institute of Functional Finance for Development (IFFD), and is Associate Editor of the *Review of Political Economy*. Her research focuses on macroeconomics, monetary and financial economics, and political economy, and she works specifically on the topics of modern monetary theory, critiques of neoliberalism, financial fragility and instability (crises), the regulation of banking systems, and development finance.

Gary Dymski is Professor of Applied Economics at the Leeds University Business School, UK. His research focuses on discrimination and redlining in credit markets, financial exclusion, regional and national economic development, financial instability and financial crisis, banking and financial regulation, and the problems of hegemony and power in global finance. He holds a PhD in economics from the University of Massachusetts–Amherst, USA.

Enzo Gerioni has a PhD in economics from the University of Campinas, Brazil. He has been a researcher at the Centro de Estudo de Relações Econômicas Internacionais (CERI), and co-authored the book *Teoria Monetária Moderna: a chave para uma economia a serviço das pessoas* (2020, Nova Civilização). His main areas of interest are Modern Money Theory (MMT), the theory of the monetary circuit, endogenous money, and economic growth.

Annina Kaltenbrunner is Professor of Global Economics at Leeds University Business School, UK. Her research focuses on financial processes and relations in emerging capitalist economies. She holds a PhD from the School of Oriental and African Studies, University of London.

Sylvio Antonio Kappes is Assistant Professor of Economics at the Federal University of Ceará, Brazil, and Visiting Professor of the Graduate Program in Economics at the Federal University of Rio Grande do Sul, Brazil. His main areas of research are central banking, monetary policy, income distribution, and stock-flow consistent models. His work has been published in a number of peer-reviewed journals, such as the *Review of Political Economy*, the *Journal of Post Keynesian Economics*, and the *Brazilian Keynesian Review*. He is co-Editor of the Elgar Series on Central Banking and Monetary Policy, together with Louis-Philippe Rochon and Guillaume Vallet. He is the Book Review Editor of the *Review of Political Economy*, and sits on the editorial boards of the *Review of Political Economy* and the *Bulletin of Political Economy*. Keppes is also a co-coordinator of the Keynesian Economics Working Group of the Young Scholars Initiative (YSI) of the Institute for New Economic Thinking (INET).

William N. Kring, PhD, is the Executive Director of the Boston University Global Development Policy Center, USA. His research and teaching interests focus on international political economy, global economic governance, international financial institutions (IFIs), and Southern-led financial institutions. He actively conducts policy-oriented research on global economic governance and works regularly with government officials and staff officials of various IFIs, particularly regional financial arrangements. He has been awarded grants by the Rockefeller Brothers Fund, the Japan Foundation Center for

Global Partnership, the Academy of Korean Studies, and the United Nations Conference on Trade and Development. His work has appeared in *World Development, Development and Change, Global Policy, Global Governance,* and *International Relations of the Asia-Pacific.*

Noemi Levy-Orlik has a BA in social sciences (economics), and her master's degree and PhD in economics (National Autonomous University of Mexico, UNAM), for which she received the Antonio Casso Medal (best economics dissertation). In 2014, she was awarded the Premio Universidad Nacional 2014 in the field of economics and administration; this is the highest recognition given to UNAM academic personnel. Levy-Orlik is a Member (numeral 77) of the Mexican Academy of Political Economy (2015), and was presented with the Recognition Sor Juan Ines de la Cruz (2019) for women professors. She is a full-time professor in the Economics Faculty, UNAM, and has attained the highest qualification for her academic performance (PRIDE, level "D"). She is a member of the Mexican National Research System (SNI, level III–highest level). Her area of academic interest focuses on monetary finance and economic development, with emphasis on heterodox economics. Levy-Orlik has written three books (one co-authored) and edited more than 16 books (including with Edward Elgar and Routledge), and she has written more than 40 book chapters and around 30 journal articles.

Gabriel Michelena is Professor of Macro-Modelling at the University of San Martín, Argentina. He is currently finishing his PhD studies at the University of Buenos Aires, and working as an advisor for the Central Bank of Argentina and as an independent consultant in economic-modeling-related issues. His work focuses on stock-flow and input–output modeling, especially the application of international economics, climate change, and gender inequality, with the goal of producing evidence for public policy decisions.

Gabriel Montes-Rojas is Professor of Econometrics at Universidad de Buenos Aires and Senior Researcher at the National Scientific and Technical Research Council (CONICET), both in Argentina. He holds a PhD in economics and an MSc in statistics from the University of Illinois at Urbana-Champaign, USA, and a BA in economics from Universidad de Buenos Aires. His topics of research are panel data, quantile regression, and network models.

Daniel Pérez-Ruiz holds a PhD in Economics from Leeds University Business School, UK. His research focuses on exchange rates and structural change in emerging and frontier markets.

Damián Pierri is a macroeconomist interested in economic theory, numerical methods, and stochastic processes. He is also an economic and financial consultant. He teaches macroeconomics at the graduate and undergraduate levels, both in Argentina and Spain. He is Visiting Assistant Professor at Universidad Carlos III, Madrid, Spain, and a research affiliate at IIEP-BAIRES. In his research, Pierri combines general equilibrium theory with the literature on stochastic processes to derive computable structures for infinite horizon non-optimal economies with representative and heterogeneous agents. He tries to extend general equilibrium theory beyond existing results to be able to characterize, numerically and empirically, macroeconomic models.

Nicole Toftum graduated in political economy from the National University of General Sarmiento (UNGS). She is finishing her MA in economic development and studying for a PhD in political economy, both at the National University of San Martín, Argentina, with a doctoral scholarship provided by the National Council for Scientific and Technological Research (CONICET). She has served as coordinator of the Financial Stability Working Group at the Young Scholars Initiative (YSI-INET) and is a member of the steering committee of the sustainable macroeconomic initiative. She teaches Advanced Macroeconomics to undergraduate students at the National University of Moreno and UNGS in Argentina.

Sebastián Valdecantos has a PhD in economics from Sorbonne Paris Nord University. He currently serves as Assistant Professor of Macroeconomics at Aalborg University (Denmark). After completing his PhD, he worked for five years at the United Nations Economic Commission for Latin America and the Caribbean. He also taught courses on macroeconomics at the National Universities of San Martín and Mar del Plata (both in Argentina). In 2020 he served as National Director of Cooperative and Mutual Development at the Ministry of Productive Development of Argentina. His research interests focus on the macroeconomic vulnerabilities of developing economies. Most of his work is undertaken through the stock-flow consistent approach.

Pablo de la Vega holds a degree in Economics and a Master's degree in Economics from the Universidad Nacional de La Plata (UNLP). He is pursuing a PhD in Economics at the same university. He is currently a researcher at the Foundation for Argentinean Development and teaches International Finance at UNLP. He has worked as a consultant at the Inter-American Development Bank. He has published scientific articles and presented papers at conferences and seminars, both nationally and internationally. His areas of interest include diverse topics such as macroeconomics, economic development, the future of work, inequality, and climate change.

Matiás Vernengo teaches at Bucknell University, USA. He was formerly Senior Research Manager at the Central Bank of Argentina (BCRA), and taught at the University of Utah and Kalamazoo College in the USA, and at the Federal University of Rio de Janeiro, Brazil. He has been an external consultant to several United Nations organizations. He has seven edited books, two authored books, and more than 120 publications in peer-reviewed journals or book chapters. He specializes in macroeconomic issues, particularly for developing countries in Latin America; international political economy; and the history of economic ideas. He is also the Emeritus Founding co-Editor of the *Review of Keynesian Economics* (ROKE), and the current book review editor and co-Editor-In-Chief of the *New Palgrave Dictionary of Economics*.

Acknowledgments

We would like to thank all the contributors to this book for their collaboration in preparing this volume to enhance the understanding of monetary policy challenges in Latin America.

We also wish to express gratitude to Edward Elgar Publishing for their enthusiastic and professional support during the development of the book.

Introduction to *Monetary Policy Challenges in Latin America*

Fernando Toledo and Louis-Philippe Rochon

Latin American countries (LACs) are facing a number of severe monetary policy challenges in the aftermath of the Global Financial Crisis and Great Recession, the post-pandemic scenario, and the war in Ukraine. Indeed, following these various crises, regional central banks must tackle an international situation characterized by inflationary pressures, output contraction, external vulnerabilities, tightness in advanced central banks' monetary policies, nominal dollar appreciation, and falling commodity prices (Bank for International Settlements [BIS], 2022; World Economic Outlook, 2022). They also face several risks and, as such, should care about the climate of uncertainty of this unusual "shock-after-shock" global context. The monetary policy challenges faced by central banks in LACs are intrinsically interrelated with the following ten stylized facts that have become even more important nowadays, given the unprecedented circumstances:

1. *LACs' central banks, international currency hierarchy, and reduced monetary policy space*

In contrast to developed countries, LACs' central banks have less monetary policy space to confront the complexity of this juncture. The subordination of regional and local currencies in the international currency hierarchy (ICH) contributes to explaining this fact (Kaltenbrunner, 2022; Bibow, 2021; Toporowski, 2021). LACs' currencies are not accepted at the global level, and in some of these economies, they are not even used in full for domestic purposes (Levy Orlik et al., 2021). As a negative consequence of ICH, LACs usually borrow from abroad in foreign currency, which not only generates currency mismatches on balance sheets (Tobal, 2014), but also lessens the monetary policy space of LACs' central banks for attending to their policy objectives.

2. *The exchange rate is a key transmission mechanism of monetary policy in Latin America*

The transmission channels of monetary policy are different in comparing advanced economies and LACs. The role of an exchange rate channel instead of the credit channel is of paramount importance in Latin America for understanding how monetary policy works in practice (Agénor and Pereira da Silva, 2019). The nominal exchange rate affects inflation and the output gap in two important ways (Agénor and Montiel, 2015). First, there exists a direct one-way relationship between the prices of imported final goods on domestic consumer prices (the pass-through effect), and second, an indirect link between aggregate demand and aggregate supply. Through its impact on the real exchange rate, the nominal exchange rate modifies relative prices and influences aggregate demand, output, and inflation. The supply side of nominal exchange rate variations is reflected in the cost of imported intermediate inputs and in the consequent adjustment of nominal wages to movements in consumer prices. LACs' central banks should be cautious of these exchange rate changes under inflation-targeting regimes because they spread the effects of variations in policy interest rates and domestic or foreign shocks to regional countries.

3.   LACs' central banks, inflation targeting, "fear of floating," and financial instability

The use of inflation targeting as a monetary policy framework is also one feature that deserves attention among some economies of the region, particularly due to its intrinsic instability related to the adoption of a floating exchange rate regime and the "fear of floating" that regional policy makers usually display. Since several LACs' central banks have taken political actions to intervene in their foreign exchange markets, they show concern about the excessive nominal exchange rate volatility, a phenomenon known as the "fear of floating" (Calvo and Reinhart, 2002). Some regional monetary authorities have also shown some "fear of appreciation," particularly when they must face a completely deregulated financial account and high nominal interest rates that attract capital inflows. High volatility of the nominal exchange rate could be detrimental in dollarized inflation-targeting LACs because greater fluctuations of this variable usually impinge on banking and financial instability.

4.   LACs' central banks, exchange rate targeting, and the risk of inflationary pressures

Some LACs' central banks use a de facto exchange rate policy that focuses on international competitiveness, economic growth, and employment generation as their main objectives. Real exchange rate targeting, or preserving a stable and competitive real exchange rate, proves to be convenient for promoting economic growth through the expansion of modern tradable sectors (Frenkel and Rapetti, 2015). The managed floating strategy (targeting the real exchange rates) also affects resource allocation, particularly if they show stability during a long last period (Frenkel and Taylor, 2006). A competitive and stable real exchange rate could boost aggregate demand and employment and promotes economic development. However, regional monetary authorities should not only consider that sustaining a competitive and stable exchange rate should be a desirable goal. They also must pay attention to its potential inflationary consequences, particularly related to higher cost-push pressures and conflicting claims outcomes (Taylor and Barbosa Filho, 2021). Bastian and Setterfield (2020) present a post-Keynesian-Structuralist (PK-S) theoretical model in a structural form that identifies how conflicting claims give place to either an equilibrium regime with a low inflation rate or a disequilibrium regime with a high and increasing inflation rate. In a similar vein, Abeles and Panigo (2015) propose a theoretical PK-S model that focuses on cost-push factors (i.e., the international commodities market). The formal contribution of this model is identifying the political and institutional factors, such as particular structural characteristics that explain the different speed and magnitude of the pass-through from the international prices of exported commodities to inflation rates in the case of small open developing economies, such as the LACs.

5. *LACs' central banks and international reserve accumulation*

International reserve accumulation as a buffer stock that reduces vulnerability to external shocks should be a more widespread practice adopted by several LACs' monetary policy makers, such as the Latin American Reserve Fund proposal (Corbo et al., 2019; Titelman et al., 2014). The configuration of the international financial system in the case of LACs has been characterized by a greater tendency toward managed floating, higher monetary policy independence, and segmented financial integration to international capital markets. The accumulation of international reserves seems to be of paramount importance given this context, and particularly in providing LACs' central banks with greater monetary policy autonomy in decision-making. The role of international reserves as buffer stock and self-insurance against the volatility of capital flows has been recognized by several scholars (Aizenman and Riera-Crichton, 2014; Eichengreen, 2006). In contrast to the experience of some Asian economies (particularly China), the main challenge for LACs' central banks is to adopt monetary policies that improve the accumulation of international reserves at a faster pace.

6. *LACs' central banks' vulnerability to global liquidity shocks, and the transmission of the Global Financial Cycle*

The higher vulnerability to the different phases of the Global Financial Cycle (GFCy) and the global liquidity changes are two topics that have increased the attention of LACs' central banks during the last few years. Monetary policy shocks in the financial centers are one of the main determinants of GFCy (Miranda-Agrippino and Rey, 2021; Jordà et al., 2018). The monetary policy international spillovers from financial centers to Emerging Markets and Developing Economies (EMDEs; including LACs) are transmitted through different channels, such as the commercial and financial ones. A fall in US monetary policy interest rates stimulates a greater appetite for risk among global investors, who decide to reallocate their financial funds mostly to developing economies. Thus, lower policy interest rates in the US trigger nominal appreciation in small open economies driven by portfolio flows and cross-border lending (Bonizzi and Kaltenbrunner, 2021; Yilmaz and Godin, 2020). These external funds are reverted when the Federal Reserve announces an increase in its nominal interest rate policy. In such a case, we observe increases in global risk aversion that stimulate flight-to-quality behavior and higher exchange rate market pressure in LACs, even though these economies show solid macroeconomic fundamentals (Kohler, 2021; Botta, 2021).

7. *LACs' central banks, capital controls, and macro-prudential regulations*

The need to apply capital controls and macro-prudential measures that increase financial stability has also been of greater concern in LACs' central banks' policy agendas, particularly after the Global Financial Crisis of 2007–08 (Bastourre and Zeolla, 2018). Since the 1990s, there has been a rapid transformation in international finance that has brought financial globalization to unprecedented levels. LACs have not escaped this general trend. These processes, far from generating the benefits predicted by theory, led early to debt, currency, and financial crises. After the international economic crisis of 2008–2009, both the practices toward the liberalization of the financial account and the conventional theory on the subject tended to be revised (Pasricha and Nier, 2022). Driven by the experience of developing countries, a reassessment of capital flow management measures arose in which Latin America actively participated (Grabel, 2016). However, despite some re-regulations, the degree of capital and financial account management in LACs is currently below that of other comparable emerging economies. So, this is one other important monetary policy challenge that LACs' central banks face.

8. *LACs' central banks and the need for coordination of monetary and fiscal policies in high-inflation economies*

The historical record of high inflation and the lack of coordination of monetary and fiscal policies have been of paramount importance, particularly in Argentina (Heymann, 2015). This economy is nowadays reporting a change of regime from chronic to high inflation. The control of nominal variables has become a serious problem for policy makers. Inflation expectations are de-anchored, and monetary and fiscal policies face serious difficulties coordinating them in a virtuous way. Disorder in relative prices expresses some of the hurdles faced by monetary authorities, which must confront several limitations in terms of the degree of maneuver of their policy instruments to stabilize the economy. One of the main monetary policy challenges that Argentina faces is thinking about the design and implementation of a stabilization program that improves the credibility of policy announcements and minimizes the sacrifice output ratio (Calvo and Végh, 1999). The coordination between fiscal and monetary policies seems to be of critical importance to accomplish this goal.

9. LACs' central banks, external debt, and greater financial vulnerabilities

LACs' central banks should also care about the composition of total debt, public and private, especially to avoid currency mismatches and the resulting negative social implications linked to greater exchange rate market pressures (Goldberg and Krogstrup, 2018). The distinction between external and domestic debt is of vital importance, particularly for LACs. External debt generally implies greater challenges for monetary policy makers. They do not only take care of the generation of fiscal surplus to accomplish their obligations. They also need to guarantee continuous access to foreign currency (Moreno-Brid, 2003). Excessive external debt profiles usually correlate with currency crises and lower growth paths. They also relate to currency mismatch issues and greater financial vulnerabilities. So, the main monetary policy challenge that LACs' central banks realize here is to regulate and monitor external debt indicators at macro and micro dimensions, while also promoting the financial depth of local currency bonds.

10. LACs' central banks, climate change, and the green finance agenda

Climate change, sustainable growth, and green finance have been other key topics of LACs' monetary policy makers' agendas (CAF, 2022). Climate change and the conservation of natural capital are the main environmental challenges facing society. Latin America is a continent that emits in proportion to its economic activity and its population. Funding for activities that catalyze transformation in LACs is critical to achieving both its climate goals and other development goals. Climate change and the policies to combat it will affect the financial system through its physical impacts and through the changes inherent to the transition itself. Understanding how banks are adapting to this new environment is critical to fostering a dynamic transition in a stable environment. The Network of Central Banks and Supervisors for the greening of the financial system has developed a set of models that make it possible to establish different scenarios of the relationship between the economy and climate change with a special focus on financial risks (Economic Commission for Latin America and the Caribbean [CEPAL], 2022).

THE STRUCTURE OF THE BOOK

This book includes contributions that analyze the main monetary policy challenges in LACs. The chapters show the paramount importance of identifying some of the topics that deserve attention by central banks in the region in a synergic way. The goal of the compiled material is not only to list the problems but also to invite policy makers to reflect on the numerous ways in which monetary policy and related issues could be thought of.

Part I of the book is titled "Alternative Views about Central Banks and Monetary Policy in LACs" and comprises two chapters. In Chapter 1, Sebastián Valdecantos assesses the prescriptions of the Integrated Monetary Policy Framework (IPF) of the International Monetary Fund using an empirical stock-flow consistent model for Argentina, a country that for the last ten years has been suffering a balance of payments crisis. One possible representation of the IPF is designed and counterfactually tested for the years 2016 and 2017, when Argentina was indeed a net recipient of foreign financial flows. The goal is to examine whether this suggested policy mix would have generated more sustainable dynamics than observed ones, ending in a currency crisis in 2018. This author makes some reflections on which lessons about the IPF can be generalized to other small open economies and which results should be understood as specific to the Argentinian context. In Chapter 2, Simone Deos and Enzo Gerioni suggest that the ICH literature can be inconsistent with the endogenous money approach when related to basic elements, such as the nature of money, its distinguishing characteristics, and consequently monetary and mainly fiscal policies—the last of which is almost completely neglected in the ICH literature. Going further, and focusing on the Brazilian economy, they observe that both monetary and fiscal policies are autonomously set by governments that issue their own sovereign currency, despite different degrees of freedom and sovereignty related to conditions that are specific to each economy.

Part II of the book, "Monetary Policy Transmission Channels in LACs," includes three chapters. In Chapter 3, Esteban Pérez Caldentey and Matías Vernengo argue that the adoption of inflation targeting was a result of a policy shift that began with the Washington Consensus, and that materialized sequentially in increased financial openness and greater exchange rate flexibility. These authors sustain that, in the case of an open economy, the use of inflation targeting leads to incoherent and contradictory results that severely question its alleged superiority over other monetary policy frameworks. Finally, they posit the need for comprehensive regulatory frameworks to deal with the complex dynamics and transmission mechanisms that characterize economies that have a high degree of financial openness, such as those of Latin America. In Chapter 4, Noemi Levy Orlik revises the discussion of the views of monetary policy dominant during the 21st century, looking at how developed and developing economies were affected, specifically in Mexico. Also, she analyzes the alternative views that have been strengthened considering the COVID-19 crisis. Levy Orlik suggests that central banks will continue to determine an objective rate of interest, used as a policy instrument, guided by different goals. Considering the 2008 Global Financial Crisis and the COVID-19 crisis, short- and long-term liquidity requirements need to be considered by the central bank reaction function, which means that the central bank ought to recognize the need to stabilize the yield curve. To pursue this objective, the monetary and fiscal authorities need to resume coordination around economic growth objectives and financial stability. In Chapter 5, Gabriel Michelena and Fernando Toledo analyze the bust GFCy transmission to EMDEs through a Neo-Kaleckian model of growth, inflation, income distribution, and external debt. These authors calibrate and simulate the model to evaluate the effects of this phase of GFCy spread on income distribution, capacity utilization, and real exchange rates. They propose several monetary policy rules to examine how financial centers' monetary spillovers could be mitigated during the bust GFCy stage. These scholars find that external financial shocks conducted by GFCy to EMDEs could be magnified or dampened out, depending on the kind of monetary policy rules followed by EMDEs' central banks.

Part III of the book is titled "Monetary Policies and Exchange Rates in LACs" and includes three chapters. In Chapter 6, Annina Kaltenbrunner, Gary Dymski, and Daniel Pérez-Ruiz discuss whether exchange rates should be managed by laying the foundations for defining what they term the "Policy Target Exchange Rate." These authors support their discussion with experience from Latin America since exchange rates in this region are among the most important policy variables and the idea of exchange rate targeting has been widely discussed. Their aim is to build the groundwork for a post-Keynesian theoretical approach to the challenges of exchange rate management. In Chapter 7, Nelson H. Barbosa-Filho shows how some sensible economic assumptions create two nonlinearities in the economy through a simple formal model, one between the real exchange rate and growth and the other between the real exchange rate and inflation, which then makes an exogenous inflation target set boundaries to the real exchange rate and economic growth itself. In Chapter 8, Gabriel Montes-Rojas and Nicolás Bertholet present empirical evidence on the short- and medium-run contractionary effects of exchange rate shocks and currency devaluations for bi-monetary (i.e., highly dollarized) countries. These scholars estimate a vector autoregression model with quantile heterogeneity for Argentina during the period January 2004–December 2018, with four macroeconomic variables (exchange rate variations, inflation, economic activity, and nominal wage growth). The empirical results show a 30 percent price pass-through effect and a bimodal effect on output, with both positive and negative effects. Wages adjust less than prices, with the consequent effect that real wages have a negative elasticity of 0.23 with respect to exchange rate shocks. Further analysis of the multivariate responses shows that the negative effect on output is associated with a decline in real wages: a 1 percent fall in real wages after a currency devaluation produces a 2.3 percent decline in output.

Part IV of the book, "Monetary Policies, International Reserves, and Sustainable Finance in LACs," contains two chapters. In Chapter 9, William N. Kring highlights the unique and important role that the Latin American Reserve Fund (FLAR) plays in advising member countries on macroeconomic stability efforts and in responding to balance of payments and liquidity challenges. This author remarks how adaptability is one of the FLAR's keys to success over its history and demonstrates how members broadened FLAR's scope and bolstered the mechanism's lending capacity to US$6.8 billion in response to the COVID-19 crisis. The chapter concludes with a brief discussion of how further efforts toward regional integration and the expansion of existing efforts, such as FLAR, could help to further foster financial stability in the region. In Chapter 10, Pablo G. Bortz and Nicole Toftum review the alternatives available to Emerging Market Economies (EMEs) to finance the investment required to mitigate and adapt to climate change. Since the requirements dwarf the financial capabilities of the public sector in EMEs, these scholars explore possible funding channels, focusing on international financial markets. They identify potential obstacles to a smooth and sustainable finance provision, including the influence of the GFCy on credit supply, risks related to currency mismatch and creditworthiness assessment, and mispricing of risks. The review also identifies the challenges to the exporting profile and, therefore, the sustainability of the balance of payments of EMEs. Finally, they provide some reflections on the limits of domestic private capital markets to bridge the "environmental financial gap" and call for the deeper involvement of specialized and official financial institutions.

Part V of the book is titled "Monetary Policies, Central Banks, Income Inequality, and Fiscal Policies in LACs" and encompasses four chapters. In Chapter 11, Jorge Carrera, Pablo de la Vega, and Fernando Toledo assess the fiscal policy responses of EMDEs' governments to unexpected shocks that increase income inequality. These scholars focus on the relationship between income inequality and public expenditure, progressive taxation, and public debt. They aim particularly at the strategic use of public debt to finance greater public expenditure targeted to lessen the negative effects of hikes in income inequality. To this end, these authors estimate dynamic panel models for 49 EMDEs with annual data for the 1990–2015 period. They find that the marginal effect of inequality on the public debt is increasing in the share of the executive term completed, and it becomes statistically significant after completing 85 percent of the corresponding term. This finding is robust to different empirical specifications and is more pronounced in LACs and in economies with higher external liabilities. In Chapter 12, Damián Pierri studies the connection between monetary policy and capital markets in Argentina since 2019. After the sudden stop observed in 2018, there were several fundamental changes in the design of economic policy, especially following the 2019 national election, which implied a turnover in the ruling party. These changes have major implications for the relative behavior of Argentina with respect to other middle-income countries. Having a clear diagnosis is essential to anticipate the future macroeconomic outlook of the country, considering especially the limitations to restoring macroeconomic stability implied by COVID-19. In Chapter 13, Sylvio Antonio Kappes analyzes the four most important items in the Brazilian Central Bank balance sheet: on the asset side, the international reserves and the treasury bills; and on the liabilities side, the repurchase agreements and the treasury account. This author observes that these four items evolved due to the same policy decisions and institutional features. Their evolution began with the decision to accumulate international reserves. A second decision, regarding the sterilization of the liquidity created by this first incident, explains the increase in both repos and treasury bills. Finally, the legal framework connects the first decision to the increase in the treasury account. In Chapter 14, Alfredo Schclarek Curutchet empirically explores the relationship between external debt and growth for 20 Latin American and Caribbean countries. Using a dynamic system generalized method of moments panel estimator, he finds that higher (lower) total external debt levels are associated with lower (higher) growth rates, and that this negative relationship is driven by the incidence of public external debt levels, and not by private external debt levels. This scholar does not find evidence of non-linear effects for these relationships.

REFERENCES

Abeles, M., and Panigo, D. (2015). "Dealing with Cost-Push Inflation in Latin America: Multi-Causality in a Context of Increased Openness and Commodity Price Volatility", *Review of Keynesian Economics* 3(4): 517–35.

Agénor, P.R., and Montiel, P. (2015). *Development Macroeconomics*. Princeton University Press.

Agénor, P.R., and Pereira da Silva, L.A. (2019). *Integrated Inflation Targeting. Another Perspective from the Developing World*. Bank for International Settlements.

Aizenman, J., and Riera-Crichton, D. (2014). "Liquidity and Foreign Asset Management Challenges for Latin American Countries", *NBER Working Paper* 20646.

Bank for International Settlements (BIS). (2022, June). *Annual Economic Report*. BIS.

Bastian, E., and Setterfield, M. (2020). "Nominal Exchange Rate Shocks and Inflation in an Open Economy: Towards a Structuralist Inflation Targeting Agenda", *Cambridge Journal of Economics* 44(6): 1271–99.

Bastourre, D., and Zeolla, N. (2018). "Regulación de la cuenta capital en un mundo financieramente complejo: evolución reciente y perspectivas en América Latina", *Serie Estudios y Perspectivas* No. 52, CEPAL.

Bibow, J. (2021). "Evolving International Monetary and Financial Architecture and the Development Challenge. A Liquidity Preference Theoretical Perspective", in Bonizzi, B., Kaltenbrunner, A., and Ramos, R. (eds): *Emerging Economies and the Global Financial System Post-Keynesian Analysis*, 101–15, Routledge.

Bonizzi, B., and Kaltenbrunner, A. (2021). "A Minskyan Framework for the Analysis of Financial Flows to Emerging Economies", in Bonizzi, B., Kaltenbrunner, A., and Ramos, R. (eds): *Emerging Economies and the Global Financial System Post-Keynesian Analysis*, 43–55, Routledge.

Botta, A. (2021). "Financial Liberalization, Exchange Rate Dynamics and the Financial Dutch Disease in Developing and Emerging Economies", in Bonizzi, B., Kaltenbrunner, A., and Ramos, R. (eds): *Emerging Economies and the Global Financial System Post-Keynesian Analysis*, 181–96, Routledge.

CAF (2022, December). *Energía, agua y salud para un mejor ambiente.* Banco de Desarrollo de América Latina.

Calvo, G.A., and Reinhart, C.M. (2002). "Fear of Floating", *Quarterly Journal of Economics* 117(2): 379–408.

Calvo, G., and Végh, C. (1999). "Inflation Stabilization and BoP Crises in Developing Countries", in Taylor, J., and Woodford, M. (eds): *Handbook of Macroeconomics*, Vol. 1, Part C, 1531–1614. Elsevier.

Corbo, V., de la Torre, A., García, E., Guidotti, P., Langoni, C., Levy-Yeyati, E., Ortiz, G., Perry, G., Rojas-Suárez, L., and Velasco, A. (2019). *Hacia un FLAR de alcance regional.* Informe del grupo de trabajo sobre estabilidad financiera regional. http://flar.com/wp-content/uploads/2019/05/Hacia-un-FLAR-de-alcance-regional_0-1.pdf

Economic Commission for Latin America and the Caribbean (CEPAL) (2022, November 10). *Evento COP27: Acción climática - Una visión desde la Banca Central, multilateral y comercial.*

Eichengreen, B. (2006). "Insurance Underwriter or Financial Development Fund: What Role for Reserve Pooling in Latin America?", *NBER Working Paper* 12451.

Frenkel, R., and Rapetti, M. (2015). "The Real Exchange Rate as a Target of Macroeconomic Policy", in Calcagno, A., Dullien, S., and Priewe, J. (eds): *Development Strategies: Country Studies and International Comparisons*, 81–92, UNCTAD.

Frenkel, R., and Taylor, L. (2006). "Real Exchange Rate, Monetary Policy and Employment", *DESA Working Paper* No 19.

Goldberg, L., and Krogstrup, S. (2018). "International Capital Flow Pressures", *Working Paper* 2018/030, International Monetary Fund.

Grabel, I. (2016). "Capital Controls in a Time of Crisis", *Working Paper Series* No 146, PERI/UMASS.

Heymann, D. (2015). "Inflation in Argentina. An Eventful Experience". Banking History. http://bankinghistory.org/wp-content/uploads/Heymann.pdf

Jordà, O., Schularick, M., Taylor, A., and Ward, F. (2018). "Global Financial Cycles and Risk Premiums", *Federal Reserve Bank of San Francisco Working Paper* 2018-05.

Kaltenbrunner, A. (2022). "International Monetary and Financial Hierarchies: Macroeconomic Implications for Emerging Market Economies", *Ensayos Económicos* No. 79. Banco Central de la República Argentina.

Kohler, K. (2021). "Post Keynesian and Structuralist Approaches to Boom–Bust Cycles in Emerging Economies", in Bonizzi, B., Kaltenbrunner, A., and Ramos, R. (eds): *Emerging Economies and the Global Financial System Post-Keynesian Analysis*, 56–69, Routledge.

Levy Orlik, N., Bustamante, J., and Rochon, L.-P. (2021). *Capital Movements and Corporate Dominance in Latin America. Reduced Growth and Increased Instability*. Edward Elgar Publishing.

Miranda-Agrippino, S., and Rey, H. (2021). "The Global Financial Cycle", *Centre for Economic Policy Research* DP16580.

Moreno-Brid, J.C. (2003). "Capital Flows, Interest Payments and the Balance-of-Payments Constrained Growth Model: A Theoretical and Empirical Analysis", *Metroeconomica* 54(2–3): 346–65.

Pasricha, G., and Nier, E. (2022). "Review of the Institutional View on the Liberalization and Management of Capital Flows — Background Note on Capital Flows and Capital Flow Management Measures — Benefits and Costs", *IMF Policy Paper* 2022/009, International Monetary Fund.

Taylor, L., and Barbosa Filho, N. (2021). "Inflation? It's Import Prices and the Labor Share!", *Institute for New Economic Thinking Working Paper Series* No. 145.

Titelman, D., Vera, C., Cavallo, P., and Pérez Caldentey, E. (2014). "Un fondo de reservas regional para América Latina", *Revista de la CEPAL* No. 112, CEPAL.

Tobal, M. (2014). "Prudential Regulation, Currency Mismatches and Exchange Rate Regimes in Latin America and the Caribbean", *CEMLA Research Papers* 17.

Toporowski, J. (2021). "The Transmission Mechanism of Financial Crisis to Developing Countries: Why the 'Global Financial Crisis' Wasn't Global", in Levy Orlik, N., Bustamante, J., and Rochon, L.-P. (eds): *Capital Movements and Corporate Dominance in Latin America. Reduced Growth and Increased Instability*, 24–37. Edward Elgar Publishing.

World Economic Outlook (2022). *Countering the Cost-of-Living Crisis*. International Monetary Fund.

Yilmaz, S.-D., and Godin, A. (2020). "Modelling Small Open Developing Economies in a Financialized World: A Stock-Flow Consistent Prototype Growth Model", *Working Paper* 5eb7e0e8-560f-4ce6-91a5-5, Agence Française de Développement.

PART I

Alternative views about central banks and
monetary policy in LACs

1. Assessing the new "integrated policy framework": a counterfactual analysis of the case of Argentina

Sebastián Valdecantos

INTRODUCTION

After decades of advocating for the adoption of flexible exchange rate regimes, in the last ten years, the International Monetary Fund (IMF) seems to have taken a more permissive stance toward developing countries' central banks adopting foreign exchange interventions and capital flows management as tools to mitigate the effects of volatile cross-border financial flows on their domestic economies (IMF, 2018, 2022). More recently, IMF staff members have developed a new "integrated policy framework" built upon a New Keynesian model that seems to support this broader open-mindedness regarding policymaking in developing countries (Basu et al., 2020). Specifically, it is claimed that small open economies can achieve macroeconomic stability and economic growth through a combination of an inflation-targeting monetary policy, interventions in the foreign exchange market, some restrictions on capital inflows, and the use of the macroprudential policy.

This chapter assesses the prescriptions of this policy framework using an empirical stock-flow consistent model for Argentina, a country that for the last ten years has been suffering a balance of payments crisis. One possible representation of the integrated policy framework proposed by Basu et al. (2020) is designed and counterfactually tested for the years 2016 and 2017, when Argentina was indeed a net recipient of foreign financial flows. The goal is to examine whether this suggested policy mix would have generated more sustainable dynamics than observed ones, ending in a currency crisis in 2018. Based on the experiment results, we offer some reflections on which lessons about the integrated policy framework can be generalized to other small open economies and which results should be understood as specific to the Argentinean context.

THE CONTEXT

In December 2015, a new government with a center-right orientation took office. The previous two periods (from 2007 to 2015) were characterized by a heterodox administration of the macroeconomy, alongside an inward-oriented government that implemented distributive policies to boost private domestic consumption. The key pillars of the policy mix were: i) keeping the nominal exchange rate stable; (ii) keeping interest rates low to accommodate an expansionary fiscal policy; (iii) not taking external debt to prevent foreign meddling with domestic policy issues; and (iv) preventing the leak of domestic savings resulting from the low return of domestic financial assets (due to the negative real interest rates) through capital controls on outflows.

When the new government took office in December 2015 it immediately launched a massive liberalization package (the first element being the foreign exchange market) that resulted in a very fast increase in foreign indebtedness. Foreign investors were willing to purchase the bonds of a country that not only exhibited very low levels of indebtedness but was now managed by a market-friendly government. Simultaneously, a massive increase in the private sector's acquisition of foreign assets occurred, as it could now channel its savings into foreign exchange-denominated assets with practically no restrictions. To attract foreign financial capital and to undermine the leak of foreign exchange, the Central Bank increased the issuance of short-term bills paying high interest rates. However, in 2018 global financial markets stopped lending to Argentina, as they interpreted that its growth model was not sustainable. Consequently, the Central Bank started to sell part of its foreign reserves stock, which was insufficient to prevent two devaluations in a matter of months. A major collapse could only be prevented by appealing to the IMF, giving Argentina the largest bailout in its history (US$57 billion). In a little more than a year, however, the IMF also convinced itself of the unsustainability of Argentina's trajectory and decided not to disburse the last installment of the standby agreement. Devoid of any form of financing, suffering a continuous leak of foreign exchange, and with almost no more Central Bank firepower, the coalition in power lost the 2019 elections, leaving gross domestic product (GDP) 2.5 percentage points below the level inherited in 2015 and having almost doubled the rate of inflation.

The failure of the macroeconomic program implemented by the center-right coalition raises the question of whether it could have been possible to implement a mainstream policy mix with more successful results than the ones observed. The integrated policy framework is an interesting starting point for an initial exploration of this question, as it takes a more moderate stance,

mainly concerning the administration of the financial account, compared to the fully fledged liberal approach followed by the government.

THE "INTEGRATED POLICY FRAMEWORK"

The prototype model developed by Basu et al. (2020) is motivated by the recognition that the Mundell–Fleming approach fails to describe some of the main features of emerging and developing economies. It consists of a small open economy with three sectors (the tradable differentiated goods sector, the commodity sector, and the non-tradable housing sector) with sticky prices and a flexible (albeit not fully) exchange rate. Commodity prices are exogenous, and the country is exposed to stochastic shocks on them. There is also a financial sector that borrows from the rest of the world to provide credit in domestic currency to the private non-financial sector. The authors also claim that the search for "optimal policies" in emerging and developing economies must account for a series of externalities that might render economic policy inefficient. These externalities are the following:[1]

- Keynesian aggregate demand externality: by this externality, the authors refer to the fact that households do not fully internalize the effects of the consumption decisions on aggregate demand, the reason being the price stickiness.
- Pecuniary aggregate demand externality: the economy's exposure to currency mismatches is affected by the private sector's not internalizing the effects of its individual actions on aggregate demand, the exchange rate, and the tightness of the external borrowing constraint *ex post*.
- Financial terms of trade externality: the external premium that the economy pays to borrow from abroad is affected by the individual borrowing decisions of the private sector, which do not internalize the impact of their behavior on the aggregate risk premium.

The model considers four key policy tools: monetary policy, capital controls, foreign exchange interventions, and macroprudential policy. Monetary policy is conducted by the setting of the (short-term) interest rate. It affects the economy through the behavior of the private sector when making consumption, production, and borrowing decisions. The effect that interest rates have on the exchange rate monetary policy can also influence net exports. Capital controls are modeled as taxes on inflows that discourage overborrowing (the authors claim that modeling capital controls as quantity restrictions on inflows or outflows would have similar effects; see Basu et al., 2020, 8, fn. 2). Foreign exchange rate interventions are used in a context of an adverse shock to the foreign appetite for domestic currency debt to reduce the need to increase the interest rate, therefore enhancing monetary autonomy. Macroprudential policy is designed as taxes on domestic banks' lending to the private sector and is similar in spirit to capital controls, as they are intended to curb overborrowing.

The model is defined in a New Keynesian framework, implying that agents' behavior is modeled following constrained intertemporal optimization problems. Households maximize a linear welfare function that depends positively on consumption and negatively on labor subject to a budget constraint that incorporates many of the key relevant variables for an emerging and developing economy (such as the exchange rate and international prices) as well as the policy tools of the "social planner" (such as tax rates and the interest rate). The tradable sector firms are assumed to operate in imperfectly competitive markets with sticky prices, which level results from the profit maximization problem. Banks are assumed to lend to households based on the funding obtained from the rest of the world. The amount of the loans granted to the private sector also results from a profit maximization problem, which is subject to the financing obtained from the rest of the world. The "social planner" then sets the policy instruments in such a way that the overall utility function is maximized given the constraints and the externalities with which the economy is faced.

THE MODEL

To examine the performance of a policy combination along the lines of the integrated policy framework described in Basu et al. (2020), the structure of an empirical stock-flow consistent model for Argentina estimated for the period 2004Q1–2021Q4 is used. The model's technical details can be found in Valdecantos (2022). Figure 1.1 describes the main elements of the model and the transmission channels that drive the model's dynamics. Being a post-Keynesian demand-led model, it is convenient to describe the main transmission mechanisms at play through the components of aggregate demand. Real GDP (y) is determined by consumption (c), investment (inv), public consumption (g), exports (x), and imports (m). The variables inside the boxes are exogenous, meaning that they can be affected by policy decisions, structural or institutional changes, or events originating in the rest of the world. The variables that appear without a box are endogenously determined by the combination of other model variables. The arrows in the diagram denote causation, and the sign attached to each arrow indicates the sign of the causal effect (for instance, investment has a positive effect on GDP).

The primary source of consumption is disposable income (yd), which is in turn determined by wages (w), and taxes (T^H). Although it is not shown in the figure for simplicity, disposable income is divided into a lower and an upper class to account for the possibility of different propensities to save. A wealth effect is also considered, incorporating net wealth (nw) as an additional

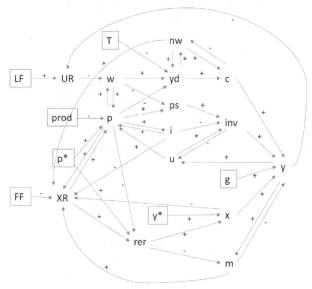

Source: Author's elaboration.

Figure 1.1   *Structure of the model*

component. While taxes are an exogenous government policy tool, financial wealth and wages are endogenous processes determined within the model. Wages depend on the rate of unemployment (*UR*) and prices (*p*), which are endogenous. Unemployment, in turn, is determined by the labor force (*LF*) and the level of activity (*y*). Prices are affected by international prices (*p**), the nominal exchange rate (*XR*), the interest rate (*i*), and unit labor costs, which are given by the ratio of wages to productivity (*prod*). A positive relationship between output and prices is included to incorporate the New Keynesian imprint of Basu et al.'s (2020) framework. This is done through the rate of capacity utilization (*u*).

The investment equation takes a Neo-Kaleckian structure, implying that the main drivers of capital accumulation are the profit share (*ps*) and capacity utilization (*u*). The profit share is endogenously determined by the combination of wages and prices, which are given by all the above factors. This implies that, in turn, shocks to the determinants of wages and prices also have implications on income distribution. The rate of capacity utilization depends on the level of activity (*y*) and investment (*inv*). The interest rate is also included in the investment equation to allow monetary policy to be transmitted to economic activity (along the lines of the dynamic IS curve characteristic of the New Keynesian approach). Following the spirit of the Taylor rule, the interest rate is assumed to be a function of inflation and the output gap.

Regarding the external sector, international trade flows are modeled following the standard approach, where exports are defined as a function of the level of activity of the rest of the world (y^*) and the real exchange rate (rer), and imports as a function of the domestic level of activity and the real exchange rate as well. The real exchange rate, in turn, is an endogenous variable given by the nominal exchange rate (XR) and both domestic and foreign prices. The nominal exchange rate is, in turn, determined by a variety of factors that make up the excess demand for foreign exchange, such as international trade flows, the flows of foreign financing (FF), and the private sector's demand for foreign assets, which is a function of net wealth (nw), the domestic interest rate, and inflation.

Before specifying how the integrated policy framework provisions are fitted into the model, it is worth making two clarifications regarding Figure 1.1. First, the stock-flow consistent nature of the model implies that, because of these transactions, the private sector, the government, and the rest of the world register a financial balance (net lending). While sectors running surpluses accumulate financial assets, sectors running deficits either reduce their holdings of financial assets or increase their liabilities. The holding of these assets and liabilities bears interest payments that, in turn, affect sectors' income in the subsequent periods. For simplicity, these stock-flow interactions are not included in Figure 1.1, but it is important to keep in mind that the accounting structure of the model always ensures the fulfillment of budget constraints. Second, from Figure 1.1 there is a variety of feedback effects that can render the parameters of the behavioral equations (e.g., consumption, investment, wages, prices, exports, imports, etc.) biased due to simultaneity. To prevent this problem, lags of the endogenous variables are included instead of contemporaneous relationships whenever needed.

OPERATIONALIZING THE INTEGRATED POLICY FRAMEWORK: AN INITIAL EXPLORATION

As mentioned above, the integrated policy framework consists of four main policy instruments: monetary policy, capital controls, interventions in the foreign exchange market, and macroprudential policy. To make the structure of the model as consistent as possible with the New Keynesian nature of the framework under consideration, we define a pseudo-Phillips curve where price changes are a function of the output gap, GAP (defined as the deviation of capacity utilization from its trend level), lagged inflation (a proxy of inflation expectations), and a series of variables related to cost-push factors, such as the nominal exchange rate (XR), energy prices (p^E), and international prices (p^*).

It is worth mentioning that the interest rate was also found to be significant, with a positive effect on prices (most likely reflecting the fact that the interest rate is a cost in the production process), which can undermine the capacity of contractionary monetary policy to rein in inflation. In contrast, the output gap was not found to be as statistically significant as the cost-push factors, and the size of its effect on prices is small in comparison. Since there is evidence of cointegration between prices and their determinants, an error correction term is also included:

$$\Delta ln(p_t) = 0.50 \; \Delta ln(p_{t-1}) + 0.07 \; \Delta GAP_{t-1} + 0.20 \; \Delta ln(XR_t)$$
$$+0.14 \Delta ln(p_t^*) + 0.03 \Delta ln(p_t^E) + 0.09 \; \Delta ln(i_t) - 0.87 \; EC_{t-1}$$

As inflation is defined as the percentage change of prices ($\pi = \Delta ln(p_t)$), $\bar{\pi}$ the inflation target, a standard interest rate rule can be written as follows, where θ represents the degree of monetary policy smoothing, $\bar{r}$ is the "natural" real interest rate, and μ^G and μ^π reflect the Central Bank's aversion to output and inflation deviations from their optimal levels. The interest rate role is calibrated with the following values: $\theta = 0.5$, $\bar{r} = 0.02$, $\bar{\pi} = 20$, $\mu^G = 0.5$, and $\mu^\pi = 0.5$:

$$i_t = \theta i_{t-1} + \left(1 - \theta\right)\left[\bar{r} + \pi_t + \mu^G \; GAP_t + \mu^\pi(\pi_t - \bar{\pi})\right]$$

Figure 1.1 depicts the transmission channels of the interest rate to aggregate demand and, in turn, to prices. First, increases in the interest rate negatively affect investment, thereby inducing a negative output gap that (slightly) eases the pressure on inflation. A similar effect could have been included in the consumption equation, but the interest rate was found to be insignificant. Therefore, that transmission channel was removed from the model. Second, increases in the interest rate induce appreciations of the nominal exchange rate through the (fall of the) domestic demand for foreign assets and the (increase in the) flows of foreign financing. Despite not being as strong as the income effect, exchange rate appreciation has an impact on international trade flows and, in turn, on aggregate demand.

The second policy tool of the integrated policy framework is the capital controls on cross-border financial inflows. These controls could be modeled in a wide variety of ways, ranging from market-based (e.g., taxes) to non-market-based mechanisms (e.g., quantitative restrictions), and following diverse criteria to define the threshold above which capital inflows become risky or undesirable. We arbitrarily define the approach to modeling capital controls, leaving a more complete analysis for future research. Hence, we establish a rule whereby financial flows, which take the form of public external debt (ED^G), are allowed to enter the country to the extent they finance the current account deficit ($-CA$). However, as Basu et al. (2020) explain, it is possible that in moments of financial stress, either in the domestic economy or in global markets, international investors are not willing to finance the budget deficit. We assume that these events are exogenous and denote them by $z = 1$. In such a scenario we follow Basu et al. (2020) and assume that the Central Bank intervenes to avoid the need to increase the interest rate, thereby maintaining (in theory) the monetary autonomy of the country. Thus, capital controls and foreign exchange market interventions are modeled jointly as follows:

$$\Delta ED_t^G = \begin{cases} -CA_t & z = 0 \\ 0 & z = 1 \end{cases}$$

$$-\Delta FA_t^{CB} = \begin{cases} 0 & z = 0 \\ -CA_t & z = 1 \end{cases}$$

Since the model does not explicitly reflect the banking sector (encompassed in the private sector), macroprudential policy is left out of the analysis. Basu et al. (2020) claim that macroprudential policy plays a similar role to capital controls, so we consider this omission not severe enough and carry on with the experiment. Not being part of the key policies of the "integrated framework," we keep fiscal policy unchanged with respect to the baseline scenario, which consists of the macroeconomic program implemented by the government in power in the period 2016–19.

Before presenting the results of the experiment, it is worth keeping in mind that, while the integrated policy framework was developed within a New Keynesian theoretical system representing an abstract economy, the exercise presented in this chapter is based on an empirical stock-flow consistent model estimated for a specific country with its own structural and institutional features. Although the behavioral equations were estimated by prioritizing statistical accuracy and precision, the starting point when defining their functional form has a strong post-Keynesian flavor, as seen from the description in Figure 1.1. The New Keynesian elements incorporated into the model are the ones described in this section.

ASSESSING THE INTEGRATED POLICY FRAMEWORK

Now we are prepared to examine the integrated policy framework performance along the lines defined in this chapter. The experiment is applied to the period 2016–19 to compare it with the failed market-friendly approach implemented by the administration of the center-right government in power, whose main features and results were explained in the introduction to this chapter. To counterfactually assess the performance of the proposed policy approach, two guiding questions are worth asking. First, would the integrated policy framework as defined here, and under the same circumstances that the economy faced, have delivered better results in terms of economic activity and inflation and macro-financial stability? Specifically, are there any signs suggesting that the 2018 crisis would have been avoided under the proposed policy combination? Second, if there are elements to answer the first question affirmatively, can the integrated policy framework be considered an "optimal" policy mix, or are there any clear signs of weaknesses indicating that other alternatives would potentially leave the economy better off?

Figures 1.2 and 1.3 show the trajectories of some of the key main variables of the economy. At first glance, compared to the actual evolution of the economy, the integrated policy framework as designed in this chapter produces:

• A higher interest rate, which helps to reduce inflation, not so much through the aggregate demand channel but through lower demand for foreign assets, which in turn eases the pressure on the exchange rate;
• As a result of the latter, more stable exchange rate dynamics, avoiding the strong devaluations of the second half of 2018 and 2019;
• Lower inflation, albeit not as stable as an inflation-targeting regime would aim at;
• A slightly higher level of activity toward the end of the simulation brought about by the lower inflation, which produces a higher purchasing power for the private sector. In line with the higher activity, the unemployment rate is slightly lower;
• Lower cross-border financial flows—both inflows increasing external indebtedness and outflows taking the form of acquisition of foreign assets by the domestic private sector; and
• A higher current account deficit, explained by the increased imports that result from the higher activity.

The model shows that the higher policy interest rate observed during the second half of 2016 and the beginning of 2017 results from the strict pursuits of an inflation-targeting regime. The Central Bank then decides to cut interest rates after a few periods of monetary tightening. Toward the middle of 2017, however, the interest rate rule dictates the Central Bank to set the policy rate at a level that is very close to the one observed, the reason being the success at bringing inflation down. Given the relatively low sensitivity of aggregate demand components to changes in the interest rate, it is the higher nominal exchange rate stability that allows the monetary authority to tame inflation and, therefore, reduce the monetary tightening. Note that by the middle of

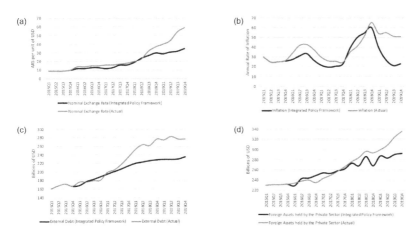

Figure 1.2   Performance of the "integrated policy framework," part 1

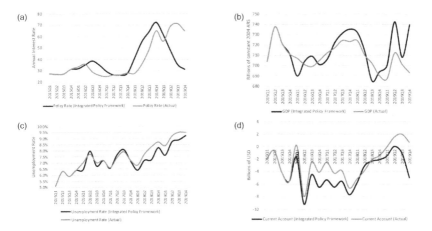

Figure 1.3   Performance of the "integrated policy framework," part 2

2017, both scenarios exhibit the same policy rate, but in the case of the integrated policy framework, inflation is 5 percentage points lower. In this sense, it could be argued that this policy approach provides superior results to the path that was taken.

The dynamics of inflation until the end of 2017 seem to be mainly driven by cost-push factors and, specifically, nominal exchange rate variations (other supply-side factors like the price of utilities also play a central role, but they are identical in both scenarios and, thus, do not explain the differences between them). The importance of the exchange rate in explaining price dynamics has already been pointed out by many scholars at the theoretical level (Díaz-Alejandro, 1963; Krugman and Taylor, 1978; Vernengo, 2005; Vera, 2014) and empirically in the case of Argentina (Zack et al., 2018; Montes-Rojas and Toledo, 2021). In our simulation of the integrated policy framework, it is observed that, until the end of 2017, external indebtedness is lower than in the baseline (actual) scenario due to the rule establishing that the country takes no more debt than what is needed to finance the current account deficit. This reduces the depreciation pressures on the exchange rate. Simultaneously, the acquisition of foreign assets by the private sector starts out higher (implying an upward pressure on the exchange rate) and ends lower (implying lower depreciation pressures).

But there is still one more element that plays out and determines that the nominal exchange rate is more appreciated and contributes to the disinflation. Recall that one of the provisions of the integrated policy framework is that foreign exchange reserves were constant unless there was a low foreign appetite for domestic financial assets. This implies that the stock of foreign reserves is constant across the sample (since we are not assuming a scenario where the country is faced with an external financing constraint) compared to the actual situation where the Central Bank acquired a massive number of reserves in line with the higher external indebtedness. A lower acquisition of foreign reserves by the Central Bank implies a higher supply of foreign exchange, which, in a flexible exchange rate closure, leads to a more appreciated exchange rate.

The more appreciated nominal exchange rate leads also to a more appreciated real exchange rate (despite the lower inflation rate), which tends to boost imports. The latter are also stimulated by the income effect derived from the higher level of activity induced by the lower inflation rate. Consequently, the current account balance worsens to reach a deficit equal to 6 percent of GDP, putting into question the sustainability of the integrated policy framework as designed in this chapter.

At the beginning of 2018, the economy is disrupted by a surge in inflation. In this case, the depreciation of the exchange rate is not the cause but the consequence of the jump in the inflation rate. Toward the end of 2017, real GDP is as high as in 2015. Since in the integrated policy framework there is an interest rate rule establishing that, to cool down the economy, the Central Bank must increase the policy rate, in 2018Q1 an increase from 27 percent to 40 percent is made (while in the actual scenario it was kept at 27 percent). As discussed above, this has inflationary consequences since the interest rate is a production cost that, together with other supply-side factors, determines the price level. Hence, instead of preventing the rise in inflation, the Central Bank ends up producing it. Higher inflation increases the demand for foreign assets, thereby inducing an exchange rate depreciation. The combination of these factors leads the economy to the short (though deep) recession observed in the drop in real GDP. It is worth mentioning that this "crisis" is not to be compared to the one that actually occurred in 2018Q2; while the latter was a crisis produced by over-indebtedness combined with the full liberalization of the financial account, the former is endogenously triggered by the structure of the reaction function of the Central Bank (which could be defined and calibrated in a different manner and which can eventually be chosen not to be followed if it is evident that its strict pursuit will trigger a crisis).

After the economy falls into recession, the Central Bank eases its monetary stance, which, for the reasons explained before, also helps reduce the inflation rate. From the middle of 2018 to the end of the simulation, the private sector's demand for foreign assets exhibits more stable dynamics. External indebtedness is also steadily growing, in line with the current account deficit, which, as in the actual scenario, is reduced mainly due to the increase in exports driven by the exogenously higher agricultural exports (compared to the low level registered in 2018 because of the severe drought that affected the country). In the absence of new monetary policy shocks, such as the one that took place in 2018Q1, the nominal exchange rate depreciates at an average rate of 5 percent quarterly, in line with the quarterly rate of inflation. Toward the end of the sample, the economy has a higher level of activity, a lower rate of unemployment, and a higher current account deficit, again putting into question the sustainability of the policy combination. Still, the avoidance of the currency crises of 2018 and 2019 and the consequent significantly lower rate of inflation makes the integrated policy framework a superior alternative to the one used by the government of that time.

CONCLUSIONS

After decades of advocating for full financial account liberalization, the IMF seems to have nuanced its view on the issue and now appears comfortable with some degree of regulation of cross-border capital flows. The "new integrated policy framework" developed by IMF staff members explicitly incorporates capital controls alongside other policies in what they consider an optimal policy mix in that it solves some of the externalities that characterize policymaking in emerging and developing economies. As their proposal is an abstract contribution, the goal of this chapter was to operationalize the proposed framework in the context of a specific country (Argentina) in a period characterized by a financial account surplus (2016–17). The exercise was appealing because the policy program deployed ended up in a severe crisis, which gives us the possibility of counterfactually testing the hypothetical performance of the integrated policy framework.

The simulations made through an empirical stock-flow consistent model suggest that a macroeconomic program along the lines of the integrated policy framework would have outperformed the policy mix pursued by the government, mainly due to the more stable exchange rate dynamics that the lower external indebtedness brings about (with the consequent lower capital flight in a context of financial stress), the most important achievement being the prevention of the 2018 and 2019 currency crises. As a result, inflation dynamics are also lower, thereby inducing a higher level of activity through higher real incomes in the private sector. Conducting monetary policy through an interest rate rule does not necessarily contribute to taming inflation, as the effect ends up being ambiguous (a higher interest rate weakly reduces inflation, generating a negative output gap through the drop in investment, but it also fuels inflation through higher financing costs for firms). Finally, instead of focusing on "optimality" (from the perspective of minimizing the effect of externalities), we highlight that, under the integrated policy framework, the economy exhibits a persistently high current account deficit that can hardly be considered sustainable.

However, several points should be kept in mind before drawing bold conclusions. First and foremost, the exercise presented in this chapter is highly speculative, as it consists of a counterfactual analysis based on one of multiple possible ways of designing the instruments of the integrated policy framework. Second, the Lucas critique is always a threat to these analyses, either when they are counterfactual or when they are prospective. The exercise offered in this chapter should therefore be taken as a thought experiment that can be used to motivate a broader research agenda, rather than a conclusive diagnostic of the macroeconomic policy combination under study. Still, thought experiments are very useful in social sciences where the laboratory is reality itself. Policy mistakes based on unrealistic assumptions, inaccurate diagnoses, and incomplete (and sometimes wrong) identification of transmission channels can have grave consequences for society.

NOTE

1.   Basu et al. (2020) also mention the "terms of trade externalities" and the "pecuniary production externality" in their analysis. However, we do not take these into account in the analysis in this chapter. The "terms of trade externalities" are discarded by the authors themselves, as they consider that its relevance for policy purposes is unclear. The "pecuniary production externality" is not considered here because the model used does not incorporate land prices.

REFERENCES

Basu, M. S. S., M.E. Boz, M.G. Gopinath, M.F. Roch, and M.F.D. Unsal. 2020. "A conceptual model for the integrated policy framework." IMF Working Paper No. 2020/121.

Díaz-Alejandro, C. 1963. "A note on the impact of devaluation and the redistributive effect." *Journal of Political Economy*, 71(6): 577–80.

International Monetary Fund (IMF). 2018. "The IMF's institutional view on capital flows in practice. Prepared by the staff of the IMF for the G20." www.imf.org/external/np/g20/pdf/2018/073018.pdf (accessed July 2022)

International Monetary Fund (IMF). 2022. "Review of the institutional view on the liberalization and management of capital flows." IMF Policy Paper No. 2022/008.

Krugman, P., and L. Taylor. 1978. "Contractionary effects of devaluation." *Journal of International Economics* 8(3): 445–56.

Montes-Rojas, G., and F. Toledo. 2021. "External shocks and inflationary pressures in Argentina: a post-Keynesian-structuralist empirical approach." *Review of Political Economy* 34(4): 789–806. https://doi.org/10.1080/09538259.2021.1993001

Trajtenberg, L., S. Valdecantos, and D. Vega. 2015. "Los determinantes de la inflación en América Latina: un estudio empírico del período 1990–2013." In A. Bárcena, A. Prado, and M. Abeles (eds), *Estructura Productiva y Política Macroeconómica: enfoques heterodoxos desde América Latina*, 163–90, Libros de la CEPAL.

Valdecantos, S. 2022. "Endogenous exchange rates in empirical stock-flow consistent models for peripheral economies: an illustration from the case of Argentina." *Journal of Post-Keynesian Economics* 45(4): 636–66.

Vera, L. 2014. "The simple post-Keynesian monetary policy model: an open economy approach." *Review of Political Economy* 26(4): 526–48.

Vernengo, M. 2005. "Money and inflation: a taxonomy." Department of Economics of the University of Utah Working Paper Series, No. 2005–14.

Zack, G., M. Montané, and M. Kulfas. 2018. "Una aproximación a las causas del proceso inflacionario argentino reciente." In M. Kulfas and G. Zack, *Pensar la Economía Argentina*, X–X, Siglo XXI Editores.

2. Macroeconomic policy under a managed floating exchange rate regime: a critical appraisal of the international currency hierarchy literature

Simone Deos and Enzo Gerioni

INTRODUCTION

The concern of economists with external constraints in the periphery is not a novel one.[1] Even the term "periphery" has long been employed to describe economies that are structurally dependent on the external sector, in opposition to "center" economies that have developed productive capabilities. This dichotomy between periphery and center is at the core of the origins of the Latin American Structuralist School, which has been a major influence for most heterodox economists in this region of the world. Development and growth constraints in the context of the periphery are the main object of Latin American Structuralism.

Currently, one of the most important strands in heterodox economics that openly embraces the influence of Structuralism is what we call throughout this chapter the "International Currency Hierarchy" (ICH) literature. Although there are similarities between ICH and Structuralism, their arguments regarding the existence of an external constraint in peripheral economies are essentially very distinct. While Structuralism has been mainly concerned with the productive capabilities of the peripheral economies, the ICH literature is focused on asymmetries of the international monetary system (IMS) and its consequences over peripheral countries. Even the dichotomy between periphery and center, we should note, is not exactly the same. In the ICH literature, the center–periphery relation is established relative to countries that issue peripheral currencies and countries that issue central currencies rather than the difference in productive capabilities.[2]

The other major influence openly embraced by the ICH literature is the post-Keynesian school.[3] Uncertainty, expectations, and liquidity preference theory are key elements in their theoretical framework, which is used to analyze monetary, fiscal, and exchange rate policies in the periphery of the IMS. The asymmetrical hierarchy of currencies in the system, according to the main argument of the ICH, would be responsible for the higher volatility of the exchange rates at the periphery, lack of autonomy for monetary and fiscal policies, and, ultimately, would be an obstacle to the implementation of broader development policies. The attempt to unify in some way these two schools of thought can be clearly detected in the name "Keynesian Structuralism,"[4] which is often adopted by authors of the ICH literature (see Prates, 2015; Paula et al., 2017; Fritz et al., 2016, 2018).

The theoretical framework proposed in the ICH literature has been largely disseminated by heterodox macroeconomists in Brazil. However, while ICH's main objects are monetary issues, and most ICH researchers identify themselves as post-Keynesians, one can hardly find any mention of the endogenous money approach, which is an essential feature of modern post-Keynesianism. Therefore, the purpose of this chapter is to debate whether or not the argument that peripheral countries do not have macroeconomic policy autonomy in a managed floating exchange rate regime remains valid when analyzed under the endogenous money approach. To be clear, we consider throughout this chapter the case of countries that have monetary sovereignty. A monetarily sovereign government in the modern monetary theory's (MMT) perspective is one that solely defines the official money of account, issues the currency denominated in its own money of account, imposes non-reciprocal obligations denominated in its own money of account (tax), and has the prerogative to decide what it accepts in payments and what it delivers in payments for its own obligations, goods, and services (Wray, 2015; Mitchell et al., 2019). That stated, one should notice that, from this perspective, to have monetary sovereignty, a country has to issue its public debt—entirely or in majority—denominated in its own currency.

The chapter begins with a brief overview of the ICH literature and its main concepts. Once they are established, we go through the main arguments regarding the constraints on monetary and fiscal policies of peripheral countries. Next, we present the circuitist/endogenous money approach for open economies and its implications for a central bank's ability to set and keep the targeted interest rate in an exchange rate regime with substantial interventions—the *dirty* floating. Following up, we make a critical appraisal of the arguments contained in the ICH literature in light of the endogenous money approach, considering that most peripheral economies actually operate a managed floating exchange rate regime.

PERIPHERAL CURRENCIES AND MACROECONOMIC POLICY CONSTRAINT

The ICH literature is openly influenced by both Latin American Structuralists and post-Keynesians (Fritz et al., 2016, 2018), and is deeply embedded in the current heterodox economics in Brazil and other countries. One could safely point to the Institute of Economics at the University of Campinas (Unicamp; Brazil) as a stronghold of the ICH literature, with many professors being some of the most important early (see Miranda, 1997; Carneiro, 1999) and current researchers in this literature.[5] As the Institute of Economics at Unicamp is one of the most influential research and teaching institutions of heterodox economics in Brazil, it comes as no surprise that ICH has been far-reaching in Brazilian heterodox macroeconomics.

The well-known center–periphery relation in a modified (monetary) version is at the base of the ICH. According to their analysis, the gradual erosion of the Bretton Woods system during the 1970s—financial and monetary market openings and deregulations with the *pari passu* abandonment (for the majority of the countries) of the fixed exchange rate regime—increased the deleterious impacts of the asymmetrical IMS that were kept at bay by the stricter regulations of the post-Second World War period. While the asymmetrical hierarchy in the IMS is not identified as a recent phenomenon, the end of Bretton Woods—meaning the end of the gold-dollar standard with fixed exchange rates—and financial globalization would be blamed for the narrower autonomy of the macroeconomic policy of countries at the periphery.

Asymmetry of the International Monetary System

The asymmetry of the IMS is responsible for the differences between countries that issue peripheral currencies, the country that creates the top central currency (the United States), and those that are at intermediate positions. Other terms employed in ICH's papers to describe the same hierarchy are "Northern" and "Southern"—"Northern" meaning the United States, which is at the top, but also other countries that issue currencies that have an intermediate position, as they are also liquid, yet with smaller liquidity premiums relative to the key one (Fritz et al., 2018). In earlier works of the ICH, the most common terms to describe this phenomenon were "convertible" (central) and "non-convertible" (peripheral) currencies (see Carneiro, 1999; Prates, 2005), but these have since fallen out of use. Some other variations can be found, but all with the meaning stated above.[6]

The distinction between central, intermediate, and peripheral currencies is rooted in the capacity of national currencies to perform "the three functions of money on the international scale: means of payment, unit of account (and denomination of contracts), and store of value (international reserve currency)" (Paula et al., 2017, p. 187). Implicit in this argument is the idea that money is what performs the three functions simultaneously. On the one hand, central and intermediate currencies are national currencies that are able to settle payments, denominate prices (and contracts), and store value beyond domestic borders. However, among central currencies, some are only partially able to perform on an international scale—they are called intermediate currencies—and the key currency of the system (the American dollar, currently) is the only one that fully performs all three functions of money on a global scale. On the other hand, peripheral currencies cannot fully perform any of the three functions of money on an international scale and often have limited use even domestically. But, according to the ICH, not all peripheral currencies are exactly the same; a few are partially able to perform internationally—although on a very reduced scale—and the majority are barely accepted within their own national territory.

It is worth noting that, since a few peripheral and intermediate currencies are able to partially perform the three functions of money internationally, the line dividing both groups may be blurred rather than clearly marked like it is in the extreme cases. The existence of this spectrum in the hierarchy, instead of a binary division, is recognized and pointed out by many authors in the ICH literature.[7] However, while there is a recognition that the hierarchy is more of a spectrum, the analytical framework of the ICH adopts a simplifying assumption of a binary division—in which all peripheral currencies are taken as unable to perform on an international scale at any level[8]—and generalize the conclusions regarding macroeconomic policy autonomy at the periphery. As useful as this simplification may be, it clearly overlooks the diversity within the peripheral currencies' group and results in substantial loss of accuracy to analyze the reality of many economies.

The key reason why a peripheral currency is not able to perform the functions of money internationally is the lack of liquidity at the international level. Thus, in the simplified division, the central currency is considered to be the liquid currency, and peripheral currencies are considered to have a negligible degree of international liquidity. Consequently, the demand for peripheral currencies would be very unstable and often dependent on the business cycle. In periods of increased global liquidity (low interest rate in center currency economies and a good degree of confidence), investors search for higher yields in emerging markets, making the demand for peripheral currencies temporarily grow (Paula et al., 2017). Because the opposite is also true, when global liquidity and the degree of confidence decrease, the demand for peripheral currencies fades away. We must distinguish the market liquidity—which fluctuates with global liquidity—from the structural international liquidity of the currency that remains unchanged (or changes at a much slower pace than global liquidity). The ICH literature is mainly concerned with the latter.

Therefore, although peripheral currencies may seem to become more liquid during periods of high global liquidity, their structural liquidity remains unchanged. As a result of being issuers of structurally illiquid assets, monetary authorities of peripheral economies end up offering high yields in an attempt to establish a more stable demand for their national currency. In other words, a stricter monetary policy is employed in peripheral currency economies to compensate for the lack of liquidity and to attempt to provide some stability to the exchange rate (Prates, 2015; Paula et al., 2017; Fritz et al., 2018; Bonizzi et al., 2019).

Monetary Policy and Exchange Rate

The fundamental link between being at a low level in the currency hierarchy and the lack of macroeconomic policy autonomy envisaged by the ICH literature is given by the necessity to at least partially control the exchange rate— meaning that central banks in peripheral countries have to be proactive at the foreign exchange market. There is a shared understanding among subscribers of the ICH literature that countries at the periphery cannot (and should not) let the exchange rate freely float because of the substantial deleterious effects it would inevitably bring to the economy. But besides that, controlling the exchange rate to maintain a competitive and stable level is considered to be the "main target that peripheral emerging economies should pursue to achieve external competitiveness" (Paula et al., 2017, p. 196).

It is argued that even with the end of the Bretton Woods system and, consequently, the ascent of the flexible exchange rate as the predominant regime in center countries, the periphery (understandably, from the ICH standpoint) remains wary of letting the exchange rate float freely. Controlling, at least partially, the exchange rate would also be beneficial because it would curb the uncertainty of most agents in the economy. Although many peripheral economies officially adopt a floating regime—as has been the case in Brazil since 1999—in practice, interventions in the exchange rate market are frequent and substantial. This is often referred to as the "fear of floating," a term found in the conventional economic literature (Calvo and Reinhart, 2002) and adopted in the ICH literature (Fritz et al., 2016; Paula et al., 2017). As Rodrik (2006) points out, since the early 1990s, central banks of developing countries (roughly the peripheral currency issuers) have been accumulating foreign reserves at a much faster pace than developed countries (roughly the central and intermediate currency issuers).[9]

Given the acknowledged reality that a flexible exchange rate regime simply does not exist in practice at the periphery, two strands of arguments are developed in the ICH literature to explain the lack of monetary policy autonomy. The first is that peripheral countries lack monetary policy autonomy because domestic goals have to be overlooked to set an interest rate that is more adequate to keep the exchange rate from going too high or too low—and this would have to be done only by means of the monetary policy, independently of the constraints in the external sector.[10] The high volatility of the exchange rate involves costs and risks for peripheral countries that would far exceed the ones faced by central countries, including inflation, international competitiveness loss, financial fragility, and slow economic growth (Paula et al., 2017; Conti et al., 2014).

When there is high global liquidity and investors are searching for higher yields at the periphery of the IMS, the absence of interventions in the foreign exchange market and the maintenance of interest rates at the same level by central banks would lead to an (excessive) appreciation of the domestic currency. This, in turn, could reduce international competitiveness,[11] decrease net exports, and slow economic growth. It also may lead to domestic private agents borrowing at lower interest rates in foreign markets, leading to increased indebtedness in foreign currency, potentially causing a problem of currency mismatch. Conversely, during low global liquidity periods, investors tend to leave peripheral economies in case the monetary authorities do not increase the basic interest rate, which would imply depreciation of the domestic currency, leading to higher inflation and uncertainty. In summary, for the ICH literature, central banks at the periphery would be, in principle, either forced to intervene in the exchange market or to reset the basic interest rate with the exchange rate as the primary objective. Then, according to this reasoning, all domestic goals of the monetary policy at the periphery would be secondary concerns that only occasionally can be addressed. In this sense, the monetary policy at the periphery is considered reactive to changes in the external sector, reflected (not only, but mainly) in the exchange rate. Thus, it cannot be autonomous.[12]

The second strand of arguments of the ICH for the lack of monetary policy autonomy is that substantial interventions in the foreign exchange market by the central bank cannot be performed because they would impair its ability to set the short-term interest rate. Before exposing the reasoning coming from the ICH literature which suggests why, in this scenario, the central bank monetary policy is impaired, one should first explain how these operations—usually called sterilizations—are de facto performed by central banks. The mechanism is the following: during a period of high global liquidity, central banks at the periphery purchase foreign currency at the foreign exchange market to prevent appreciation of the domestic currency. In this intervention, the central bank pays for the foreign currency by crediting high-powered money (reserve balances) in the banking sector. This increased amount of reserve balances in the monetary market would then create a downward pressure on the interest rate of the interbank system that can only be avoided with a sterilization operation. Sterilization is carried out with the central bank selling government securities from its portfolio to drain the added reserve balances and offset any potential undesired impact on the interest rate. In similar fashion, during low global liquidity periods, the central bank sells foreign currency from its portfolio to prevent domestic currency depreciation. However, the sale of foreign currency ends up draining reserve balances from the banking sector, bringing about an upward pressure on the interest rate. In this case, central banks purchase government securities in the monetary market to inject reserve balances to offset any potential undesired impact on the interest rate.

In the ICH literature, however, sterilization is understood as a policy decision of the central bank, and not as a regular operation currently performed de facto by contemporary central banks to keep the short-term interest rate at this targeted level. It is important to highlight that, if sterilization was a policy decision—meaning that the monetary authority, for any reason, could choose not to sterilize the reserve balances created to pay for the dollar it is purchasing (in the case of inflows)—there would be changes in the monetary base leading to undesired changes in the basic interest rate. If one assumes that position (e.g., that the central bank could decide not to sterilize, or could be "forced" to that), one has to conclude that interest rate setting would be a result of foreign currency flows rather than being autonomously set by the central bank. Following this reasoning, one should ask, why would the central bank forego the sterilization strategy and altogether monetary policy autonomy? The plain reason pointed out by ICH would be the excessive "fiscal cost"[13]—the increase of the public debt entailing interest payments—of sterilizing exchange market interventions.

As clearly stated by Prates (2010), that would happen when the central bank is driving monetary policy with the primary objective of controlling or reducing the volatility of the exchange rate:

> Furthermore, in the Brazilian economy case, during this period [January 2003–June 2007], the impossibility of the Central Bank to control, simultaneously, the basic interest rate and the nominal exchange rate in this context was taken to the limit because of two specificities …
> The adoption of a more aggressive purchase of currency—with the objective of influencing the exchange rate trajectory—with partial sterilization of its monetary impacts would put the inflation targeting regime anchored in the maintenance of a high basic interest rate at risk. (p. 33, our translation)

According to the passage above, the central bank could perform (or be forced to perform) a partial sterilization of the foreign currency flows. As a result, in a context of surplus in the overall balance of payments, the interest rate could be forced downward. Of course, this would jeopardize the operation of the inflation target regime, since the central bank would not be able to freely raise the interest rate according to the level indicated by the Taylor rule.[14] And more than that, if the central bank allows the short-term interest rate to escape from the targeted one, substantial instability in the national financial system should be expected, since all financial transactions are done based on a short-term interest rate that is at the base of the yield curve. Hence, if the central bank, concerned with the "fiscal situation," decides (for any reason) not to sterilize and leave the short-term interest rate to vary—a situation that, as far as we know, has never happened in countries that adopt *dirty* floating regimes with inflation targets—that could bring about important financial distress, besides its effects on the inflation target regime.

Fiscal Policy Constraint

Unlike the emphasis given to the link between exchange rate volatility (and the necessity to, at least partially, control it) and the monetary policy (and the necessity to have it as a tool to create a more stable demand for the peripheral currency), the constraint on fiscal policy appears in the ICH literature as an afterthought, only comprehensible when taking into account the prior considerations about exchange rate and monetary policy. The analysis of fiscal policy autonomy is based on the important assumption that fiscal policy is subordinated to monetary and exchange rate policies in the context of an inflation targeting regime and the need to keep the exchange rate at a competitive level in a *dirty* floating regime (Fritz et al., 2018). As for the ICH, monetary and exchange rate policies are the most relevant macroeconomic policies for price stabilization and economic development, respectively, whereas the fiscal policy role is basically limited to accommodating the other two macroeconomic policies.

To begin, we must go back to the sterilization issue. As the ICH literature considers sterilization as a policy decision under the monetary authorities' discretion, when there is foreign reserve net inflow and the central bank intervenes in the foreign exchange market to prevent domestic currency appreciation, the monetary authority has to choose between sterilizing or not. To put it clearly, the central banks' choice would be to (i) carry on sterilization and keep its ability to maintain the short-term interest rate at the targeted level, or (ii) forego sterilization to avoid increasing public debt and fiscal costs. Under the assumption that fiscal policy is subordinated to monetary policy, it is argued that the role of fiscal policy is heavily constrained by the necessity to sterilize.

One can see this relation very straightforwardly stated in an overview of the ICH literature presented by Palludeto and Abouchedid (2016):

> the accumulation of reserves ... results in additional pressure on public finances and also reduces the potential for other development policies because it reduces the financial resources of domestic authorities. The cost of reserve restricts the role of fiscal policy, which is to act in times of low economic activity and promote sustainable aggregate economic growth. (p. 80)

Therefore, according to the ICH, fiscal policy in peripheral economies cannot be autonomously conducted by the government at the risk of leading public finances to a point at which the central bank may be forced not to sterilize.[15] Fiscal policy has to be run passively, with the objective of reducing pressure on public finances and allowing for sterilization. Otherwise, there is the risk of running out of financial resources. One can identify in the ICH literature a trade-off between the government being able to set the interest rate and having fiscal policy autonomy in peripheral economies, as stated by Fritz et al. (2018):

> As peripheral emerging economies have to implement foreign reserve accumulation as a defensive and precautionary response to enhance their capacity of restraining speculative attacks in times of capital flows reversals, the need to sterilize the monetary impact of that policy (to counter the downward pressures on the policy rate) results in fiscal costs due the high interest rate differentials. (p. 216)

Another constraint on fiscal policy presented in the ICH literature is the discipline imposed by the globalized financial markets. Due to the volatile demand for peripheral currency and the deleterious effects of an abrupt depreciation of the national currency, the governments of peripheral countries would be subject to important pressures from international investors to which they would have to comply. Even considering that international investors adopt a mistaken economic theory (from a heterodox point of view) to reach their conclusions, they still could require governments at the periphery to adopt a fiscal policy based on sound finance doctrine, creating a self-fulfilling prophecy. Governments in peripheral economies that do not comply with the imposed discipline would be at constant risk of a capital flight (Fritz et al., 2018). Vergnhanini and Conti (2017) succinctly explain that "[not] much is needed to cause the 'flight to liquidity' movement ... Any action that goes against 'market discipline' and the so-called 'sound finance' may lead to a self-fulfilling prophecy of currency depreciation" (p. 27).

Although this argument seems to be instinctive at first sight, what does it mean theoretically? How exactly would a negative budget result, or an increasing public debt/gross domestic product (GDP) relation, trigger a capital flight?

Considering all else equal—domestic and international interest rates—the reversing of the interest rate differential that could trigger international capital to leave a peripheral economy would mean that the risk spread increases in response to fiscal indicators. In other words, fiscal policy autonomy would be constrained because peripheral economies' governments are disciplined by foreign investors. If the government does not comply with the markets, increasing risk spread would lead to either higher basic interest rates—to compensate for the risk spread—or to a capital flight, domestic currency depreciation, high inflation, and, possibly, an external crisis.

A CRITICAL APPRAISAL OF THE ICH LITERATURE IN LIGHT OF THE ENDOGENOUS MONEY APPROACH

The lack of macroeconomic policy autonomy, argued in the ICH literature, has been a major topic of debate in Brazilian heterodox economics regarding policy prescription, including many researchers who subscribe to post-Keynesianism. However, some elements in their core argument, presented above, seem to be out of touch with the endogenous money approach.

Endogenous Money Approach in the Open Economy and the ICH Literature

While the endogenous money approach is a well-known and essential feature in modern post-Keynesian strands—and this approach encompasses not only acknowledging that the commercial banks create money endogenously, but also that central banks exogenously set interest rates and must act in the monetary market, buying and selling reserves/government bonds to keep the targeted interest rate—its extension to incorporate the external sector is still not unequivocally acknowledged. This extension is established through the compensation principle,[16] which extends not only the endogenous money approach, but also the circuitist logic to the open economy. After a brief presentation of the compensation principle, we proceed to make a critical appraisal of the ICH main arguments.

According to the compensation principle, inflows or outflows of foreign currency do not impair a central bank's ability to set the interest at the level it believes is the most appropriate, whether it is a floating, managed floating, or even fixed exchange rate regime. Even in peripheral economies that are forced by the asymmetrical hierarchy of the IMS to control their exchange rate to some extent, the compensation principle should still be valid.

To explain the compensation principle, we assume a fixed exchange rate regime for the purpose of simplicity. The central bank establishes a fixed rate of conversion from the domestic currency to a target foreign currency (most likely the American dollar). The overall balance of payments result—surplus or deficit—would create a tendency for nominal variations of the exchange rate, forcing the central bank to intervene in the foreign exchange market. If there is a surplus, the central bank purchases foreign currency by crediting reserve balances at the banking sector. At the initiative of this sector, excess reserve balances are utilized to buy interest-yielding assets (government securities) or pay their interest-bearing debt (if it is an asset-based or overdraft economy, respectively),[17] rather than held as bank reserves—a non-interest-yielding asset (Lavoie, 2001; Angrick, 2017). This process is triggered by the banking sectors' simple and logical decision to seek a higher return for their assets. One should note that while individual banks may use the credited reserve balances to purchase assets other than government securities, for the whole sector the credited reserve balances inevitably end up as government securities or as payment of debts with the government.[18]

Therefore, sterilization is not subject to a discretionary policy decision of the central bank. On the contrary, it is part of the reflux mechanism through which reserve balances created by the central bank in the foreign exchange market intervention flow back to the same central bank through the purchase of government securities by the banking sector. The central bank acts passively in the sterilization process, simply accommodating the demand of the banking sector for interest-yielding assets—public bonds. Instead of a change at the monetary base that would be caused by the exchange market intervention, there is an automatic compensation at another item on the central bank's balance sheet.[19] As a consequence, every foreign exchange market intervention is automatically sterilized at the banking sector's own initiative, under the normal functioning of the central bank—and independently from any macroeconomic policy decision (Serrano and Summa, 2015).

One important recognition to be made is that, from the monetary authority's perspective, and considering—for the sake of simplicity—a fixed exchange rate regime, while sterilization can go on limitlessly in the case of an overall balance of payments surplus, a tendency to deficits in the balance of payments would be limited by the amount of foreign currency at the disposal of the central bank to sell at the exchange market. So, in the deficit case, it is most likely that the central bank would either raise the basic interest rate to reverse the deficit or forfeit the fixed conversion of the domestic currency into foreign currency, effectively abandoning the fixed exchange rate regime. One should note that this is not a limit of the sterilization process itself, but rather a limit of the fixed exchange rate regime given by the total amount of foreign reserves previously accumulated.

On the other hand, in a *clean* flexible exchange rate regime, the absence of a central bank's interventions in the foreign exchange market means that reserve balances will not be created and, subsequently, the banking sector will neither be able to buy the additional amount of government securities nor cancel part of their debt with the government. In other words, the quantity of money—monetary base—remains endogenous without the explicit operation of the compensation principle. As to the more real managed floating regime, or *dirty* floating, the compensation principle operates in the same way as in the fixed exchange rate regime, the difference being the amount of intervention in the foreign exchange market carried out by the central bank.

One can notice that there is a very marked contrast between the compensation principle and the ICH literature. In fact, sterilization's being a part of the normal functioning of the central bank (compensation principle) or being a policy decision of the central bank dependent on the state of public finances (ICH literature) may seem like a subtle difference, but it is essential for conclusions about monetary policy autonomy. Differently from the ICH argument, in reality there is no such thing as non-sterilized or partially sterilized foreign exchange market interventions. Even a managed floating regime with substantial interventions in the exchange market does not affect the central bank's autonomy to exogenously set and keep the interest rate at the level it believes to be the most appropriate.

In light of the compensation principle, as we could notice, there is no trade-off between monetary policy autonomy and fiscal policy autonomy. An increasing (or already very high) public debt/GDP ratio is not a threat to the sterilization process, which is automatically triggered by the banking sector looking for yields in the monetary market, independently of the fiscal situation. In other words, it is not that a peripheral economy with a high public debt/GDP ratio, and/or with negative budget results, has to choose either being able to set the interest rate or having an active fiscal policy.

In the case of countries that issue public debt denominated in foreign currency, unlike monetarily sovereign countries, there is the possibility of government default, and the monetary authority could be forced to increase the interest rate to roll the government's debt. So, while many peripheral economies issue their public debt in foreign currency—and do not have monetary sovereignty in the MMT's sense—one can point to other peripheral economies that issue public debt mainly or totally denominated in its own currency.[20] In other words, issuing public debt denominated in foreign currency is not a defining feature of the set of economies that has been currently called peripheral economies. Also, as sterilization is part of the normal functioning of modern central banks, being merely the operation of exchanging reserve balances in excess for government securities, differently from what has been posed by the ICH literature, it does not impair the implementation of an active fiscal policy.

It is also important to emphasize that the validity of the compensation principle is not disproved by the fact that the central banks of peripheral economies take into consideration, or even set their monetary policy decisions based on the overall balance of payments results and, consequently, on the exchange rate tendency. It would be expected that an outflow of foreign currency would trigger a more restrictive monetary policy—mostly to raise the cost of leaving—but not as a result of the foreign currency outflow forcing the basic interest rate upward (Lavoie, 2001). The autonomy of the central bank to make monetary policy decisions, its ability to set and keep the short-term interest rate where it decides, is preserved even when there are substantial interventions in a managed floating exchange rate regime.

Fiscal Discipline

Besides the understanding—criticized above—that sterilization drains financial resources from the governments and constrains monetary and fiscal policies, there is also the argument that globalized financial markets impose fiscal discipline on peripheral economies. As presented above, among some authors there is an implicit idea that recurrent budget deficits and/or increasing (or already high) public debt/GDP ratio would cause a higher risk spread, narrowing or even reversing the interest rate differential. Calvo et al. (1996) suggested a similar mechanism, referring to the impact of the sterilization process:

> since sterilization involves increasing the number of domestic bonds to offset the currency inflow, it results in an increase in public debt. Eventually, this policy could result in a rise in public debt so large as to undermine the credibility of policymakers, especially if the public begins expecting a partial repudiation of the debt-expectations that may well halt the inflows altogether. (p. 134)

With a strict interpretation of this line of reasoning one would paradoxically conclude that an overall balance of payment surplus in a managed floating regime would lead to an increased perception of risk from international investors caring about the soundness of their portfolio. We consider that a more robust explanation for the increasing risk spread charged by investors should take into account the foreign reserve position of the central bank relative to the foreign currency denominated debt (Medeiros and Serrano, 2001).

Going further with the reasoning, one can pose the following question: If the international investors are subscribers of the sound finance doctrine, would they be compelled to withdraw their capital from "fiscally undisciplined" economies because they believe it to be too risky? To address this question, Jorge and Bastos (2019) analyzed the auctions of the Brazilian National Treasury in the 2000s and found no evidence that it was "threatened" by the market. Specifically regarding the international investors, the author concluded that "downgrades of international agencies *did not* cause a persistent pressure on auction rates nor a persistent change in the amount of bonds sold to the market" (Jorge and Bastos, 2019, p. 10, emphasis in original)

So, from what is stated above, it is not a stretch to understand that international investors are not likely to give up a higher yield on their capital because of their commitment to sound finance doctrine. Therefore, in our view, the "discipline of the market" argument, which is often used to justify the lack of macroeconomic policy autonomy, cannot simply be invoked in the case of all peripheral countries. Perhaps a more specific analysis would be able to pinpoint in which cases the argument is valid, but certainly it is not appropriate to make this argument for the whole periphery.

CONCLUSION

The concern with external constraints and vulnerabilities, especially at the periphery, is mandatory. We acknowledge that the external sector vulnerability is a key limiting factor for the countries that are in general defined as peripheral economies. In this sense, the ICH literature has deepened the analysis about the external vulnerabilities related to monetary and financial dimensions of these economies and the limitations they bring about, enlarging the traditional debate about the relation between center and periphery focused on incomplete productive capabilities.

However, at this point, it remains rather unclear in which sense being at the bottom of the ICH's currencies pyramid would be a constraining factor to monetary and, especially, fiscal policies. The lack of mention of money endogeneity in a broad sense—as was treated above—in the ICH literature led us to believe that a critical appraisal of the fundamentals behind their core argument in light of the endogenous money approach would be interesting. That could even lead to a reappraisal of what is money in a monetary economy of production.

As stated in this chapter, our research has found elements in the ICH literature that are inconsistent with the endogenous money approach. As a result, our conclusion is that the ICH literature's main discussion, about macroeconomic policy autonomy, would greatly benefit from a clearer statement regarding this essential feature of contemporary post-Keynesianism.

NOTES

1. The authors thank Fabiano A. S. Dalto, Alex W. A. Palludeto, and Fernando Toledo for their thoughtful comments and suggestions on an earlier version of this chapter. Usual disclaimers apply.
2. Hereafter, mentions to periphery (or peripheral countries) and center (or center countries) refer to the ICH's concepts focused on monetary asymmetries of the IMS.

3.   See Lavoie (2011) about the existence of multiple strands within
     post-Keynesianism.
4.   Do not mistake it for Palley's term, structural Keynesianism, which refers to
     another strand of post-Keynesianism (Lavoie, 2014). Also, to the best of our
     knowledge, there has not been a critical appraisal of the fundamentals behind
     their core argument in light of the definition of money and of the endogenous
     money approach. As we argue in this chapter, macroeconomic policy limitations
     invoked by the ICH literature seem inconsistent with money endogeneity and,
     consequently, ought to be scrutinized before being incorporated into policy
     recommendations.
5.   As it would take us far from our objective and would not significantly change
     the proposed debate, we do not go into a detailed discussion of whether or not
     the ICH literature is a school of thought. It is important to note, though, that the
     authors who are identified as part of the ICH literature have, to some extent,
     a homogenous theoretical framework with only small differences between them.
6.   One should note that this hierarchy is not the same as the one proposed by
     Minsky (1986) and followed by others such as Wray (2015) and Bell (2001). The
     Minsky hierarchy is about domestic money: state money on top, banking money
     in the middle, and other debts at the bottom layers of the hierarchy (or pyramid).
7.   See Conti et al. (2014) and Paula et al. (2017).
8.   The difficulty in pinpointing whether some national currencies pertain to the
     group of central or peripheral currencies can be perceived by inconsisten-
     cies between different authors in the classification of some currencies—the
     Australian dollar, for example. This could possibly be related to the lack of
     a clear determination of the causes for the hierarchy. See Kaltenbrunner (2015)
     and Conti et al. (2014) for two very different explanations for the existence of the
     international currency hierarchy.
9.   This is not only due to interventions to control the exchange rate, but is also part
     of an issuance strategy of the central bank of developing countries to prevent
     external debt crises.
10. Current account balance and the amount of foreign reserves.
11. The emphasis on the effect of the exchange rate appreciation on external compet-
     itiveness is discussed in much more detail in the New Developmentalism school.
     The essence of the discussion focused on deindustrialization remains very similar
     in the ICH literature, as one can see in Fritz et al. (2016, 2018).
12. According to the ICH literature, some monetary policy autonomy could be
     achieved with the imposition of capital controls that reduce speculative flows
     to and from peripheral economies. By hindering exchange rate volatility, capital
     control measures subsequently allow more freedom for monetary policy (Fritz et
     al., 2016, 2018).
13. The discussion about the "fiscal cost" of sterilization will be carried out in more
     detail in the following subsection.
14. There is no suggestion in the ICH literature that the inflation targeting regime is
     the most adequate or even that it works properly.
15. Palludeto and Abouchedid (2016) point out the exception when foreign reserve
     accumulation is accompanied by GDP growth due to net export growth.
     Public finances, in this case, would not be necessarily constrained by reserve
     accumulation.

16. The terms "compensation thesis" (Lavoie and Wang, 2012), "compensation view" (Angrick, 2017), and "Banque de France view" (Lavoie, 2014) can also be found in the literature.
17. See Lavoie (2014) for a detailed explanation about the difference between asset-based and overdraft economies.
18. Part of the reserve balances are kept as central banks' compulsory reserve requirements. Banks also hold a minimal amount for settlements with the government and with other banks.
19. Which item compensates for the lack of changes in the monetary base depends on the institutionality and relation of each central bank and banking sector. See Angrick (2017) for examples of the compensation principle taking place in different Asian economies.
20. As it is in Brazil, for instance, where public debt in its majority is denominated and settled in Reais, the local currency.

REFERENCES

Angrick, S. (2017). Global liquidity and monetary policy autonomy: an examination of open-economy policy constraints. *Cambridge Journal of Economics*, 42 (1): 117–35.

Bell, S. A. (2001). The role of the state and the hierarchy of money. *Cambridge Journal of Economics*, 25 (2): 149–63.

Bonizzi, B., Kaltenbrunner, A., & Michell, J. (2019). Monetary sovereignty is a spectrum: modern monetary theory and developing countries. *Real-World Economics Review*, 89: 46–61.

Calvo, G. A., Leiderman, L., & Reinhart, C. M. (1996). Inflows of capital to developing countries in the 1990s. *Journal of Economic Perspectives*, 10 (2): 123–39.

Calvo, G. A., & Reinhart, C. M. (2002). Fear of Floating. *The Quarterly Journal of Economics*, 117(2): 379–408.

Carneiro, R. (1999). Globalização Financeira e Inserção Periférica. *Economia e Sociedade*, 8 (2): 57–92.

Conti, B. M., Prates, D. M., & Plihon, D. (2014). A hierarquia monetária e suas implicações para as taxas de câmbio e de juros e a política econômica dos países periféricos. *Economia e Sociedade*, 23 (2): 341–72.

Fritz, B., De Paula, L. F., & Prates, D. M. (2016). Hierarquia de moedas e redução da autonomia de política econômica em economias periféricas emergentes: uma análise Keynesiana-estruturalista. In F. Ferrari Filho & F. H. B. T. Terra (eds), *Keynes: Ensaios sobre os 80 Anos da Teoria Geral*. Porto Alegre, 177–202, Tomo Editoria.

Fritz, B., De Paula, L. F., & Prates, D. M. (2018). Global currency hierarchy and national policy space: a framework for peripheral economies. *European Journal of Economics and Economic Policies: Intervention*, 15 (2): 208–18.

Jorge, C. T., & Bastos, C. P. M. (2019). Analysis of Brazilian National Treasury Primary Auctions in the 2000s: an MMT interpretation. Working paper number 14, IE/UFRJ.

Kaltenbrunner, A. (2015). A post Keynesian framework of exchange rate determination: a Minskyan approach. *Journal of Post Keynesian Economics*, 38 (3): 426–48.

Lavoie, M. (2001). The reflux mechanism and the open economy. In L.-P. Rochon & M. Vernengo (eds), *Credit, Interest Rates and the Open Economy: Essays on Horizontalism*, 215–42, Edward Elgar Punlishing.

Lavoie, M. (2011). History and methods of post-Keynesian economics. In E. Hein & E. Stockhammer (eds), *A Modern Guide to Keynesian Macroeconomics and Economic Policies*, 1–33, Edward Elgar Publishing.

Lavoie, M. (2014). *Post-Keynesian Economics: New Foundations*. Edward Elgar Publishing.

Lavoie, M., & Wang, P. (2012). The 'compensation' thesis, as exemplified by the case of the Chinese central bank. *International Review of Applied Economics*, 26 (3): 287–301.

Medeiros, C. A., & Serrano, F. (2001). Inserção externa, exportações e crescimento no Brasil. In J. L. Fiori & C. Medeiros (eds), *Polarização Mundial e Crescimento*, 105–34, Editora Vozes.

Minsky, H. P. (1986). *Stabilizing an Unstable Economy*. New Haven, CT: Yale University Press.

Miranda, J. C. (1997). Dinâmica financeira e política macroeconômica. In M. da Conceição Tavares & J. L. Fiori (eds), *Poder e Dinheiro: uma economia política da globalização*, 7th edn, 243–75, Editora Vozes.

Mitchell, W., Wray, L. R., & Watts, M. (2019). *Macroeconomics*. Red Globe Press.

Palludeto, A. W. A, & Abouchedid, S. C. (2016). The currency hierarchy in center–periphery relationships. In Radhika Desai (ed.), *Analytical Gains of Geopolitical Economy*, 53–90, Emerald.

Paula, L. F., Fritz, B., & Prates, D. M. (2017). Keynes at the periphery: currency hierarchy and challenges for economic policy in emerging economies. *Journal of Post Keynesian Economics*, 40 (2): 183–202.

Prates, D. M. (2005). As Assimetrias do Sistema Monetário e Financeiro Internacional. *Revista de Economia Contemporânea*, 9 (2): 263–88.

Prates, D. M. (2010). O regime cambial brasileiro de 1999 a 2008. *Textos para Discussão CEPAL – IPEA*.

Prates, D. M. (2015). *O Regime de Câmbio Flutuante no Brasil: 1999–2012: especificidade e dilemas*. Ipea.

Rodrik, D. (2006). The Social Costs of Foreign Exchange Reserves. *International Economics Journal*, 20 (30).

Serrano, F., & Summa, R. (2015). Mundell–Fleming without the LM curve: the exogenous interest rate in an open economy. *Review of Keynesian Economics*, 3 (2): 248–68.

Vergnhanini, R., & Conti, B. (2017). Modern money theory: a criticism from the periphery. *Brazilian Keynesian Review*, 3 (2): 16–31.

Wray, L. R. (2015). *Modern Money Theory: A Primer on Macroeconomics for Sovereign Monetary Systems* (2nd edn). Palgrave Macmillan.

PART II

Monetary policy transmission channels in LACs

3. Inflation targeting in open economies: the contradictions of determinacy and stability

Esteban Pérez Caldentey and Matías Vernengo

INTRODUCTION

Since 1999, more than half of Latin American countries have adopted inflation targeting regimes with the hierarchical objective of maintaining price stability within a low-inflation environment.[1] Building on previous work, we argue that this choice of monetary regime was a result of a policy shift that began with the Washington Consensus, and that materialized sequentially in increased financial openness and greater exchange rate flexibility, and eventually led to the implementation of inflation targeting.[2] We further sustain that, in the case of an open economy, the use of inflation targeting leads to incoherent and contradictory results that severely question its alleged superiority over other monetary frameworks. Finally, we posit the need for comprehensive regulatory frameworks to deal with the complex dynamics and transmission mechanisms that characterize economies that have a high degree of financial openness, such as those of Latin America. As a result, countries in the region reverted to accumulation of reserves in dollars and central bank interventions in foreign exchange markets to effectively operate their anti-inflationary policies.

Domestic conditions are the primary focus of inflation targeting. The strategy's proponents also argue that this framework is applicable to an open economy context. According to this view, managing the policy rate of interest can control both domestic spending and exchange rate upward/downward pressures on prices—that is, for demand-pull and cost-push factors. The rate of interest is also one of the determinants of financial flows. Inflation or deflation in both a closed and open economy reflect a disequilibrium between *ex ante* savings and investment. As a result, varying the rate of interest with the objective of achieving price stability also ensures its tendency toward equality with the natural rate of interest, thus ensuring that "voluntary savings" are fully used and channeled toward investment.

Hence, the case for inflation targeting and its avowed superiority over other monetary policy regimes rests on the claim that it can deliver a combination of nominal stability with a tendency toward the full employment of resources. This can be proven for a canonical inflation targeting model for a closed economy model built from very stringent conditions with the additional proviso that the monetary authorities react to any inflationary threat by increasing the real rate of interest. The extension of that model to an open economy setting shows that, even in the best of worlds, the dynamics of an open economy put in doubt the well-behaved properties of inflation targeting frameworks and justify the need for intervention in the external sector. The mainstream recommendation is to complement inflation targeting regimes with macroprudential regulation. However, the main aim of macroprudential regulation is to sever the linkage between savings and investment, and it fails to address the challenges posed by the type of open economy dynamics highlighted in this chapter.

The chapter is divided into seven sections. The second section explains that the adoption of inflation targeting regimes followed a process of financial outward orientation and increased dependency on financial flows that led Latin American countries to adopt more flexible exchange rate regimes. This view is contrary to the traditional narrative that contends that more flexible exchange rate regimes were a consequence of the decision to adopt inflation targeting frameworks. The third section provides some stylized facts on inflation targeting regimes in Latin America. Using a canonical inflation targeting model for a closed economy, the fourth section demonstrates that the stability and determinacy of an equilibrium solution are sufficient to ensure price stability and the tendency toward the full employment of resources. The fifth section extends the canonical model to an open economy. The sixth section shows that the equilibrium solution for the canonical model for an open economy is determinate and stable. Even so, simulation exercises for the open economy model yield ambiguous and incoherent results. These results illustrate the complex dynamics of an open economy even within the context of a very simple model. In the guise of a conclusion, the last section describes the transmission mechanisms that underlie these dynamics and argues for comprehensive regulatory policies beyond those associated with mainstream macroprudential regulation.

TRADE AND FINANCIAL OPENNESS LED TO THE ADOPTION OF INFLATION TARGETING

In the 1990s, Latin American governments adopted economic policies associated with the Washington Consensus and its mantra: liberalize, deregulate, and privatize.[3] Latin America became, over time, an increasingly open region to external trade and foreign finance. The countries of the region completed their adhesion to the General Agreement on Tariffs and Trade and World Trade Organization, significantly reduced their tariff rates, and opened up their economies.[4]

Around the same time, Latin American countries implemented financial liberalization policies. The arguments supporting external financial liberalization are an extension of the classical static arguments of the gains in international trade to trade in financial assets. As explained by Henry (2007: 887–8):

> In the neoclassical model, liberalizing the capital account facilitates a more efficient allocation of resources and produces all kinds of salubrious effects. Resources flow from capital-abundant developed countries, where the return to capital is high. The flow of resources in developing countries reduces their cost of capital, triggering a temporary increase in investment and growth that permanently raises their standard of living.

This set of policies made LACs' performance highly dependent on the vagaries of the external sector and particularly on the behavior of financial flows. Financial flows, including both short- and long-term flows, began to increase in the 1990s and continued their upward trend throughout the 2000s, with temporary interruptions caused by the East Asian Crisis (1997–98) and the Global Financial Crisis (2008–09), and reached a peak in 2014 (Figure 3.1).

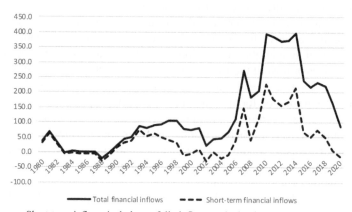

Note: Short-term inflows include portfolio inflows and other investment. Total financial inflows include short-term flows plus foreign direct investment inflows.
Source: Based on Economic Commission for Latin America and the Caribbean (ECLAC, 2021).

Figure 3.1   *Latin America: evolution of total financial gross inflows and short-term financial inflows, 1980–2021 (billions of US dollars)*

The reduction in financial flows after 2014 is explained in part by the fall in commodity prices and also responds to the declining trend in gross domestic product (GDP) growth and investment that the region experienced after 2010.[5]

This context pressured governments to adopt more flexible exchange rate regimes to accommodate this greater financial and trade openness. Reliance on financial flows, especially on short-term flows, could be disruptive to an economy. It could lead to increasing nominal and real volatility, cause unwanted contractions in the real economy through "sudden stops," and be a source of financial bubbles (Calvo, 1998, 2016). Moreover, toward the

Table 3.1   *Classification of Latin American countries by exchange rate regimes (1980, 1990, 1995, 2004, 2010, 2020)*

Year	Fixed exchange rate or "hard peg"	Intermediate regimes	Floating exchange rates
1980	Chile, Dominican Republic, Ecuador, El Salvador, Guatemala, Haiti, Honduras, Nicaragua, Panama, Paraguay, Venezuela	Mexico, Peru, Uruguay	Bolivia, Brazil
1990	Dominican Republic, Haiti, Honduras, Panama	Bolivia, Chile, Colombia, Costa Rica, Ecuador, Mexico, Nicaragua, Uruguay	Argentina, Brazil, El Salvador, Guatemala, Paraguay, Peru, Venezuela
1995	Argentina, El Salvador, Haiti, Panama, Venezuela	Bolivia, Brazil, Chile, Colombia, Costa Rica, Ecuador, Honduras, Nicaragua, Uruguay	Dominican Republic, Guatemala, Mexico, Paraguay, Peru
2000	Argentina, Ecuador, El Salvador, Haiti, Panama	Bolivia, Costa Rica, Honduras, Nicaragua, Uruguay, Venezuela	Brazil, Chile, Colombia, Dominican Republic, Guatemala, Mexico, Paraguay, Peru, Uruguay
2010	Ecuador, El Salvador, Haiti, Honduras, Panama, Venezuela	Bolivia, Costa Rica, Nicaragua	Argentina, Brazil, Chile, Colombia, Dominican Republic, Guatemala, Mexico, Paraguay, Peru, Uruguay
2020	Ecuador, El Salvador, Haiti, Panama	Bolivia, Costa Rica, Dominican Republic, Honduras, Nicaragua	Argentina, Brazil, Chile, Colombia, Guatemala, Mexico, Paraguay, Peru, Uruguay

Note: Intermediate regimes include crawling pegs, crawling bands, and stabilization arrangements.
Source: Prepared by the authors based on IMF (2020), and on the basis of official data.

middle and end of the 1990s, the experiences of Mexico (1995) and Thailand (1996) showed that adhering to a fixed exchange rate regime within a context of financial liberalization was unsustainable and led to economic and social crises. More flexible exchange rate arrangements could mitigate the impacts of these effects and lessen the possibility of crises. Flexible exchange rate regimes were defended, by the mainstream, on the basis that these provided an important shock absorber to external fluctuations preventing the passthrough of their effects to the domestic economy.

The available empirical evidence for the period 1980–2020 shows a clear shift from fixed exchange rate regimes or hard pegs to more flexible exchange rate regimes. Currently, Ecuador, El Salvador, Haiti, and Panama have this type of exchange rate regime. At the opposite end, the number of countries that have adopted floating exchange rate regimes expanded significantly (Table 3.1). Note that floating regimes did still imply some degree of intervention and fear floating.

SOME STYLIZED FACTS OF INFLATION TARGETING IN LATIN AMERICA

In response to this context of financial openness and greater exchange rate flexibility, several countries in Latin America adopted inflation targeting regimes. Inflation targeting is defined by the mainstream as a strategic monetary framework consisting of the public announcement of numerical targets for the rate of inflation, keeping in mind that the hierarchical goal of monetary policy is low and stable inflation, and maintaining a firm commitment to transparency and accountability.[6] Since 1999, more than half of Latin American countries have adopted inflation targeting frameworks (Table 3.2).

While inflation targeting proponents recognize that the primary focus of monetary policy is placed on domestic economic conditions, they argue that this monetary framework also creates the conditions that are consistent with the long-run stability of the exchange rate. According to their analysis, inflation targeting provides a superior alternative to exchange rate targeting which makes the economy more vulnerable to external conditions and lacks credibility as a nominal anchor and thus provides "little guidance to policy makers" (Bernanke et al., 1999: 250). The available evidence shows that, in fact, vulnerability to external conditions may arise in fixed, mixed, and floating exchange rate regimes. Moreover, an exercise for the period 1990–2010 for Latin America shows that 71 percent of all currency crises occurred during a period of managed or floating exchange rate regimes.[7]

In all cases, Latin American countries adopted inflation targeting regimes within a low-inflation context. Between 1971 and 1995, the rate of inflation remained, for the most part, above the two-digit level. Since 1995, the rate of

Table 3.2   Inflation targeting regimes in Latin America

Country	Adoption of target	Inflation measure	Target (2022)	Target horizon
Argentina	Jan 2017/Dec 2019	CPI	19.8% and declining	3 years
Brazil	June 1999	CPI	3.5% (+/− 1.5%)	12 months
Chile	Jan 1991	CPI	2%–4% centered at 3%	24 months
Colombia	Sept 1999	CPI	2%–4% centered at 3%	None
Guatemala	Jan 2005	CPI	4% (+/− 1%)	Medium term
Mexico	Jan 1999	CPI	3% (+/− 1%)	None
Peru	Jan 2002	CPI	1%–3%	None
Paraguay	May 2011	CPI	4% (+/− 2%)	N/A
Dominican Republic	Jan 2012	CPI	4% (+/− 1%)	24 months
Uruguay	Jan 2005	CPI	3%–6% centered at 5%	24 months
Costa Rica	Jan 2018	CPI	3% (+/− 1%)	24 months
Jamaica	Apr 2021	CPI	4%–6%	3 fiscal years

Note: The ellipsis represents data that are not available.
Source: Based on official information.

inflation at the regional level has remained below the two-digit level and even below the 5 percent level (Figure 3.2).

A country-level analysis shows a similar trend. The percentage of countries whose rates of growth of the GDP deflator and headline inflation were above 10 percent for the period 1970–95 reached 63 percent and 72 percent, respectively, declining to 9 percent and 16 percent for the period 1996–2021 (Figure 3.3). A further analysis shows that the decline in the rate of inflation between 1970–95 and 1996–2021 is also present in all the different regions of the developing world.[8]

This shows that the decline in inflation was not the result or success of a particular type of monetary framework, but was rather a worldwide phenomenon that was reflected, as expected, in the behavior of prices in Latin America and the Caribbean. The exceptions are Argentina and Venezuela, which returned to high levels of inflation in the 2000s.

The practice of inflation targeting consists of varying countercyclically the short-term policy rate of interest so that it converges to the natural rate of interest. This is tantamount to narrowing the gap between *ex ante* savings and investment. In a closed economy setting, this ensures an important result that is the basis for claiming the superiority of inflation targeting frameworks over

Source: World Bank Development Indicators (2022).

Figure 3.2   *Latin America and the Caribbean: annual consumer price inflation 1967–2021 (in percentages)*

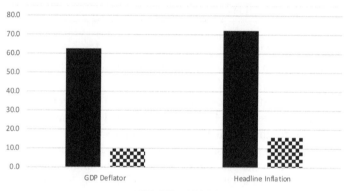

Source: World Bank Development Indicators (2022).

Figure 3.3   *Latin America and the Caribbean: percentage of countries with GDP deflator and headline inflation above 10 percent for 1970–1995 and 1996–2021*

other monetary policy regimes. This is the combination of nominal stability with the tendency toward the full employment of resources.

As shown in the following section, this result can be derived using a canonical inflation targeting model for a closed economy with all the stringent simplifications used in neoclassical economics. These include, among others, a continuum of households (which is another name for an infinitely lived consumer), competitive labor markets, ownership of firms by consumers, linear production functions (all inputs are perfect substitutes), and the literal absence of financial markets and financial frictions ("all financial considerations are swept under the rug"; Calvo, 2016, p. 56). The model consists of three equations: an aggregate demand function (IS curve), a Phillips curve, and a Taylor-based interest rate rule equation. The specification of the interest rule equation is crucial to prove that inflation targeting leads to the combination of nominal stability with the tendency toward the full employment of resources. Specifically, the monetary authorities must ensure that any rise in the rate of inflation must be offset by a concomitant increase in the real interest rate.

THE CANONICAL TARGETING INFLATION MODE: DETERMINACY AND STABILITY

The canonical targeting inflation model[9] is derived from the minimization of a central bank loss function subject to the constraints imposed by the structure of an economy. Formally, the loss function can be expressed as a standard optimal control problem according to which the path of the price level chosen is that which minimizes a quadratic loss function subject to the constraint imposed by the linear structure of the economy reflected in the Phillips and IS curves (Cecchetti and Kim, 2006: 176). Formally,

$$Min \; E_0 \sum_{t=0}^{\infty} \eta^t \left(\left(y_a - y_n \right)^2 + \beta \left(\pi_t - \pi^T \right)^2 - \gamma \left(i_t - i_{t-1} \right)^2 \right) \tag{3.1}$$

subject to

$$\pi_t = \mu E_t \pi_{t+1} + \alpha (y_a - y_n) \; \text{(Phillips curve)} \tag{3.2}$$

$$y_t^g = -\varphi \left(i_t - E\pi_{t+1} \right) + E y_{t+1}^g \; \left(\text{IS} \frac{\text{curve}}{\text{aggregate}} \text{demand function} \right) \tag{3.3}$$

To analyze the problem of determination and stability, it is useful to start from the system described by Equations 3.2 and 3.3 to which an additional interest rate rule equation is added to make the model determinate (θ_π and θ_y represent the elasticities of the nominal interest rate as a result of variations in inflation and output gaps):[10]

$$i_t = \theta_\pi \pi_t^g + \theta_y y_t^g \tag{3.4}$$

More generally, the system of Equations 3.2, 3.3, and 3.4 is a state space system and can be generalized to a system with n equations in first-order expectational differences, such as:

$$X_{t+1} = AX_t + BU_t \qquad (3.5)$$

By substituting Equation 3.4 in 3.3, and with some algebraic manipulation, we can express the expected rate of inflation and level of output at time $t + 1$ $(E_t\pi_{t+1}; E_t y_{t+1})$ as a function of the parameters of Equations 3.2, 3.3, and 3.4, and of the inflation rate and level of output at time t $(\pi_t; y_t)$. That is,

$$\begin{bmatrix} E_t\pi_{t+1} \\ EEy_{t+1} \end{bmatrix} = \begin{bmatrix} \dfrac{1}{\mu} & -\dfrac{\alpha}{\mu} \\ \varphi\theta_\pi - \dfrac{\varphi}{\mu} & 1 + \varphi\theta_y + \dfrac{\varphi\alpha}{\mu} \end{bmatrix} \begin{bmatrix} \pi_t \\ y_t \end{bmatrix} \qquad (3.6)$$

The system (Equation 3.6) has two control variables π_t y y_t^g, which means that two roots outside the unit circle are required for the system to have a unique solution. This in turn involves evaluating the system's characteristic polynomial $(p(\lambda) = \lambda^2 - \lambda Tr(A) + Det(A))$ for $\lambda = 1$ and $\lambda = -1$, which yields the following results (De la Fuente, 2000: 480–84):

$$p(1) = \theta_y\varphi \left(\dfrac{1-\mu}{\mu}\right) + \dfrac{\alpha\varphi}{\mu}(\theta_\pi - 1) > 0 \qquad (3.7)$$

$$p(-1) = 2 + \theta_\gamma\varphi + \dfrac{\alpha\theta\pi\varphi}{\mu} + \dfrac{\alpha\varphi}{\mu} + \dfrac{1}{\mu} + \dfrac{\theta_y\varphi}{\mu} + \dfrac{1}{\mu} > 0$$

From Equation 3.7 it can be easily seen that the characteristic root that corresponds to $p(-1)$ is outside the unit circle. For the system to be determined (i.e., for there to be a single equilibrium solution) it is also necessary that the second characteristic root (the one that corresponds to $p(1)$) is also outside the unit circle.

This requires that the following interest rate rule condition be met: $\theta_\pi > 1$ in Equation 3.7. In other words, the necessary and sufficient condition for the determinacy of equilibrium in an inflation targeting regime for a closed economy is that, in the face of increases in the inflation rate (π_t) or in the expected inflation rate $(E\pi_{t+1})$, the authorities react by raising the monetary policy interest rate (i_t) above the increase in the inflation rate (π_t) in such a way as to increase the real interest rate (i.e., $i_t - E\pi_{t+1}$). This is the Taylor principle.

For example, starting from an equilibrium situation where the inflation rate is equal to its target $(\pi_t = \pi^T \Leftrightarrow \pi_t^g = 0)$ and where output is equal to its natural level $\left(y_t = y_t^n \Leftrightarrow y_t^g = 0\right)$, assume that an increase in one of the components of output (either as a result of exogenous factors or from a deliberate economic policy decision) will lead to an increase in y_t above its natural level (i.e., $y_t > y_t^n$). According to Equation 3.3, this will result in an increase in the rate of inflation π_t and the expected inflation rate $E\left(\pi_{t+1}\right)$ above the target inflation rate (π^T). Under this scenario, a more than proportional increase in the interest rate of monetary policy $\left(i_t\right)$ relative to the rate of inflation will mitigate inflationary pressures in such a way that $\pi_t \rightarrow \pi^T$ and, at the same time, will make it possible to reduce output so that it approaches its natural level (i.e., $y_t \rightarrow y_t^n$; Equation 3.4 above).

The determinacy and stability of the model can be illustrated didactically by calibrating the model, including the interest rate equation (IRE), assuming $\theta_\pi > 1$ y $\theta_\pi < 1$ and with/without the IRE. The chosen values of the parameters correspond to the standard values and ranges used in the inflation targeting literature. For analytical purposes and without loss of generalization, it is assumed that $\pi^T = 0$ (i.e., the inflation target is equal to 0), an assumption that will be maintained throughout the rest of the calibration exercises. Based on these parameters, we computed the characteristic polynomial and obtained the characteristic roots (Table 3.4).[11]

As shown in Table 3.4, the canonical inflation targeting model (with IRE and with $\theta_\pi > 1$) has two unit roots outside the unit circle; therefore, the model has a unique solution and is stable. Table 3.4 also illustrates the importance of the assumption $\theta_\pi > 1$, since when $\theta_\pi < 1$, as assumed in the second calibration exercise, the model has one root inside the unit circle and another outside the unit circle and is therefore indeterminate. Obviously, without an interest rate rule there is no possibility of determinacy or stability as evidenced by the last three calibration exercises.

Determinacy and stability permit the derivation of the fundamental properties of inflation targeting frameworks on which its alleged superiority rests vis-à-vis other monetary policy regimes, namely, the coexistence of price stability with a tendency toward the full employment of resources.[12]

EXTENDING THE CANONICAL INFLATION TARGETING MODEL TO AN OPEN ECONOMY

The canonical closed economy model can be extended to the case of an open economy by introducing the nominal exchange rate into the inflation equation, and the real exchange rate into the aggregate demand function.[13]

Monetary policy challenges in Latin America

Table 3.4   *Calibration exercise for the canonical inflation targeting model*

With and without interest rate equation (IRE)	Parameters						Characteristics roots		Number and type of variable		Solution	
	μ	α	φ	θ	θ_y	θ_π	λ_i	λ_i	Predetermined	Control	Determinate or indeterminate	Stable or unstable
1. With IRE	1.00	1.00	1.0		0.5	1.5	1.50	2.00	0	2	Determinate	Stable
2. With IRE	1.00	1.00	1.0		0.5	0.5	0.72	2.78	0	2	Indeterminate	
3. Without IRE	0.99	0.34	0.5		...	...	0.66	1.50	0	2	Indeterminate	
4. Without IRE	0.99	0.50	0.5		...	...	0.60	1.60	0	2	Indeterminate	
5. Without IRE	1.00	1.00	1.0		...	...	0.38	2.60	0	2	Indeterminate	

Source: Authors' elaboration based on Adjemian et al. (2022).

The real exchange rate (q_t) enters the model in the same way as output (y_t) and the inflation rate (π_t), that is, as an expectational or control variable. The real exchange rate is specified as a function of the expected future real exchange rate (q_{t+1}), of the domestic (r_t) and external (r_t^e) real interest rate differential, and as a function of an exchange rate risk premium (z_t). Formally,

$$q_t = \phi E_t q_{t+1} - \varrho(r_t^* - r_t) + \sigma z_t \Leftrightarrow \tag{3.8}$$

$$q_t = \phi E_t q_{t+1} - \varrho\left[\left(i_t^* - E_t \pi_{t+1}^*\right) - \left(i_t - E_t \pi_{t+1}\right)\right] + \sigma z_t$$

where:

i_t = *nominal domestic interest rate*
i_t^* = *nominal external interest rate*
π_t^* = *external inflation rate*
$\phi, \sigma > 0, \varrho < 0.$

The specification of the real exchange rate is derived from the portfolio approach to the exchange rate. It postulates that arbitrage in asset markets adjusts the exchange rate. According to this approach, the exchange rate behaves no longer as the price of a good, as in the more traditional purchasing power parity (PPP) theory, but as that of an asset. That is, it responds to potential capital gains or losses in future markets. In this approach, the future exchange rate (e_t^f) is equal to the current nominal exchange rate plus its expected variation (appreciation or depreciation; i.e., $e_t^f = e_t + \Delta e_t^e$). Arbitrage in asset markets ensures that the equilibrium condition $e_t(1 + i_t) = e_t^f(1 + i_t^*)$ is met. From this it follows that $e_t = \frac{\Delta e_t^f}{(i_t - i_t^*)}$ gives way to the interest rate parity theorem in its two variants (covered and uncovered interest parity; see Taylor and Eatwell, 2000).

The first variant (covered interest parity) refers to the possibility of "hedging" against future variations in the exchange rate and thus avoids incurring in losses, and can, with due qualifications, be applicable to developed financial and futures markets. In the case of the uncovered interest parity, changes in the exchange rate can only be "hedged" by variations in the interest rate differential. Thus, the interest differential varies when expected variations in the exchange rate occur.

Starting from the strongest variant interest rate parity theorem variant, the uncovered interest rate parity, the differential between the nominal domestic and external interest rates $\left(i_t - i_t^*\right)$, is equal to the difference between the expected future and current spot nominal exchange rate $\left(E_t e_{t+1} - e_t\right)$. That is,

$$i_t - i_t^* = E_t e_{t+1} - e_t \tag{3.9}$$

This implies that interest rates (rates of return) in different financial centers can be the same even if they were not covered by a futures contract. If the covered interest parity condition is added to the uncovered parity theorem, then the equation indicates that the exchange rate established in the futures market is equal to the expected exchange rate $\left(E_t e_{t+1} = fe_{t+1}\right)$.

However, there is no reason for this condition to be fulfilled even under the assumption of perfect mobility of financial flows. In fact, perfect mobility of financial flows does not imply perfect substitution of financial assets. As Smithin (2003: 166) explains:

> In practice, even in conditions in which financial capital is completely mobile in a technical sense, this condition can only hold up to the inclusion of what is usually called a "currency risk premium" (Frankel, 1992), which is required by foreign investors if they are to hold assets denominated in the domestic currency. Even if financial capital can cross borders electronically "at the push of a button," it must still be the case that assets denominated in different currencies, and whose exchange rates are liable to change, are still not perfect substitutes. Even given "perfect capital mobility" there need not be "perfect asset substitutability." It continues to matter, in other words, precisely whose promises to pay the investor hold at any given moment (US dollars, Canadian dollars, Mexican pesos, Euros or yen).

Following this reasoning, Equation 3.9 can be modified to include a foreign exchange risk premium $\left(z_t\right)$ such that,

$$i_t - i_t^* = E_t e_{t+1} - e_t + z_t \tag{3.10}$$

From 3.10, the equation for the nominal exchange rate is obtained,

$$e_t = E_t e_{t+1} - \left(i_t - i_t^*\right) + z_t \tag{3.11}$$

And expressing Equation 3.11 in real terms yields the following expression for the real exchange rate (q_t),

$$q_t q_t = \phi E_t q_{t+1} - \varrho\left(r_t - r_t^*\right) + \sigma z_t \tag{3.12}$$

Equation 3.12 indicates that the real exchange rate increases (depreciates) in the face of increases in the external real interest rate $\left(r_t^*\right)$ and the foreign exchange risk premium $\left(z_t\right)$, and of decreases in the domestic real interest rate (r_t). It also shows that real domestic interest rates can deviate from external interest rates by a proportion equivalent to the appreciation of the real exchange rate (i.e., $r_t - r_t^* = E_t q_{t+1} - q_t \Rightarrow r_t > r_t^* = q_t < E_t q_{t+1}$).

DETERMINACY AND STABILITY IN AN OPEN ECONOMY

According to the above, the inflation targeting model for an open economy consists of the following equations,

$$\pi_t = \mu E_t \pi_{t+1} + \alpha (y_a - y_n) + \omega \Delta e_t + \varepsilon_{1t} \tag{3.2'}$$

$$y_t^g = -\varphi \left(i_t - E\pi_{t+1} \right) + E y_{t+1}^g + \delta q_t + \varepsilon_{2t} \tag{3.3'}$$

$$i_t = \theta_\pi \pi_t^g + \theta_y y_t^g \tag{3.4}$$

$$q_t = \phi E_t q_{t+1} - \varrho (r_t - r_t^*) + \sigma z_t + \varepsilon_{3t} \tag{3.12'}$$

We further assume that the real interest rate r_t is expressed in Fisherian terms as the difference between the nominal interest rate (i_t) minus the expected rate of inflation $(E_t \pi_{t+1})$. That is,

$$r_t = i_t - E_t \pi_{t+1} \tag{3.13}$$

On the other hand, the nominal exchange rate (e_t) can be expressed as the difference between the real exchange rate (q_t) and the difference between the domestic (P_t) and external price level (P_t^e):

$$e_t = q_t + P_t - P_t^e \tag{3.14}$$

Expressing the model as a system of first-order expectational differences, we have:

$$
\begin{bmatrix} 1 & \varphi & 0 \\ 0 & \mu & 0 \\ 0 & \varrho & \phi \end{bmatrix}
\begin{bmatrix} E_t y_{t+1} \\ E_t \pi_{t+1} \\ E_t q_{t+1} \end{bmatrix}
=
\begin{bmatrix} (1 - \varphi \theta_y) & \varphi \theta_\pi & -\delta \\ -\alpha & (1 + \omega) & \omega \\ \varrho \theta_y & \lambda \theta_\pi & 1 \end{bmatrix}
\begin{bmatrix} y_t^g \\ \pi_t \\ q_t \end{bmatrix}
+
$$

$$
\begin{bmatrix} 0 & 0 & 0 \\ 0 & -\omega & 0 \\ -\varrho & 0 & -\sigma \end{bmatrix}
\begin{bmatrix} r_t^e \\ q_{t-1} + \pi_t^e \\ z_t \end{bmatrix}
+
\begin{bmatrix} \varepsilon_{1t} \\ \varepsilon_{2t} \\ \varepsilon_{3t} \end{bmatrix}
$$

Establishing the determinacy/indeterminacy and stability/instability of this system requires analyzing the properties of the matrix that contains the relevant parameters:

$$
A = \begin{bmatrix} \left(1 - \varphi\theta_y\right) & \varphi\theta_\pi & -\delta \\ -\alpha & (1+\omega) & \omega \\ \varrho\theta_y & \lambda\theta_\pi & 1 \end{bmatrix} \begin{bmatrix} 1 & \varphi & 0 \\ 0 & \mu & 0 \\ 0 & \varrho & \phi \end{bmatrix}^{-1} =
$$

$$
= \begin{bmatrix} \theta_y\varphi + \dfrac{\alpha\varphi}{\mu+1} & \theta_\pi\varphi - \dfrac{\varphi(\omega+1)}{\mu} & -\delta - \dfrac{\omega\varphi}{\mu} \\[2mm] \dfrac{-\alpha}{\mu} & \dfrac{\omega+1}{\mu} & \dfrac{\omega}{\mu} \\[2mm] \dfrac{\varrho\theta_y}{\phi} + \dfrac{\alpha\varrho}{\mu\phi} & \dfrac{\varrho(\omega+1)}{\mu\phi} + \dfrac{\varrho\theta_\pi}{\phi} & \dfrac{1}{\phi} - \dfrac{\varrho\omega}{\mu\phi} \end{bmatrix}
$$

Following Brooks (2004), the necessary and sufficient conditions for the determination of a 3 x 3 square matrix are (see also Ascari and Ropele, 2009):

$|D(A)| > 1$

$|T(A) + D(A)| > M(A) + 1$

$|D^2(A) + T(A)D(A) + M(A)| > 1$

where, D = determinant, T = trace, and M = the sum of the principal minors of order 2 of the matrix A. For our particular case, the determinant (D), trace (T), and the minor main order 2 and its determinant are:

$$
D(A) = \frac{\omega + \theta_\pi(\alpha\varphi + -\varrho\omega + \omega\varphi + \alpha\varrho\delta) + \theta_y(\varphi + \varrho\delta + \omega\varphi + \varrho\omega\delta) + 1}{\mu\phi}
$$

$$
T(A) = \theta_y\varphi + \frac{1}{\phi} + \frac{(\omega + 1 + \alpha\varphi)}{\mu} - \frac{\varrho\omega}{\mu\phi} + 1
$$

$$
M(A) = \frac{\omega + \theta_y\varphi\left(1 + \omega\right) + \alpha\varphi\theta_\pi + 1}{\mu}
$$

Due to the complexity involved in obtaining an analytical solution, we proceeded to analyze the determination and stability of the system by calibrating the model according to two general scenarios.

The first scenario contemplates the case in which open economy conditions are not relevant to the trajectory and determination of equilibrium (quasi-closed economy scenario). According to this scenario, on the one hand, the parameters corresponding to the case of a closed economy are maintained at values similar to those in Table 3.4: $\mu = 1$, $\alpha = 0.34$, y $\varphi = 0.5$, $\theta_y = 0.5$, and $\theta_\pi = 1.5$. On the other hand, the parameters for an open economy are set at very small, insignificant values. For analytical purposes, ω, ϱ, ϕ, and δ are equal to 0.02.[14]

The second scenario includes an open economy context explicitly, and consists of assuming that the prevailing conditions in the external sector are as important as those of the domestic economy (open economy scenario). In this scenario r, $\mu = 1$, $\alpha = 0.34$, and $\varphi = 0.5$; $\theta_y = 0.5$ and $\theta_\pi = 1.5$; and ω, ϱ, ϕ, $\delta = 0.6$.

In both scenarios, as shown in Table 3.5, the conditions to establish the determinacy of the system are met. In addition, to complement the analysis, the characteristic vectors corresponding to the characteristic polynomial of the matrix containing the parameters were computed. The solutions when both real and complex roots are considered show that the system is stable.[15]

Once the conditions required for determinacy and stability were met, the dynamics of the open economy were analyzed by simulating its behavior through standard exogenous shocks $\left(\varepsilon_{1t}, \varepsilon_{2t,} \varepsilon_{3t} /z_t \right)$ in the inflation equation (π_t), real exchange rate (q_t), and nominal interest rate (i_t). The exercise also contemplates shocks to the real exchange rate. The shocks are specified as:

$$\varepsilon_{1t} = \rho_{1t} \varepsilon_{1t-1} + u_{1t} \tag{3.15}$$

$$\varepsilon_{2t} = \rho_{2t} \varepsilon_{2t-1} + u_{2t}$$

$$\varepsilon_{3t}/z_t = \rho_{3t} \varepsilon_{3t-1} + u_{3t}$$

where $u_{it-n} \sim N(0,1)$ and $0 \leq \rho_{it-n} < 1$. In all simulations, shocks were assumed to change by one standard deviation. All the simulations were carried out with the Dynare (2015) program. In the quasi-closed economy scenario, the parameters (ρ_{it}) associated with the inflation and the interest rate $\left(\varepsilon_{1t}, \varepsilon_{2t} \right)$ take on a value equal to 1, while in the case of the exchange rate, the parameter associated with the shock in the exchange rate $\left(\varepsilon_{3t} \right)$ has a value of 0.2. In line with the logic of the model, the shocks $\left(\varepsilon_{1t}, \varepsilon_{2t,} \varepsilon_{3t} /z_t \right)$ are uncorrelated.

In the open economy scenario, the parameters associated (ρ_{it}) with inflation and the interest rate $(\varepsilon_{1t}, \varepsilon_{2t})$ take on a value equal to 1, while in the case of the exchange rate, the associated parameter with the shock in the exchange rate (ε_{3t}) takes on a value of 1.5. In other words, in the second case, the conditions of the external sector have a greater weight in the economy than those associated with domestic conditions.

Table 3.5   *Calibration exercise for the inflation targeting model in open economies (determination and stability analysis)*

Parameters for the closed economy model					Parameters associated with the exchange rate				Variables		D	T+D	M+1	$D^2 + TD + M1$	λ_i
μ	α	φ	θ_y	θ_π	ω	δ	ϕ	ϱ	Predetermined	Control					
Quasi-closed economy															
1	0.34	0.5	0.5	1.5	0.02	0.02	0.02	0.02	0	3	102.0	154.8	3.0	1.57+e04	1.50 1.35 49.97
Open economy															
1	0.34	0.5	0.5	1.5	0.60	0.60	0.60	0.60	0	3	4.7	9.2	3.9	46.7	1.49±0.94i 1.53+0.00i r = 1.75 and 1.53

Source: Authors' elaboration based on Matlab with Dynare (2015).

The results of the simulations for both scenarios are summarized in the two correlation matrices (Tables 3.6 and 3.7) which show the responses of inflation, output, and the interest rate to the respective shocks. Following the logic of inflation targeting models (dynamic stochastic general equilibrium models), the responses of the variables of inflation, output, and the short-term interest rate to shocks are modeled in terms of deviations from their natural levels, and equilibrium is characterized by the fact that $y_t^g = 0 \iff y_t = y_n$ (*natural level of output*); $\pi_t = 0$, since it is assumed in this analysis that the inflation target $\pi^T = 0$; and $q_t = 0 \iff q_t = q_n$ (natural level of the real exchange rate).

As expected, the shocks in the inflation rate and interest rate $(\varepsilon_{1t}, \varepsilon_{2t})$ have a negative correlation with the product gap (y^g). In the same way, the inflation rate and the interest rate (π_t, i_t) have a negative correlation with the product gap (y^g), which obviously implies that the interest rate and inflation (in terms of deviations) move in the same direction. Thus, an increase in the inflation rate causes an increase in the nominal interest rate higher than the inflation rate (i.e., the real interest rate increases due to the stability condition mentioned above, $\theta_\pi > 1$), which generates a contraction in the product.

However, a shock to the real exchange rate equation, yields ambiguous results. One associated, say, with an increase in the exchange rate risk premium (as proposed in the exchange rate specification ε_{3t}/z_t) is positively correlated with inflation and the interest rate. At the same time, the real exchange rate shock has a positive effect on output, despite the rise in the interest rates.

The same phenomenon occurs with an increase in the real exchange gap, which (q_t^g) is positively correlated with the product gap (y^g), indicating that a depreciation (appreciation) leads to an increase in output above (below) its natural level. At the same time, the real exchange rate is positively correlated with the interest rate. In this case, as in the case of the shock (ε_{3t}/z_t) to the real exchange rate equation, the product increases (decreases) in the face of a depreciation (appreciation) despite the increase in the interest rate.

If the shock ceases to be transitory, unless the real exchange rate is stabilized, there will be a situation of divergence of the product with respect to its natural level. In this case, stability produces de facto unstable results.

The above analysis shows that, in an open economy, the canonical inflation targeting model has a single (determined) solution, and that this solution is stable. However, even if it is determined and stable, the model produces, in the case of an open economy with a flexible exchange rate, contradictory and incoherent results that call into question its core properties. These include, among the most important, that the output gap is both positive and negative, that variations in the nominal and real interest rate do not impact on the output

Table 3.6   *Correlation matrix for quasi-closed economy*
$\mu = 1; \alpha = 0.34, y\,\varphi = 0.5; \theta_y = 0.5; \theta_\pi = 1.5; \omega, \varrho, \phi,$
$\delta = 0.6; \rho_{it\text{-}n} = 0.6$

	y^g	π_t	i_t	rer_t	ε_{1t}	ε_{2t}	$/\varepsilon_{3t}$
q^g_t	0.83	−0.96	−0.77	1.00	...	...	...
ε_{1t}	−0.97	0.83	0.94	−0.92	1.00	...	...
ε_{2t}	−0.22	−0.55	0.23	0.35	0.00	1.00	...
$/\varepsilon_{3t}$	0.05	0.06	0.22	0.11	0.00	0.00	1.00

Source: Authors' elaboration based on Matlab with Dynare (2015).

Table 3.7   *Correlation matrix for open economy*
$\mu = 1; \alpha = 0.34, y\,\varphi = 0.5; \theta_y = 0.5; \theta_\pi = 1.5; \omega, \varrho, \phi, \delta = 0.6$

	y^g	π_t	i_t	rer_t	ε_{1t}	ε_{2t}	$/\varepsilon_{3t}$
q^g_t	0.81	−0.42	0.24	1.00	...	...	...
ε_{1t}	−0.92	0.77	0.50	−0.71	1.0	...	...
ε_{2t}	−0.21	−0.51	0.12	0.27	0.0	1.0	...
$/\varepsilon_{3t}$	0.32	0.40	0.86	0.65	0.0	0.0	1.0

Source: Authors' elaboration based on Matlab with Dynare (2015).

gap, and that the interest rate may be inoperative as an instrument to stabilize aggregate demand.

OPEN ECONOMY DYNAMICS AND REGULATION

The empirical analysis shows that the dynamics of an open economy question the well-behaved properties of inflation targeting frameworks. The open economy context puts in doubt countercyclicality and the possibility of achieving (in the best of worlds) full employment with price stability. The analysis underscores the need to control for movements in external variables, such as the exchange rate premium and the exchange rate itself, which are obviously tied to internal conditions, but also, to a great extent, to external financial conditions.

In the case of Latin America and the Caribbean, as in other parts of the developing world, the use of capital controls has been rendered extremely difficult, if not impossible, to implement due to the existing web of trade and investment agreements. As an alternative option, countries have, in general, opted to increase international reserves as the main external buffer mechanism and to a lesser degree have relied on exchange rate interventions. Between 2000 and 2021, the stock of international reserves for the Latin American and Caribbean regions expanded from US$163 billion to US$826 billion (Figure 3.4).

The open economy inflation targeting model used in this chapter exemplifies only a part of the complications introduced by the external sector. The focus has been placed on the relationship between the exchange rate premium, the real exchange rate and output, the interest policy rate, and the rate of inflation. But obviously for countries such as those of Latin America and the Caribbean, which have a high degree of trade and financial openness, there are further effects and ramifications for the rest of the sectors, including the government, financial, and non-financial corporate sectors.

The exchange rate is a key variable in the transmission of impulses that emanate from the rest of the world, especially the developed world, and to which developing countries, including Latin American ones, are highly vulnerable due to the growing dependence of the government, the financial, and

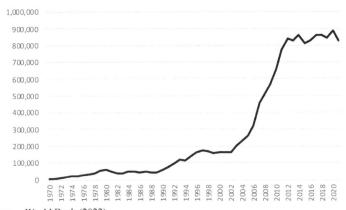

Source: World Bank (2022).

Figure 3.4   *Latin America and the Caribbean. International Reserves (including Gold), 1970–2021 (in millions of US dollars)*

the non-financial corporate sectors on international capital markets and thus on external debt for finance. Variations in the nominal exchange rate (which is directly affected by the exchange rate premium) have a statistically significant correlation with country risk: exchange rate depreciations are accompanied by increased sovereign risk. This increases the cost of external indebtedness while, at the same time, it narrows the policy space to expand aggregate demand.

Exchange rate depreciations also have negative effects on the balance sheets of financial institutions and of those in the non-financial corporate sector by increasing liabilities. These effects are compounded when collaterals are denominated in local currency, and by the fact that these sectors operate with currency mismatches (see Borio, 2019; Chui et al., 2016, 2018). In addition, the empirical evidence shows that, in the case of the non-financial corporate sector, leverage and investment exhibit a negative relationship beyond a certain threshold (Pérez Caldentey and Vernengo, 2020). Finally, exchange rates are distributive variables, and depreciation affects the real wage and has important impacts on economic growth (Pérez Caldentey and Vernengo, 2017) and inflation.

These transmission mechanisms can lead to a context of financial fragility, creating significant challenges for the management of monetary policy through inflation targeting. The existing consensus in mainstream economics recommends complementing the use of the short-term rate of interest with "macroprudential regulatory tools" to address the existence of financial vulnerabilities.

However, in practical terms, macroprudential regulation consists of a series of measures not necessarily interconnected or articulated, which focus mostly on the banking system, to limit credit expansion, improve solvency, decrease interconnectedness, and avoid excessive leverage. As explained by Shin (2010), the main objective of macroprudential regulation is to ensure that the financial system conforms to its traditional intermediary function, by severing the link between voluntary savings and investment and avoiding disruptions in the chain of causation running from savings to investment. Thus, the ultimate objective of macroprudential regulation is simply to facilitate the convergence of the market to the natural rate of interest. In this sense, it merely reinforces the logic of the inflation targeting model which, when applied to an open economy, leads to incoherent and contradictory results, as shown in this chapter.

NOTES

1.   The opinions expressed here are the authors' own and may not coincide with the institutions with which they are affiliated.

2.   See Pérez Caldentey and Vernengo (2013, 2019, 2020).
3.   See Rodrik (2006). The original Washington Consensus consisted of nine reform policies: 1) fiscal discipline; 2) reorientation of public expenditure; 3) tax reform; 4) liberalization of financial markets; 5) competitive exchange rate; 6) liberalization of trade policies; 7) openness to foreign direct investment; 8) privatization; and 9) deregulation and secure property rights (Williamson, 1990).
4.   Between 1995 and 1997 all Latin American countries except Cuba adhered to the World Trade Organization (WTO). The regional average tariff rate fell from roughly 37 percent in the 1980s to 12 percent at the beginning of the 1990s (see Moreno-Brid and Pérez Caldentey, 2010).
5.   Between 2010 and 2019 the rate of growth of regional GDP and gross formation of fixed capital fell from 6.4 percent to 0.7 percent, and from 12.8 percent to −1.1 percent, respectively.
6.   See Bernanke and Woodford (2005), Bernanke et al. (1999), and Svensson (2007).
7.   This result was obtained using the database of Laeven and Valencia (2018).

8.   *Table 3.3*   *Headline consumer price inflation for developing regions, 1970–1995 and 1996–2021 (percentages)*

Developing regions	1970–95	1996–2021
East Asia and the Pacific	8.0	3.5
Economic Commission for Africa	85.1	8.4
Latin America and the Caribbean	12.2	3.8
Middle East and North Africa	7.6	3.2
South Asia	9.4	6.1
Sub-Saharan Africa	10.9	5.5

Source: World Bank (2022).

9.   The mathematics follow the methodology of Blanchard and Khan (1980). See also Di Pietro (2011) and Duffy (2007).
10.   The Taylor rule can also be derived from an optimum monetary rule. See, for example, Svensson (1997) and Woodford (2003). Kapinos and Hanson (2011) follow a similar approach to ours.
11.   The procedure was performed using MATLAB, version 7.
12.   This is another way to express the so-called "divine coincidence" (Blanchard and Gali, 2005).
13.   Usually, much of the analysis specifies a canonical model under this hypothesis. The influence of the exchange rate is not included as an argument in the objective function of the central bank. Rather, it affects the target function through its direct impact on inflation and/or output gaps $\left(\pi_t - \pi^T \text{ and } y_a - y_n \right)$. This presupposes that monetary authorities act only when the effect of exchange rate variations is manifested in changes in these gaps (De Gregorio et al., 2005). This view is supported by the fact that the central bank should be concerned with the exchange rate, per se, only when its variation affects price stability. In addition, including the exchange rate in the objective function of the central bank can pose inconsistencies in the management of monetary policy insofar as it entails,

even implicitly, the presupposition that the monetary authority has two nominal anchors (the price level and the exchange rate; Soikkeli, 2002; Stephens, 2006). See Caputo (2009) for a discussion on the inclusion of the exchange rate in inflation targeting models.

14.   The parameter $\alpha = 0.34$ is derived from neoclassical microeconomic foundations (see Sienknecht, 2011).

15.   In the case of real solutions for all cases considered, there are three characteristic vectors greater than one corresponding to the three control variables $(E_t \pi_{t+1}, E_t y_{t+1}, E_t q_{t+1})$. In the case of complex roots, the determination of stability conditions first requires the transformation of Cartesian coordinates to polar coordinates, which allows for transforming any complex number from Cartesian form (i.e., $\alpha \pm i\theta$) to an equivalent trigonometric form ($r(\cos w \pm i \sin \omega)$). According to this method, the stability condition is given by the modulus of the complex number $r = +(\alpha^2 + \theta^2)^{\frac{1}{2}}$ and requires that $r > 1$.

REFERENCES

Adjemian, S., Bastani, H., Juillard, M., Karamé, F., Mihoubi, F., Mutschler, W., Pfeifer, J., Ratto, M., Rion, N. & Villemot, S. (2022), "Dynare: Reference Manual, Version 5" Dynare Working Papers 72, CEPREMAP

Ascari, G., & Ropele, T. (2009) Trend inflation, Taylor principle, and indeterminacy. *Journal of Money, Credit and Banking* 41(8), 1557–84.

Bernanke, B.S., & Woodford, M. (eds) (2005) The inflation targeting debate. NBER. University of Chicago Press.

Bernanke, B.S., Laubach, T., Mishkin, F.S., & Posen, A.S. (1999) *Inflation targeting. Lessons from the international experience.* Princeton University Press.

Blanchard, O., & Gali, J. (2005, November) Real wage rigidities and the New Keynesian Model. NBER Working Paper 11806.

Blanchard, O., & Khan, C.M. (1980) The solution of linear difference models under rational expectations. *Econometrica* 48(5), 1305–11.

Borio, C. (2019) Monetary policy frameworks in EMEs: inflation targeting, the exchange rate and financial stability. BIS Annual Economic Report 2019. Bank for International Settlements. www.bis.org/publ/arpdf/ar2019e2.pdf (accessed 15 January 2023)

Brooks, B.P. (2004) Linear stability conditions for a first-order three-dimensional discrete dynamic. *Applied Mathematics Letters* 17(4), 463–6.

Calvo, G.A. (1998) Capital flows and capital-market crises: the simple economics of sudden stops. *Journal of Applied Economics* 1(1), 35–54.

Calvo, G.A. (2016) *Liquidity in times of crisis.* MIT Press.

Caputo, R. (2009) External shocks and monetary policy. Does it pay to respond to exchange rate deviations? *Revista de Análisis Económico* 24(1), 55–99.

Cecchetti, S.G., & Kim, J. (2006) Inflation targeting, price path targeting, and output variability, in Bernanke, B.S., & Woodford, M. (eds), *The inflation targeting debate.* University of Chicago Press, 173–95.

Chui, M., Kuruc, E., & Turner, P. (2016) A new dimension to currency mismatches in the emerging markets: non-financial companies. BIS Working Paper No. 550.

Chui, M., Kuruc, E., & Turner, P. (2018) Leverage and currency mismatches: non-financial companies in the emerging markets. Special Issue of *The World Economy*: Global Trade Policy 41(12), 1–19.

De Gregorio, J., Tokman, A., & Valdés, R. (2005, August) Tipo de cambio flexible con metas de inflación en Chile: experiencia y temas de interés. *Documento de Política Económica* No 14. Banco Central de Chile.

De la Fuente, A. (2000) *Mathematical Methods and Models for Economists*. New York: Cambridge University Press

Di Pietro, M. (2011) Blanchard–Khan conditions. Mimeo.

Duffy, J. (2007) Monetary policy rules. Mimeo.

Dynare (2015) Home page. www.dynare.org/

Frankel, J.A. (1992) International capital mobility: a review. *American Economic Review*, 82, 197–202.

Henry, P.B. (2007) Capital account liberalization: theory, evidence and speculation. *Journal of Economic Literature* 45(4), 887–935.

International Monetary Fund (IMF) (2020) Annual report on exchange arrangements and exchange restrictions 2019. IMF.

Kapinos, P., & Hanson, M.S. (2011) Targets in the Taylor rule: inflation, speed, limit, or price level? Mimeo. https://onlinelibrary.wiley.com/doi/abs/10.1111/j.1465-7287 .2011.00270.x

Laeven, L., & Valencia, F. (2018) Systemic banking crises revisited. www.imf.org/ en/Publications/WP/Issues/2018/09/14/Systemic-Banking-Crises-Revisited-46232 (accessed 16 January 2023)

Morenio-Brid, J.C. & Pérez Calddentey Esteban (2010) Trade and Economic Growth: A Latin American Perspective on Rhetoric and Reality. In Mark Setterfield (ed.), *Handbook of Alternative Theories of Economic Growth*. Edward Elgar Publishing.

Pérez Caldentey, E., & Vernengo, M. (2013) Is inflation targeting operative in an open economy setting? *Review of Keynesian Economics* 1(3), 347–69.

Pérez Caldentey, E., & Vernengo, M. (2017) Wage-led, debt-led growth in an open economy. *Review of Keynesian Economics* 5(3), 307–35.

Pérez Caldentey, E., & Vernengo, M. (2019) The historical evolution of monetary policy in Latin America. In Battilossi, S., Cassis, Y., & Yago, K. (eds), *Handbook of the history of money and currency*, 1–28, Springer. https://doi.org/10.1007/978-981 -10-0622-7_44-2

Pérez Caldentey, E., & Vernengo, M. (2020) El retorno del banco central interven-cionista: El péndulo de los regímenes monetarios en América Latina. *Ensayos Económicos* 75, 5–29.

Rodrik, D. (2006) Goodbye Washington consensus, hello Washington confusion? A review of the World Bank's economic growth in the 1990s: learning from a decade of reforms. *Journal of Economic Literature* 44(4), 973–87.

Shin, H. (2010, March) Financial intermediation and the post-crisis financial system. BIS Working Paper No. 304.

Sienknecht, S. (2011) The theory of new Keynesian macroeconomics. Complementary slides for the lecture "Advanced Macoreoconmics." Department of Economics, Friedrich-Schiller-Universität, Germany.

Smithin, J. (2003) *Controversies in monetary economics*. Edward Elgar Publishing.

Soikkeli, J. (2002) The inflation targeting framework in Norway. IMF Working Paper WP/02/184.

Stephens, D. (2006) Should monetary policy attempt to reduce exchange rate volatility in New Zealand? Reserve Bank of New Zealand Discussion Paper 2006/05.

Svensson, L. (1997) Inflation forecast targeting: implementation and monitoring infla-tion targets. *European Economic Review* 41(6), 1111–46.

Svensson, L. (2007) Inflation targeting. Mimeo for L. Blum & S. Durlauf (eds), *The new Palgrave dictionary of economics*, 2nd edn Palgrave.
Taylor, L., & Eatwell, J. (2000) *Global finance at risk*. The New Press.
Williamson, J. (ed.) (1990) *Latin American adjustment. How much has happened?* Institute for International Economics.
Woodford, M. (2003) *Interest and prices*. Princeton University Press.
World Bank (2022) *World Bank development indicators*. World Bank.

4. Limitations of monetary policies in open developing economies: external capital inflows and sterilisation policies

Noemi Levy-Orlik

Central banks were created to perform the function of banker to governments,[1] followed by the roles of lender of last resort (Bagehot, 1873) and international reserves guardian. The instruments of monetary policy throughout history oscillated between the control of money supply (credits to governments and banks) and the determination of the rate of interest along with open market operations (OMOs; Keynes, 1930; Sayers, 1957). From the 1980s, the nominal short-term rate of interest became central banks' main monetary policy instrument because of the impossibility of controlling monetary aggregates in a globalised financial system with high private capital mobility (Blinder, 1998). The determination of a central bank's rate of interest has swung through "inflation objective", "exchange rate control", "liquidity provisions", and "yield curve" stability.

Historically, central banks have had a double mandate of monetary stability and sustainable economic growth, with major tension between these objectives. This discussion dates to the 18th century and the debate between the "fiduciary" and the "banking" school. The "fiduciary" school regained strength in the period of economic (and financial) deregulation and globalisation initiated in the 1970s (Eatwell and Taylor, 2000) and culminating at the onset of the 21st century, with the internationalisation of the capitalist system. In this period central banks were given autonomy in terms of their objectives and mechanisms, and adopted a single priority – the stability of prices – cancelling the central bank function of sustainable economic growth. One of the few central banks that kept both objectives is the United States Federal Reserve (Fed).

Central banks' autonomy revived the postulates of the Austro-German monetary theory (Wicksell, 1907) that operated through the central bank's determination of a monetary rate of interest[2] based on a monetary rule that ought to equate to the natural interest rate, rejecting the Quantitative Money Theory (backed by monetarists; Friedman, 1971). At the end of the 20th century,

Taylor (1993) rejuvenated Wicksell's monetary theory by proposing a monetary rule based on an "inflation objective". The Global Financial Crisis (GFC) of 2008 modified again the monetary theory, displaying a non-conventional monetary policy (NCMP, which included a programme of quantitative easing [QE] and extremely low central bank nominal interest rates) that, in 2014, the monetary authorities tried to reverse, and it resurfaced during the 2020 economic crisis caused by COVID-19.

This chapter revises the discussion of the dominant monetary policy during the 21st century, looking at its effects in developed and developing economies, specifically in Mexico. The chapter also analyses alternative views that have been strengthened in light of the COVID-19 crisis. The hypothesis is that central banks will continue to determine the short-term nominal objective rate of interest, used as a policy instrument, with different aims. Since the financial system has become increasingly complex, short- and long-term interest rates need to be incorporated into the central bank reaction function, which means that central banks ought to recognise the need to stabilise the yield curve. To pursue this objective, coordination between monetary and fiscal authorities needs to be resumed in terms of economic growth objectives. This discussion is of utmost importance in emerging economies since the yield curve can be stabilised only if the long-term financial segments are strengthened (stock market and long-term bond segments). This chapter contributes to the current discussion on revising the different theoretical views of monetary policy during the period of globalisation, showing that the policy operates differently in developed and developing economies. This highlights the limitations of the Mexican financial markets to unfold monetary policy to guarantee liquidity for economic growth.

The chapter is divided into five sections. The second section discusses briefly the different monetary policies that have been dominant during the globalisation period, specifically the "inflation objective" and NCMPs. Next, the chapter revises the new monetary policy proposition that includes the yield curve stability that should guarantee liquidity in the long-term public and private bond segments and in the stock market. The fourth section discusses central bank interventions in developing economies (e.g. Mexico) during the 21st century and argues that foreign capital entrance in developing economies is managed through central banks' liabilities, which restricts liquidity provision for economic growth, and the cost of doing so is passed on to federal governments. The final section offers the main conclusions.

MONETARY POLICIES IN THE GLOBALISATION ERA: AN ABRIDGED DISCUSSION OF THE TAYLOR RULE AND UNCONVENTIONAL MONETARY POLICY

The Inflation Objective Rule

During the process of globalisation and financialisation, the Taylor rule (1993) was proposed. It includes a set of variables that the central bank can use to account for the determination of the nominal interest rate (i_t), which are the natural interest rate (r^*_t), the inflation rate (π_t), mediated by the gaps of inflation (π_t-π^*_t) and production ($Y_t - Y^*_t$), as shown in Equation 4.1. The central bank's reaction function sets the operating monetary rate of interest, which, after deducing inflation, should equal the natural rate of interest, so long as the output and inflation gaps are zero, as in Equation 4.1.1. This rate of interest sets the groundwork to achieve full employment, given the existing resources (Modigliani and Papademos, 1975), which is a rate of economic growth free from inflationary pressures. From this perspective, inflation destabilises economic growth because wages in real terms fall, which, in turn, reduces labour supply and employment. This argument is summarised in the NAIRU concept (non-accelerating inflation rate of unemployment), which sets the rationale against loose monetary policy (and fiscal deficit), arguing that it is inefficient since it may unfold a combination of higher prices and lower output (and employment).

$$i_t = \pi_t + r^*_t + \alpha_\pi\left(\pi_t - \pi^*\right) + \alpha_y\left(Y_t - Y^*\right), \text{ where } \alpha_s > 0 \qquad (4.1)$$

$$i_t - \pi_t = r^*_t + \alpha_\pi\left(\pi_t - \pi^*\right) + \alpha_y\left(Y_t - Y^*\right) \qquad (4.1.1)$$

The theoretical grounds of Equation 4.1 lie in the Phillips and IS curves (Lavoie, 2006, among others) and in the rational expectations of interest rate theory (Hüfner, 2004, section 2.3). Regardless of Equation 4.1's robustness, the Taylor rule does not explain how the inflation target (π^*) and the potential output (Y^*) are set (Smithin, 2007; Epstein and Yeldan, 2005; Parguez and Seccareccia, 2000), nor does it clarify the natural interest rate (Smithin, 2007).

Despite the theoretical flaws of the Taylor rule, it operates differently in developing open economies, particularly in Latin America, because of the productive structures' exposure to the external market. In these economies, prices are affected by the exchange rate and a magnified passthrough effect of exchange rate movement to domestic prices. The latter is explained by two channels (see Lafleche, 1996; Hüfner, 2004). The first is a direct short-term channel, which relates exchange rate variations (undervalued exchange rate) with higher prices of intermediate and final imported goods that pushes up the consumer price index, noting that the impact of the exchange rate variation on prices is generally not proportional (generally magnified in Latin American economies) due to non-demand factors (distributional conflicts between the main capitalist classes). The other channel is indirect and indicates the effect of exchange rate variations on the composition of demand and production. Higher imported prices (undervalued exchange rate) should induce a process of import substitution that involves higher domestic production of goods and that has not occurred in Latin America due to the region's weak productive and social structures.

Considering the above factors, it is argued that these economies favour over-valued exchange rates because their productive structures have not been able to develop and compete on equal terms with developed economies. This argument goes back to the process of Industrialisation by Substitution of Imports (ISI), on the basis of which, it is argued, Latin American economies remain highly dependent. This has been reflected by highly inelastic export demand prices and imports income-prices (Economic Commission for Latin America and the Caribbean [CEPAL], 1949). In addition, overvalued exchange rates reduce the weight of external debts.

In emerging and developing economies, the effects on inflation of the rate of exchange depend on the weight of imports in domestic inflation (ω; first independent term in Equation 4.2) and the movement of the real exchange rate (q; second independent term in Equation 4.2):

$$\omega^c_t = (1 - \omega)\,\pi_t + \omega\,(q_t - q_{t-1}) \tag{4.2}$$

Consequently, new variables intervene in the determination of the rate of interest in open developing economies, which are the current expectations for the future nominal exchange rate (Es_{t+1}), the international rate of interest (i'_t) and a risk premium (ϕ; Svensson, cited in Hüfner, 2004). The big assumption is that the uncovered interest parity theory operates:[3]

$$i_t + i'_t + Es_{t+1} + \varphi \tag{4.3}$$

Therefore, central banks need to consider the international rate of interest and the current expectation of the future rates of exchange in their monetary policy determination. Furthermore, in open developing economies with high import coefficients, central banks have an intermediate objective, which is exchange rate stability, on the basis of which is promoted foreign capital inflows, which is attained through high interest rate margins (with respect to international financial centres) along with exchange rate sterilisation mechanisms (during periods of high instability).

In more general terms, it is argued that, although monetary policy based on "inflation targets" coincides with low and stable inflation rates (from the 1990s onwards), it does not explain this phenomenon. Price stability is explained by the conditions of valorisation of the neoliberal era, particularly the breakdown of the labour market (wage reduction, lower benefits, and labour flexibility) that has led to the pauperisation and precarisation of the working conditions (summarised by a horizontal Phillips curve; Bellofiore et al., 2011), along with the reduction of manufactured prices resulting from China's entry into the international market.

Moreover, the Taylor rule promoted capital market inflation because the central bank interest rate guarantees floor yield rates (above inflation) and the market mechanism determines ceiling yield rates (Bernanke, 2005), allowing large corporations to obtain financial gains in the circulation sphere. Under these conditions, debt volume surged under the expectations that financial securities prices would go up (financial inflation), which took place so long as net capital inflows to the capital market were positive. Finance was detached from productive activity, developing financial bubbles followed by their corresponding financial burst and economic recession. In this context, the 2008 GFC and economic recession took place.

The 2008 GFC imposed a new monetary policy era. In the aftermath of the 2008 recession, developed economies did not resort to long-term expansionary fiscal policy because it was assumed to include a threat of higher debt-to-GDP coefficients (Carstens, 2015, 3), unfolding what has been called NCMP. Meanwhile, developing countries maintained their monetary policy to attract foreign capital, which generated large capital inflows to the public bond market, while non-financial corporations issued bonds in the international market, keeping domestic equity markets depressed (Pérez Caldentey and Favreau-Negron, 2021; Levy and Bustamante, 2021).

Non-conventional Monetary Policies

The United States financial crisis that burst in October 2008 spread very rapidly to other developed countries due to the enormous volume of cross-border capital. The US's immediate answer was the reduction by the Fed of the target interest rate to levels close to zero, along with a massive programme of financial asset purchases, known as QE, which had several stages and spanned between 2008–14.[4] The authorities' main objective was to reverse financial market deflation and prevent it from spreading to the productive sector.

The asset purchase programme was very extensive, taking place between November 2008 and April 2014 (the NCMP period of duration). During this time, Fed assets increased nearly five times and, more importantly, its composition changed (Monaghan, 2014). From 2008 to 2009, the traditional assets linked to financial institution loans dropped significantly and were replaced by mortgage-backed securities and long-term securities. Another noteworthy element is that the central bank target interest rate dropped to levels close to zero, which not only reduced long-term interest rates[5] but also flattened the yield curve, which revived stock market activity (see more in the next section).

Post-2008 GFC economic policies did not restore employment to the pre-crisis level, nor did they promote robust and sustained economic growth.[6] Although NCMPs managed to stop the recession, they induced a poor economic recovery, with stops and starts, without recuperating the jobs lost during the recession and abandoning the 6.5 per cent unemployment target as a guide for raising interest rates (Monaghan, 2014).

The most important success of the NCMPs was the reactivation of the stock market because of the reduction of long-term interest rates and the flattening of the yield curve, along with very low short-term lending rates (due to target interest rates near zero); altogether this activated investors' "risk appetites", which channelled credits to the acquisition of financial securities (the S&P 500 index increased 80 per cent in 2009–14). In addition, financial securities based on raw material prices (oil, copper, etc.) soared, inducing large capital inflows to Latin America moved by "carry trade" because of the large interest margins and the relatively stable exchange rate (even overvalued). Therefore, Latin American shared developed economies' "excess liquidity", which also had destabilising effects, such us higher import coefficients and short-term capital flows that, in turn, raised Latin American external debt. Once the Fed decided to reverse its NCMP, its sole announcement depreciated the exchange rates in the region, even before increasing the Fed's target interest rate (December 2015).

Another relevant characteristic of the Latin American region was the wide and unrestricted financial market openness that took the form of net capital inflows significantly above external current account's deficit and the region's economic absorption capacities. These capital inflows induced financial deepening that was absorbed by non-bank instruments, particularly government bonds. The domestic bond market widened and became the principal public source of finance, and thereby its domestic component increased. However, private bonds and capital markets remained shallow and, in that way, the external private debt continued to rely on the external market. A major outcome of the increased capital inflows is that the composition of the external debt was modified, relying mostly on the private sector, especially the private non-financial sector. Additionally, given the large influx of foreign capital, central banks' international reserves soared and required liquidity management policies on the central bank liability side through monetary and bonds regulatory deposits that, in turn, increased the returns of financial institutions that operated in Latin American national spaces.

In 2014, the Fed announced the end of the NCMP, followed almost immediately by an external capital reversal from developing to developed economies ("flight to safety"), although the Fed target interest rates increased one year later (December 2015). In Latin America, this generated exchange rate depreciation and higher interest rates that, altogether, increased the weight of domestic and external debt. This was followed by economic recessions, especially in the southern region of the continent, where economies are led by export models based on raw materials, and affected to a lesser extent the export-led countries that are based on manufactures (Central America). Long before the 2020 crisis, Latin American economies were experiencing economic recession that only deepened during the COVID-19 pandemic.

NEW MONETARY POLICY PROPOSAL

The economic crisis generated by the COVID-19 emergency, coupled with the unresolved 2008 GFC, opened a wide discussion as to what economic policy is required to resume sustainable and robust economic growth.[7] In light of these two crises, it is evident that government spending – specifically fiscal deficit spending – is essential, along with long-term stable liquidity that ought to guarantee sufficient liquidity for economic growth and avoid capital market inflation coupled with the loosening of inflation targets.

Michell and Toporowski (2019), following Keynes and Henderson's (1929) pamphlet *Can Lloyd George Do It?*, argue that monetary policies in place prior to the GFC cannot be reimposed. On the one hand, central banks cannot continue to operate as a Monetary Policy Commission that determines an interest rate, combined with OMOs, to enforce the target interest rate and act as a government cashier that manages reserves and issues bank notes ("inflationary targets" monetary policies). On the other hand, NCMPs cannot continue either, since the rentiers have been the main beneficiaries (as in Lloyd George's times) over families and productive activity requirements. Furthermore, developed central banks' assets accumulated during the last two crises cannot be reduced without provoking deflation in the financial and banking sectors.

These authors argue that NCMPs mean that central banks buy bonds retained by financial institutions, banks, other central banks, and wealthy people. The payment of these transactions requires that central banks open reserve accounts in commercial banks, which represents the selling bond institutions. Commercial bank reserves augment their balance sheet and amplify in an equivalent volume but do not modify public wealth (families, enterprises, and financial institutions) since there is an exchange of bonds for bank deposits.

It should be recalled that the expansion of liquidity in banks (and other institutions) was due to the increased bank deposits along with a low short-term interest rate; this was followed by long-term bond acquisitions that raised bond and share prices, even though financial instruments' returns shrank (returns in relation to market price), and ended with financial gains. An additional factor of the "excess of liquidity" period is that capital movement to emergent and developing economies increased significantly in search of higher returns (see further discussion in the next section).

Summing up, the "excess of liquidity" did not expand families' incomes, employment, or investment spending. Its main impact has been a new finance composition in big corporations that moved from short- to long-term finance, causing a relatively illiquid position in market capital.

The main lessons of NCMP are that capital market liquidity can be regulated, even under conditions of financial globalisation. Central banks, via the determination of a target interest rate and OMOs, can modify long-term interest rates to match the yield curve shape. Thus, central banks can intervene in capital markets and administer long-term liquidity in public and private financial markets. In this context, central banks recover the function of "market maker" by acknowledging that they intervene in the yield curve; for this, they need to forecast the different terms of interest that compose the yield curve, as well as market participants (non-bank financial institutions, banks, and even large non-financial corporations), and public and private instruments.

The central bank role of "market maker" is supposed to prevent key financial market liquidity from "drying up" and, in so doing, guarantee the forecasted returns in long-term securities for public and private bond markets (which include private corporations willing to be regulated by the central bank). This argument is not new since the central bank "market maker" role in the UK goes back to the 19th century.

In modern globalised financial markets, central bank intervention can limit asset price volatility, especially in instruments used as collateral. In doing so, this guarantees bond holders' liquidity and market participants' certainty (government and corporations), easing investment spending planning. On that note, it is possible to resume government and central bank coordination around economic growth objectives (fiscal policy and ways of generating liquidity, monetary policy).

Fiscal and monetary authority coordination is a fundamental issue that stabilises the capital markets, securing liquidity for the process of economic growth. The issuance of new financial instruments in domestic markets can be absorbed by market participants, highlighting that speculation can be discouraged through stabilising the yield curve.

The objective of central banks in determining the interest rate and setting forecasts of the yield curve is to reach an agreement with the Treasury authority (government authority) based on economic growth and productivity objectives, without excluding price stability that, however, ought to be looser in comparison to the periods of "inflationary targets". In short, the central bank must accept that it intervenes in the yield curve and guarantees liquidity to achieve stable economic growth.

THE CENTRAL BANK OF MEXICO IN THE 21ST CENTURY

Banco de Mexico (BdeM) started to operate in January 1994 as an autonomous entity with the sole objective of stabilising prices; this occurred in a context of advanced financial system deregulation and globalisation. In the same year, the North American Free Trade Agreement was enacted, and Mexico experienced its first neoliberal financial crisis – a debt crisis that took place in December 1994. In 1997, the derivative market was created and culminated in the pension fund privatisation process that strengthened institutional investors; this was followed by the internationalisation of the stock market. Between 2008 and 2013, the Mexican peso became the most traded emerging currency in the international exchange markets (Levy, 2017); since then, it has been displaced only by China's yuan.

As a result of the BdeM's autonomy mandate, monetary policy started to operate under an inflation targeting scheme. In the first stage (1995), it operated through a policy of "accumulated stocks in the current account of commercial banks at the central bank", which was very similar to the Fed's policy of "non-borrowed reserves" (Ramos-Francia and Torres-Garcia, 2005). This period was considered transitional, and it aimed to reduce the intermediate annual inflation targets to signal a convergence to low and stable inflation within a free-floating exchange rate and healthy public finance regime (Heath and Acosta, 2020). The second stage (2001) set a permanent inflation target established around 3 per cent (+/− 1 per cent).

In these years, BdeM's operational objectives switched from monetary aggregates (monetary base) that lasted a very short period (1994) to the determination of the objective interest rates. In 1995, a 28-day zero-average reserve requirement system was imposed in which, at the end of the maintenance period, the central bank charged interest at twice the 28-day rate on all negative accumulated balances. In 2003, the zero-average reserve requirement moved to a zero-daily basis, applying the same penalties to deficit balances based on the one-day interbank interest rate. Finally, in January 2008, a target interest rate was imposed.[8]

The evolution of the rates of interest during the first period of BdeM's autonomy shows a drastic reduction; however, also in these years, the yield curve flattened – that is, the different rates of interest did not show significant differences with the equilibrium interbank interest rate (TIIE), indicating that between 1999 and 2002, the bond market was not very robust. This in part can be explained by the effect of the 1994 financial crisis and the transition period towards an inflation targeting policy (Figure 4.1a).

During the second period (starting in 2003), when an inflation target was based on a daily interest rate (1-día tasa intermedia interbancaria de equilibrio -TIIE), with lows gaps with the remaining bonds interest rates (Cetes 28, 91, 191 days), the yield curve continued to be flat (Figure 4.1). In the third period, an "objective interest rate" was applied, significantly widening the gap between short- and long-term rates. This indicates that the bond market diversified and strengthened, becoming an import source of public sector finance and reducing public external debt. However, the Fed's unconventional monetary policy reversal, announced in 2014 and implemented in December 2015, together with Donald Trump's election to the US presidency, generated high levels of uncertainty, again flattening the yield curve between 2016 and

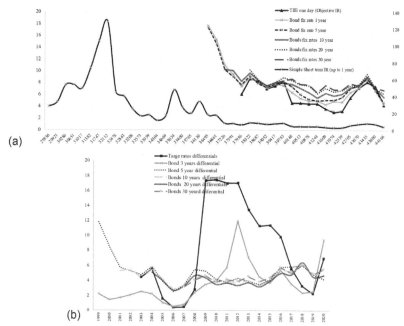

Note: (a) Average monthly rates of interest (%); (b) Margins calculated on the basis of the difference between the Mexican and the USA rates.
Source: (a) Own calculation based on Banco de Mexico data; (b) Own calculations based on Banco de Mexico and Fed Reserves Economia Data (https://fred.stlouisfed.org Economic Research Division Federal Reserve Bank of St. Louis 9).

Figure 4.1   (a) Short and Long-Term Interest rates; (b) Interest rates margins Mexico–US (%)

2019; the bond market still has not achieved maturity. Finally, in 2020, the interest rate margins widened yet again, signalling that the financial system uncertainty generated from the COVID-19 crisis in Mexico was not different from other financial markets:

The trend of the Mexican bond market yield curve and the different dated instrument gaps is explained mostly by the Mexican and US short-term rates for less-than-one-year bond differentials, which increased considerably between 2009 and 2014 (Figure 4.1b). This indicates that external capital inflow is elastic to Mexican interest rates and, more importantly, creates positive expectations for long-term bonds purchases. From the above we can infer that, although the Mexican monetary policy is affected by foreign (US) interest rate movements, the bond market deepened without achieving these results in the stock market.

The main effect of BdeM's autonomy was the reinforcement of foreign capital inflows as the central bank's largest asset, whose counterpart has been BdeM liquidity management through the liability side (Table 4.1). Based on BdeM's balance sheet, I argue that developed and developing countries' monetary policies differ in various respects. First, the 1994 Mexican financial crisis was followed by a contraction of the central bank assets to GDP (Table 4.1, section A), indicating that the 1995 financial rescue scheme took place through public trusts (FOBAPROA-IPAB) that socialised the rescued corporation scheme costs, followed by foreign capital taking control of the bankrupt corporations. Second, BdeM's assets became highly dependent on foreign capital inflow, especially after the GFC (Table 4.1, section A). Third, BdeM continued to operate with negative net internal credit to GDP through sterilisation mechanisms (Table 4.1, section B). Here we confirm that BdeM is issuing sterilisation mechanisms to stabilise the monetary base to attain exchange rate stability.

In this context, federal government credits were annulled (which started to fall long before the BdeM autonomy act was passed); and although central bank credit to commercial banks continued, it was drastically diminished, and bank liquidity was granted through repo agreements (Table 4.1, section A). Moreover, the public sector and – less so – financial institutions (banks) turned into BdeM lenders (Table 4.1, section B). The sterilisation mechanisms were based on central bank bonds (BREMS) and monetary regulation liabilities that included monetary regulation deposits based on federal government bonds and those of other public agencies, and commercial private and public banks' liquidity restrictions (Table 4.1, section B).

Consequently, the main sterilisation mechanisms were based on government bonds that the central bank located in commercial banks to reduce their liquidity, backed by Treasury Current Deposits at the central banks with "other deposits", and less so by direct banks' monetary regulatory deposits at the

Table 4.1   *Central banks' assets and liabilities and regulatory instruments (%)*

Section A: Assets side, with respect to total assets (%)

	Total assets to GDP	Foreign assets	Public securities	IPAB securities	Credits	Repos[a]	International organisation, participation	Others
1990–94	9.8	42.1	22.0	0.0	20.1	6.0	0.8	9.0
1995–99	7.7	52.7	1.6	0.0	29.4	0.0	0.8	15.4
2000–08	9.6	64.7	0.0	0.0	19.4	4.7	0.4	10.8
2009–14	13.8	86.0	0.0	4.1	1.7	5.7	0.2	2.3
2015–20	17.2	88.5	0.0	0.0	0.3	10.1	0.2	0.9

Section B: Liabilities composition with respect to total liabilities (%)

			Monetary regulatory deposits (MRD)					
	NIC to GDP[b]	Regulatory bonds	MRD[c]	hold in Government bonds	hold by bank deposits	BRM IE[d]	FBP, FMV, and FO[e]	Others
1990–94	−0.7	0.0	5.6	5.6	0.0	0.0	5.4	42.6
1995–99	−1.9	0.0	8.4	5.9	2.5	0.0	5.7	39.7
2000–08	−3.0	0.2	27.2	7.7	19.5	0.0	0.3	5.6
2009–14	−7.2	0.0	46.3	32.8	13.2	0.3	0.0	4.5
2015–20	−8.1	0.0	34.1	26.1	5.6	2.5	0.0	9.9

Section C: Regulatory instruments (% GDP)

	TCAE[f] and MRD in federal government bonds		MRD of banks[g]		Liabilities MRD and
	TCAE[d]	MRD government bonds	BREMS	MRD banks	BREMS
2000–05	1.3	0.6	2.2	2.0	4.8
2006–14	1.8	3.7	0.2	2.1	6.3
2015–20	2.2	4.7		1.4	6.1
2000–20	1.8	3.1	0.8	1.9	5.8

Notes: [a] Debtors on repo securities; [b] NIC: Net Internal Credits; [c] Monetary Regulatory Deposits; [d] Monetary Regulatory Deposits immediate enforceability; [e] BP-FMV-FO and IPAB: Fobaproa, Fameval, Oficial Trusts and IPAB finance; [f] Treasury Current Account and other deposits; [g] Monetary Regulatory deposits of banks and other deposits of credit institutions.
Source: Author's calculation based on Banco de Mexico data.

central banks. In addition, during the first ten years of the 21st century, BdeM issued bonds (BREMS) that financial institutions were required to obtain to reduce their liquidity. The BdeM balance sheet reveals that, throughout the period of analysis, the Treasury Currency Account averaged a 1.8 per cent surplus to GDP (Table 4.1, section C) even though the government was enti- tled to a 1.5 per cent deficit in relation to the authorised government spending. This indicates that the Mexican government did not use fully the financial resources to which it was legally entitled, particularly when renouncing the plan to expand government spending through borrowing resources. BdeM reg- ulatory liabilities' purposes increased, based mainly on government bonds that increased more than seven times between 2000 and 2020. On the other hand, commercial bank deposits, due to monetary regulations, shrank from 2 per cent to 1.4 per cent of GDP. And central bank regulatory bonds (BREMS) were important sterilisation operations for a short period. It is argued that financial institutions prefer to hold government or central bank bonds rather than trans- ferring liquidity to the central bank (Capraro and Pánico, 2020, 2021).

Specifically, the burden of the sterilisation mechanism since 2006 has been laid on federal government and non-financial entities. In particular, in 2015–20, the total deposits of the treasury current account at the central bank and the monetary regulation deposits based on governments represented 6.9 per cent of GDP, whereas monetary regulation deposits based on commercial banks' government deposits at the central banks totalled 1.4 per cent of GDP. These sterilisation mechanisms positively influence banks' returns (Capraro and Pánico, 2020, 2021).

Although BdeM liquidity management attained financial depth (total liabili- ties to GDP – M4/GDP) during 2000–20, its results were poor since total debts represented only half of the GDP total value and, more importantly, money and near money increased faster than total debts (Table 4.2). In addition, the liabilities composition changed, bank instruments stagnated, and public bonds increased. Thereby, the excess of liquidity resulting from the foreign capital inflows from the US QE monetary policy was neutralised by the central bank sterilisation mechanism, limiting the expansion of credits in the Mexican financial system. It is important to mention that the bond market (based on public instruments) expanded, and it became an important source of public spending finance.

The Mexican consolidated banking system balance sheet shows that bank assets to GDP expanded slowly despite the foreign excess liquidity after the GFC; the holding of bonds was around 30 per cent of total assets, while the current credits ratio was around 43 per cent of total assets to GDP (Table 4.2). In this context, it is argued that central bank sterilisation boosted commercial banks' bond holding, which is part of BdeM's policy to limit financial system liquidity at the expense of government bond issuance instead of transferring

Table 4.2   Monetary aggregates and total consolidated bank assets and liabilities to GDP (%)

	2000–05	2006–14	2015–20
M4/GDP	32.7	44.8	55.1
M1/GDP	10.4	14.1	19.9
M4–M1/GDP	22.3	30.8	35.2
Bank instruments	8.7	8.5	9.0
Bonds	13.5	22.3	26.1
Public bonds	3.4	10.6	15.6
Financial institution bonds	3.6	6.5	6.9
Repos	6.5	5.2	3.7
Commercial bank assets	31.0	36.4	40.6
Availabilities	3.8	4.1	3.5
Securities	10.0	11.0	9.7
Operations with values and derivatives	2.7	3.3	3.7
Total credits	13.2	15.7	20.9
Current credits	12.2	15.2	20.4
Commercial	9.4	9.4	13.0
Enterprises	3.9	6.8	9.7
Financial entities	0.4	0.6	0.9
Government entities	5.1	2.1	2.4
Consumption	1.3	3.3	4.0
Housing	1.5	2.5	3.4
Bank liabilities	28.6	32.7	36.4
Traditional deposits	15.4	17.6	22.2
Interbank loans	2.5	1.4	1.7
Operation with values and derivatives	8.9	9.9	8.1
Other liabilities	1.5	3.3	3.4

Source: Author's calculation based on information from Banco de Mexico and the Comisión Nacional Bancaria y de Valores.

liquidity to their central bank accounts' acquired government bonds. It can be argued that bank credits expanded during the QE period, but the reason for these growing figures was that bank credits plummeted after the 1994 crisis and started to recuperate in 2000; thus, their ratios in terms of GDP were still low (Table 4.2).

CONCLUSIONS

Monetary policies with the same objective take different forms in developed and developing countries and have different results. The rates of interest became the main monetary policy instrument guided by "inflationary targets" in the era of economic globalisation and internationalisation. In developed economies, the Taylor rule guaranteed minimum returns in the financial market, coupled with high credit availability that, together, augmented debt volumes coupled with financial inflation, whose result was a financial bubble that burst in October 2008.

Developed economies (in Latin America) also adopted the Taylor rule, but focused on the stabilisation of the exchange rate. Thereby, the central banks' interest rate (operational instrument) was constantly above the international interest rate (US) and, thus, was highly sensitive to the international market rate of interest movement to guarantee large volumes of foreign capital. Positive expectations were coupled with foreign capital whose main outcome was the expansion of the bond market (in particular, the public sector segment). The Mexican financial market deepened, but financial dependency increased, as did the external current account deficit, limiting economic growth.

I further argue that monetary policy guided by "inflationary objectives" coincides with the contention of inflation in developed and developing economies but is related to wage reduction along with a process of precarisation and pauperisation of the workforce at a global level, as was China's entrance to the international trade arena, which lowered manufacturing costs.

The GFC led to modifications in monetary policy, including imposing non-conventional instruments, reducing the objective rate of interest to a level near zero, and bringing down long-term interest rates. The interest rate reductions came along with wide programmes of central bank asset acquisition, not only by banking institutions, but also by financial non-banking institutions and some non-financial corporations. The central banks diversified their asset holding and, more importantly, acted as financial "market makers".

The UCMP results in developed economies were not the expected ones. Even though deflation in the financial market was reversed and did not spread to the productive sector, and big corporations were rescued, economic growth was feeble. It is widely accepted that the structural problems that led to the 2008 GFC and economic recession have not been resolved. In this context, it is further argued that central banks cannot go back to monetary policy guided only by "inflationary objectives", and if central bank balance assets are reduced, this can spark deflationary pressures in the financial market. Moreover, resolving the COVID-19 economic crisis of 2020 and, in general, the capitalist structural crisis (evident from 2008) requires a new economic policy based on monetary and fiscal coordination and guided by an economic growth objective. In this context, the central bank needs to stabilise long-term rates of interest, acknowledge that the yield curve needs to be stabilised, and, in this way, guarantee liquidity in all financial market segments, including the long-term private securities segment. Inflationary objectives still need to be considered by the monetary authorities, but with more flexible objectives, including inflation rates around 4–6 per cent.

In developing and emerging economies, the high volume of net foreign investment has been confronted with sterilisation policies that generate negative net internal credit, reducing the available resources for government spending (surplus Treasury Current Account at the central bank) and monetary regulation deposits based on government bonds. Commercial banks are being subsidised by BdeM's regulation liabilities, whose costs are beared by the federal government.

In this context, developing and emergent Latin American economies need to deepen their financial markets based on domestic debts that will finance public and private spending. The domestic private bond and share markets need to expand so that central banks will be able to perform the "market maker" function, control the yield curve, and guarantee liquidity in the different financial segments.

ACKNOWLEDGEMENTS

This chapter is part of the research project PAPPIT IN 306120. This chapter benefited from comments by Carlo Pánico and Christian Dominguez. Any remaining errors are my sole responsibility.

NOTES

1.   The Bank of England (BofE) is the oldest central bank (1694) in the world and was created to help the English government, which was at war with France. Keynes (1930, vol. 2, 135) reminds us that the BofE was the result of a stock market bubble and, since then, has been inseparable from the complex of securities trading in London (cited in Michell and Toporowski, 2019).
2.   Wicksell (1907) put forward a monetary policy guided by monetary interest signalled by a natural rate of interest (that guarantees full employment), the former being modified by inflationary pressures (signs of the economy overheating) and gold reserve changes.
3.   Mántey (2011), based on Calvo and Reinhart's (2002) "fear to float" proposal, argues that, in Latin America, the uncovered interest rate parity theory does not hold. She concludes that exchange rate stability is an intermediate monetary policy objective that is attained through interest rate movements and direct control of the exchange rate.
4.   For further information on how it was organised, see: www.forbes.com/sites/greatspeculations/2015/11/16/quantitative-easing-in-focus-the-u-s-experience/#5ad6136d3013.
5.   The long-term interest rate (ten-year bonds) fell significantly from 2009. In the US, UK, and eurozone, the rates were below 4 per cent and 2 per cent, and in Japan, below 2 per cent. In 2015, these rates were near 0 per cent in the eurozone, 2 per cent in Japan and the US, and below 2 per cent in the UK (Bloomberg, cited in Carstens, 2015).

6. This represents the percentage change in US GDP (annual rates), from the US Bureau of Economic Analysis. Data on the US unemployment rate (%) are from the US Bureau of Labor Statistics. For both data sets, see Monaghan (2014).
7. This section is constructed based on Michell and Toporowski (2019).
8. In this scheme, BdeM equates to the excess or the missing liquidity of the interbank market through open market operations. This operation can take the form of credit if liquidity is short, or deposits when liquidity is excessive, securing the objective interest rate set by the funding interest on Day 1 (Heath and Acosta, 2020).

REFERENCES

Bagehot, W. (1873). *Lombard Street: A Description of the Money Market*. http://socserv.mcmaster.ca/econ/ugcm/3ll3/bagehot/lombard.html
Bellofiore, R., Garibaldo, F., and Halevi, J. (2011). The global crisis and the crisis of European neomercantilism. *Socialist Register*, 47, 121–40.
Bernanke, B. (2005). *The Global Saving Glut and the U.S. Current Account Deficit*. Virginia Association of Economists.
Blinder, A. (1998). *Central Banking in Theory and Practice*. MIT Press.
Calvo, G.A., and Reinhart, C.M. (2002). Fear of floating. *Quarterly Journal of Economics,* 117(2), 379–408.
Capraro, S., and Pánico, C. (2020). *¿Podemos defendernos de los efectos persistentes de la crisis and fortalecer la economía?* Universidad Nacional Autónoma de México.
Capraro, S., and Pánico, C. (2021). Monetary policy in liberalized financial markets: the Mexican case. *Review of Keynesian Economics*, 9(1), 109–38.
Carstens, A. (2015, 20 April). *Challenges for emerging economies in the face of unconventional monetary policies in advanced economies*. Stavros Niarchos Foundation Lecture, Peterson Institute for International Economics.
Eatwell, J., and Taylor, L. (2000). *Global Finance at Risk*. New York: The New Press.
Economic Commission for Latin America and the Caribbean (CEPAL) (1949). El desarrollo económico en América Latina y algunos de sus principales problemas. In R. Bielschowsky (ed.), *Cincuenta años pensamiento en la CEPAL, Texto seleccionados*, 69–129. FCE-CEPAL.
Epstein, G., and Yeldan, E. (2005). Beyond inflation targeting: assessing the impacts and policy alternatives. In G. Epstein and E. Yeldan (eds), *Beyond Inflation Targeting: Assessing the Impacts and Policy Alternatives*, 1–27. Edward Elgar Publishing.
Friedman, M. (1971). Un marco teórico para el análisis monetario. In J. Gordon (ed.), *El Marco Monetario de Milton Friedman. Un Debate con Sus Críticos*, 13–79. La red de Jonas.
Heath, J., and Acosta, J. (2019). Reflexiones y perspectivas 25 años de la autonomía del Banco de Mexico. *Investigación Económica*, 78(310), 11–39. https://doi.org/10.22201/fe.01851667p.2019.310.71545
Hüfner, F. (2004). *Foreign Exchange Intervention as a Monetary Policy Instrument*. New Economic Studies.
Keynes, J.M. (1930). *The Treatise on Money* (Vol. 1). Cambridge University Press.
Keynes, J. M. (1930). The Treatise on Money. The applied theory of money (Vol. II). Cambridge, in *The Collected writings of John Maynard Keynes*, Vol. 6, The Royal Economic Society 1971, 2013.

Keynes, J.M., and Henderson, H.D. (1929). *Can Lloyd George Do It? An Examination of the Liberal Pledge.* W.C.I.

Laflèche, T. (1996). The impact of exchange rate movements on consumer prices. *Bank of Canada Review*, No. 1996–97(Winter), 21–32.

Lavoie, M. (2006). A post-Keynesian amendment to the new consensus on monetary policy. *Metroeconomica International Review*, 57(2), 165–92. https://doi.org/10.1111/j.1467-999X.2006.00238.x

Levy, N. (2017). Financiarización y Modelo de Acumulación: La evolución de las deudas y el sector externo de la economía Mexicana. *Análisis Económico*, 32(79), 53–75.

Levy, N., and Bustamante, J. (2021). The unique development of non-financial corporations in Latin America. In N. Levy, J. Bustamante, and L.P. Rochon (eds), *Capital Movements and Corporate Dominance in Latin America*, 89–105. Edward Elgar Publishing.

Mántey, G. (2011). La política de tasa de interés interbancaria y la inflación en México. *Investigación Económica*, 70(277), 37–68.

Michell, J., and Toporowski, J. (2019). *Can the Bank of England do it? The scope and operations of the Bank of England's Monetary Policy.* Working Paper 12 November 2019, Progessive Economy Forum.

Modigliani, F., and Papademos, L. (1975). *Targets for monetary policy in the coming years.* Brooking Papers on Economic Activity.

Monaghan, A. (2014, 29 October). Fed calls time on QE in the US – charts and analysis. *The Guardian.* www.theguardian.com/business/economics-blog/2014/oct/29/the-fed-to-call-time-on-qe-in-the-us (accessed 21 May 2021)

Parguez, A., and Seccareccia, M. (2000). The credit theory of money: the monetary circuit approach. In J. Smithin (ed.), *What Is Money?*, 101–23. Routledge.

Pérez Caldentey, E., and Favreau-Negron, N. (2021). Capital flows, the role of non-financial corporations and their macroeconomic implications: an analysis of the case of Chile. In N. Levy-Orlik, J.A. Bustamante-Torres, and L.-P. Rochon (eds), *Capital Movements and Corporate Dominance in Latin America*, 89–105. Edward Elgar Publishing.

Ramos-Francia, M., and Torres-Garcia, A. (2005). *Reducción de la inflación a través de un esquema de objetivos de inflación: la experiencia Mexicana.* Banco de México Working Paper 2005-01.

Sayers, R.S. (1957). *Central Banking after Bagehot.* Clarendon Press.

Smithin, J. (2007). A real interest rate rule for monetary policy? *Journal of Post Keynesian Economics*, 30(1), 101–18.

Taylor, J.B. (1993). Discretion vs Policy Rules in Practice. *Carnegie-Rochester Conference Series on Public Policy*, 39, 195–214. https://doi.org/10.1016/0167-2231(93)90009-L

Wicksell, K. (1907). The influence of the rate of interest on price. *The Economic Journal*, 17(66), 213–20.

5. Global financial cycle and monetary policy rules: a Neo-Kaleckian model for emerging markets and developing economies

Gabriel Michelena and Fernando Toledo

INTRODUCTION

This chapter presents an extension of Bortz et al.'s (2018) Neo-Kaleckian model to examine situations in which the use of Post-Keynesian Activist Monetary Policy Rules (PKAMPR) serves to decouple the transmission of the boom-and-bust Global Financial Cycle (GFCy) phases on Emerging Markets and Developing Economies (EMDEs), particularly in Latin American countries (LACs).[1] These PKAMPR could help to lessen the incidence of external financial shocks that operate mainly through the balance of payments (BoP) dominance. This idea refers to the prevalence of external shocks in the case of EMDEs and LACs, which conveys from the real side (i.e., an improvement in the terms of trade, related to the trade channel) and from the financial side (i.e., a greater incidence of global push factors or GFCy, linked to the financial channel).

There exists a critical relationship between nominal short-run interest rates set by peripheral economies' monetary authorities and the nominal short-run interest rate policy set in financial centers—for instance, the United States. The fall in the Federal Reserve's (FED's) short-run nominal interest rate engenders a greater appetite for risk among global investors, who decide to reallocate their financial funds mostly to EMDEs and LACs (i.e., the beginning of the boom phase of the GFCy).

In the absence of capital controls and PKAMPR, we find an appreciation of nominal exchange rates in these economies, some initial deflationary tendencies (under certain conditions), improvements in external competitiveness (if the Marshall–Lerner condition holds), greater net exports, and negative effects on the current account (through the nominal exchange rate appreciation and a greater weight of external debt service obligations). In this vein, according to

Bortz et al. (2018), in a debt-burdened regime, the bust phase of GFCy is detrimental to the degree of capacity utilization, the wage share, and the inflation rate in EMDEs.

Moreover, when the FED decides to reduce its monetary policy instrument, EMDEs' and LACs' monetary authorities could be tempted to cut their own nominal short-run interest rates to offset the resulting increase in the global appetite for risk and to minimize some of its negative consequences. However, this strategy could face significant bounds: if EMDEs' and LACs' central banks lower their nominal interest rates by a significant amount to fight against the boom GFCy effects, this monetary policy decision could have harmful effects through the validity of the Uncovered Interest Parity condition, especially in the presence of imperfect currency substitution. Additionally, capital gross inflows could abruptly turn into outflows due to the excessively low nominal interest rates that occur in EMDEs and LACs, leading to greater exchange rate market pressures.

The chapter structure is as follows. The next section introduces a review of the related literature, with an emphasis on BoP dominance in EMDEs and LACs, its relationship with the GFCy, its transmission through the bust phase, the relevance of the nominal exchange rate channel, and some considerations about the PKAMPR approach. The third section incorporates the analytical extension of the original model based on Bortz et al. (2018). Next, we add the main monetary policy rules discussed in the Bortz et al. (2018) extended model, followed by the main endogenous equations of interest for the empirical analysis. Sixth, the chapter discusses some empirical results based on the calibration and simulation of this extended Neo-Kaleckian model, highlighting the importance of examining the GFCy bust phase and different PKAMPR to ease financial distortions created by global push factors and negative spillover transmission. The final section presents the conclusions.

RELATED LITERATURE

BoP dominance is an important tool to evaluate how EMDEs and LACs show a different degree of vulnerability to external trade and financial shocks. According to Cimoli et al. (2016: 13), the BoP dominance is relevant in some EMDEs and LACs since: "it is not possible for workers to have their desired wage share, for firms to have their desired profit share in output, and for the economy to have a stable current account to [gross domestic product] GDP ratio at the same time." Similarly, Abeles and Panigo (2015: 533) suggest that: "A new open economy 'impossibility trinity' or 'trilemma' seems to follow from our formal analysis, whereby only two of the following three objectives sought out—domestic price stability, exchange-rate competitiveness, and income equality—could be attained."

Henceforth, economic growth, income distribution, and the external equilibrium could be conflicting policy economic aims if we consider BoP dominance issues in EMDEs. So, the BoP dominance notion is of paramount importance given its relationship with the GFCy literature, particularly when we consider the relevance of the financial interdependence channel (Centro de Economía Internacional, 2003).

The monetary policy international spillovers from financial centers to EMDEs and LACs are transmitted through different channels, such as financial and external trade channels. A fall in the US monetary policy interest rate stimulates a greater appetite for risk among global investors, who decide to reallocate their financial funds mostly to developing economies. Thus, lower policy interest rates in the US trigger nominal appreciation in small open economies driven by portfolio flows and cross-border lending (Bonizzi and Kaltenbrunner, 2021; Yilmaz and Godin, 2020).[2] These external funds are reverted when the FED announces an increase in its nominal interest rate policy. In such a case, we observe increases in global risk aversion that stimulates flight-to-quality behavior and higher exchange rate market pressures in EDMEs, even though these economies show solid macroeconomic fundamentals (Kohler, 2021; Botta, 2021).

There exists a considerable pass-through from changes in global financial conditions toward EMDE and LAC economies, particularly on exchange rates, asset prices, the risk premium, and credit growth (Miranda-Agrippino and Rey, 2021; and Jordà et al., 2018). In recent decades, empirical evidence has shown that push factors—particularly the monetary stance of the US—have been the major drivers of the ebb and flow of capital movements to EMDEs and LACs (Chari et al., 2020; Rey, 2013).

Aidar and Braga (2020) examine the extent to which push factors linked to global liquidity play a major role—compared to country-specific factors—in changes in the risk premium for a set of developing countries during the 1999–2019 period. These authors find evidence that the common factors behind the set of country-risk premiums can be explained by financial variables, namely, the US interest rate and the Chicago Board Options Exchange Market Volatility Index. Aldasoro et al. (2020) suggest that, for the GFCy, short-term cycles dominate, and they point out that the EMDEs that allow the build-up of macroeconomic imbalances and financial vulnerabilities (i.e., credit expansion, currency overvaluation, and economic overheating), and get most of their capital inflows in the form of debt, are significantly more likely to experience a crash after episodes of capital inflow surges.

At the same time, the exchange rate channel of monetary policy has been remarked as one of the main transmission conduits of the GFCy and global push factors' incidence in EMDEs and LACs. According to Brandao-Marques et al. (2020: 4): "Our first key result is that transmission through interest rates generally does work in EMDEs. The estimates of the impact of monetary policy shocks resemble those for advanced economies once we take the exchange rate channel—a key part of transmission in EMDEs—properly into account."

Last, but not least, the small elasticity of private consumption and private investment to changes in monetary policy instruments imposes challenges to the effectiveness of inflation targeting adopted by several EMDEs' and LACs' central banks (Damill and Frenkel, 2009), leading us to ask about the need to discuss the relative effectiveness of different monetary policy rules. The shallow financial depth of local banking systems in some EMDEs and LACs works against the proper functioning of this monetary regime.

Still, traditional Taylor rules assume that central banks could effectively achieve the "Divine Coincidence" using their main monetary policy instrument: the short-run nominal interest rate. Through the validity of the Taylor principle, the monetary authorities could eliminate any positive output gap by raising the real interest rate via short-run nominal interest rate increases. Overheating situations are then eradicated, and the inflation target is effectively accomplished. The New Consensus or New Keynesian literature allows some Taylor rule extensions to attend—for instance, financial stability considerations, such as the nominal exchange rate, the prices of real and financial assets, some credit indicators, and interest rate spreads (Woodford, 2012). There exists an agreement among some New Keynesian economists that suggests how EMDEs and LACs could embrace two objectives—two instruments frameworks—that is, inflation control and external competitiveness with an inflation targeting monetary policy regime and a managed floating exchange rate regime, respectively (see Airaudo et al., 2016; Ghosh et al., 2014; Bofinger and Wollmershäuser, 2003).

Nevertheless, the PKAMPR has other goals than these traditional or extended Taylor rules. Instead of focusing on the inflation–output trade-off through the existence of a hybrid New Keynesian Phillips curve, the PKAMPR emphasizes the need to guarantee a short-run business-cycle-oriented fine-tuning in terms of attaining several desirable economic and social goals, such as nominal stabilization, full employment, wage increases, external sector equilibrium, and financial stability. Several variants of PKAMPR have been inspired by the contributions of Terra and Arestis (2017), Tily (2009), Atesoglu (2008), Palley (2007), and Fontana and Palacio-Vera (2007).[3]

According to Terra and Arestis (2017: 61):

> the interest rate has five transmission channels: the portfolio channel; the credit channel; the wealth effect; the exchange rate channel; and the expectations channel. Every time the central bank changes the interest rate it impacts one or more of these transmission channels; thus, they reach the immediate goals of monetary

policy, namely, the stability of prices, exchange rate, liquidity, financial system, and expectations. All of them affect the immediate goals of monetary policy and thereby effective demand. Because they impact effective demand, they are essential for reaching the ultimate objective of the Post Keynesian monetary policy, that is, the full-employment economic growth.

Based on these arguments, we calibrate and simulate the Bortz et al. (2018) model for two opposite regimes: a profit/debt-led regime and a wage-led regime that is less reliant on capital flows and imports. After identifying two baseline scenarios according to the calibration of each of these two alternative regimes, we proceed to simulate an increase in external risk perception—proxied by changes in the threshold variable d^T—to capture the bust phase of the GFCy. We examine the dynamics of the endogenous variables following the Bortz et al. (2018) model to determine the impacts of three PKAMPR and to evaluate their effects in terms of their magnifying or dampening influence measured as the GFCy transmission to EMDEs.

THE FORMAL EXTENSION OF THE BORTZ ET AL. (2018) MODEL

The model described in Bortz et al. (2018) assumes the existence of four institutional agents in this economy: households, firms, a central bank, and the rest of the world (ROW). To provide a clear exposition, we split this section into four blocks: distribution, aggregate demand, debt, and monetary policy.

Distribution

We suppose a small open economy that produces one homogenous good fit for consumption, investment, and export purposes with a fixed-coefficient production function of the Leontief kind (Cimoli et al., 2016), in conditions of imperfect competition, with the existence of idle capacity as a norm:

$$Y = \min(\alpha_L \bullet L, \ \alpha_K \bullet K, \alpha_M \bullet M) \tag{5.1}$$

where the unit requirement associated with each input ($\alpha_L, \ \alpha_K, \alpha_M$) multiplies the respective factor endowments labor, L; capital, K; and imported inputs, M.

The wage-setting curve that rules workers' nominal wage demands is:

$$\hat{w} = \ \phi_w \bullet (\psi_w - \psi) \tag{5.2}$$

The growth rate of nominal wages depends on the bargaining power of workers—captured by the term ϕ_w, which is exogenous to the model, and the discrepancy between the wage share targeted by workers and the actual wage share. The price-setting curve is, in turn:

$$\hat{p} = \zeta \cdot (\psi - \psi_f) \tag{5.3}$$

where ζ is the exogenous bargaining power of firms, and ψ_f is the wage share targeted by firms.

A reasonable assumption for ψ_f would be to link it negatively to the real exchange rate, q, as in Blecker (2011):

$$\psi_f = \kappa - \delta \cdot q \tag{5.4}$$

where k is the autonomous wage share that can be interpreted as a long-term value determined by history and institutional factors.

Considering that, and excluding the labor productivity growth from the equation, the wage share dynamics equals:

$$\hat{\psi} = \hat{W} - \hat{P} \tag{5.5}$$

Replacing the wage-setting function (5.5), we get the following expression:

$$\hat{\psi} = \phi_w \cdot (\psi_w - \psi) - \zeta \cdot (\psi - \kappa + \delta \cdot q) \tag{5.6}$$

In terms of the model extension proposed in this paper, Equation 5.6 provides the connection between the labor market and the BoP.

Aggregate Demand

Given that there are no domestic banks in the model and that only firms have access to foreign borrowing, smoothing consumption possibilities are limited, and most agents are liquidity-constrained, with their current income having a prominent influence on their consumption decisions. We adopt a simple approach to savings decisions, considering different savings propensities according to the source of income (wages, dividends, and profits). For the sake of simplicity, we embrace the Kaldorian approach of workers consuming all their income and rentiers saving it. Therefore, household savings are inversely related to wage share:

$$S_h = s \cdot Y = (1 - \psi) \cdot Y \tag{5.7}$$

Hence, the total saving rate of the private sector—firms and households—is as follows:

$$\sigma_h = \frac{S}{K} = (1 - \psi) \bullet u \tag{5.8}$$

where $u = \frac{Y}{Y}$ is the full capacity-to-output ratio.

Investment decisions, in turn, depend on expected profitability and financial restrictions. Our investment function tries to capture several factors involved in the decision-making process. The first one is the impact of output on investment, akin to an accelerator effect, which has good empirical support both for advanced and developing countries. The second factor is related to the domestic borrowing cost faced by firms and captured by the real interest rate term. Finally, the last term includes the weight of external debt in investment decisions. We consider a threshold d^T below which the economy is in a debt-led regime (Bortz et al., 2018), whereas above it the economy is debt-burdened, because of higher default risk and interest payments on external debt:

$$g = \frac{I}{K} = g_u \bullet u - g_\iota \bullet (\iota - \hat{p}) - g_d \bullet (d - d^T) \tag{5.9}$$

The current account expressed in foreign currency is:

$$b = \frac{B}{K} = -b_u \bullet u + b_f \bullet u^* + b_q \bullet q - b_d \bullet \iota^* \bullet d \tag{5.10}$$

We assume that the economy is a net debtor from the ROW since it only includes interest payments on external debt to foreign investors. The current account deteriorates with rising capacity utilization, and it improves with rising foreign capacity utilization. It is also affected by interest payments, captured by the parameter b_d. Moreover, we add the term b_q to account for the Marshall–Lerner condition, reacting upon the driver of exchange rate movements.

In a Keynesian fashion, the capacity utilization adjusts to conciliate the eventual discrepancies between investment decisions, saving decisions, and the current account. We therefore attain:

$$\hat{u} = \lambda \bullet (g + b - \sigma_h) \tag{5.11}$$

After appropriate substitutions and reordering terms, we get:

$$\hat{u} = \lambda \bullet \left[\begin{array}{c} (-g_\iota \bullet (\iota - \hat{p}) - g_d \bullet (d - d^T) + b_f \bullet u^* + b_q \bullet q - b_d \bullet \iota^* \bullet d) \\ + u \bullet (b_u + g_u - (1 - \psi)) \end{array} \right] \tag{5.12}$$

So, changes in the capacity utilization rate depend positively on the impacts of profitability, economic activity upon investment, and external demand.

Debt

Changes in capacity utilization, as a proxy for growth prospects and pull factors, are one variable influencing—attracting or repelling—gross capital flows. We also differentiate between investors by distinguishing "chartist" and "fundamentalist" agents (Spronk et al., 2013; Lavoie and Daigle, 2011; Moosa, 2003; Harvey, 1993; Frankel and Froot, 1990; Cutler et al., 1990).

Chartists follow recent trends, which in normal times are influenced by interest rate differentials, while fundamentalists invest according to their view of the state of fundamentals, forgiving the redundancy. In our model, what they see is the level of external indebtedness—normalized by the capital stock—relative to some critical value, of a conventional nature, that can vary from country to country.

That is what the parameter d^T tries to capture, and this is the parameter through which international financial conditions (i.e., the boom-and-bust phases of the GFCy) make their entrance. What seemed a perfectly reasonable indebtedness level in a lax financial environment may look thoroughly unsustainable in tighter financial markets. The domestic conditions of EMDEs and LACs have little influence on the determination of this threshold. Expressing d in variation rates, we have:

$$\hat{d} = \mu(\iota - \iota^* - \varphi) + (1 - \mu)(d^T - d) \tag{5.13}$$

Then, we move forward to exchange rate determination. Here, we assume one possible closure for the external sector in which central banks freeze the foreign reserves and let the exchange rate float freely. Under these conditions, the exchange rate must move following the change in foreign reserves supply so that:

$$\hat{r} = -\frac{\dot{F}}{F} \tag{5.14}$$

The foreign reserves supply equals the current account result plus the net inflow of external debt, which could be either positive or negative in value:

$$\dot{F} = B + \dot{D} \tag{5.15}$$

where the dot above the variable represents the change with respect to time $\dot{x} = \frac{\partial x}{\partial t}$, and $\dot{D}$ is the net change in capital flows.

With the real exchange rate dynamic being equal to the difference between the nominal exchange growth and the inflation rate:

$$\hat{q} = \hat{r} - \hat{p} \qquad (5.16)$$

After appropriate substitutions and reordering terms, we finally get:

$$\hat{q} = -\left(\frac{(b_0 - b_u \bullet u + b_f \bullet u^* + b_q \bullet q - b_d \bullet \iota^* \bullet d) \bullet}{\vartheta + \mu(\iota - \iota^* - \varphi) + (1 - \mu)(d^T - d)} \right)$$
$$- \zeta \bullet (\psi - \kappa + \delta \bullet q) \qquad (5.17)$$

Monetary Policy Rules

The present model's version brings in the central bank and the monetary policy as a key stabilizing factor. In the previous work (Bortz et al., 2018), we intentionally omitted this institutional sector, and we rested on the self-stabilizing forces among income distribution, growth, and foreign debt.

Now our goal is different, given that we want to test how distinct monetary schemes contribute to amplifying the volatility in prices and activity created by the GFCy. In our simplified version of a central bank, the monetary authority intervenes in the money market using the nominal short-run interest rate as its main policy tool, in line with the current consensus in the discipline (Tadeu Lima and Setterfield, 2008; Woodford, 2003).

Henceforth, we will present three options for the interest rate policy. In all cases, the policy rate evolves according to a determined target (ι^T), which varies according to each rule:

$$i = \beta_i \cdot (\iota^T - \iota) \qquad (5.18)$$

The price stability target usually relates to strict inflation targeting monetary policy regimes and simplified Taylor rules:

$$\iota^T = \beta_p \cdot \left(E(\hat{p}) - \widehat{p^T} \right) \qquad (5.19)$$

The full-employment target PKAMPR relates to Atesoglu (2008) and Palley (2007):

$$\iota^T = \beta_u \cdot (u - u^t) \qquad (5.20)$$

The real exchange rate target links to Bofinger and Wollmershäuser (2003):

$$\iota^T = \beta_q \cdot (q - q^T) \tag{5.21}$$

In all cases, β is the adjustment parameter and it is used to smooth the response of the interest rate with respect to changes in the variable included in the policy rule.

THE BORTZ ET AL. (2018) MODEL REDUX

In this section, we present a simplified version of the Bortz et al. (2018) model, getting rid of redundant parameters to gain simplicity in the analysis and the simulations. We dropped all the parameters and exogenous variables that will not contribute to the calibration and simulation of this new version of the model:

$$\hat{\psi} = \psi \cdot (1 - \zeta) - \zeta \cdot \delta \cdot q \qquad \textit{(Distribution Locus)}$$

$$\hat{u} = \lambda \left[\begin{array}{c} \left(-g_d \cdot (d - d^T) - g_i \cdot (i - \hat{p}) + b_q \cdot q - b_d \cdot i^* \cdot d \right) \\ + u \cdot \left(b_u + g_u - (1 - \psi) \right) \end{array} \right] \qquad \textit{(Activity Locus)}$$

$$\hat{q} = - \left(\begin{array}{c} \left(- b_u \cdot u + b_q \cdot q - b_d \cdot i^* \cdot d \right) \cdot \\ \vartheta + \mu \cdot (i - \varphi) + (1 - \mu) \cdot (d^T - d) \end{array} \right)$$
$$- \zeta \cdot (\psi + \delta \cdot q) \qquad \textit{(Exchange Rate Locus)}$$

$$i = \beta_i \cdot (\iota^T - \iota) \qquad \textit{(Monetary Policy Rule)}$$

CALIBRATION, SIMULATIONS, AND RESULTS

We calibrated the main parameters to simulate the model presented above and to analyze its empirical properties. The procedure used to calibrate and simulate the model can be summed up according to the following sequence.

We selected a range of initial values, with four criteria in mind: (1) the need to achieve a convergent solution; (2) data from Social Accounting Matrices for developing countries (Aguiar et al., 2016); (3) that the potential solutions do not lack economic meaning; and (4) best guess estimation criteria.

A prime goal of this exercise is to analyze the reaction of the system to the bust GFCy stage, and its response to different monetary policy options, given a particular priority to the PKAMPR kind. Specifically, we tested to which extent different interest rules affect the dynamic behavior of the economic system.

In the simulations, we tried to replicate the bust GFCy stage in a stylized way. Our main assumption is that the GFCy lasts, on average, eight years, before reversing (see Aldasoro et al., 2020). Once we obtained the values for the set of variables and parameters, we simulated the equation system comprised of the equations of the model redux. We used the Forward Euler methodology (Langtangen, 2012). To solve the system in the interval of $t \in (0, T]$, we searched for a solution to u, d, q and ψ at discrete points in time $t_i = i\Delta t$, $i = 1, 2, ..., n$.

$$\hat{u}(t_k) = f(u(t_k), t_k) \tag{5.22}$$

The main idea of the Forward Euler scheme is to proxy each variable growth rate through the following equation:

$$\hat{u}(t_k) \cong \frac{u(t_{k+1}) - u(t_k)}{\Delta t} = \frac{u_{k+1} - u_k}{\Delta t} \tag{5.23}$$

Replacing 5.22 into the left-hand side in Equation 5.23 removes the derivative and leaves one equation where the only unknown is u_{k+1}. Equation 5.24 is solved recursively, fixing initial values for the endogenous variables of the model:

$$u_{k+1} = u_k + \Delta t f(u_k, t_k) \tag{5.24}$$

One of the main contributions of model analysis provided by Bortz et al. (2018) rests in the development of several accumulation regimes that connect debt, output, and income distribution. Simulating all the possible regimes would be well beyond the scope of this chapter. As previously mentioned, we will consider two opposite configurations. On the one hand, we will consider a profit/debt-led regime (PDR), where utilization responds negatively to changes in income distribution and positively to debt. On the other hand, we will focus on a wage-led regime (WLR) where output and wage share vary in the same direction, and in which we soften the impact of debt on capital accumulation and the effect of utilization capacity on the current account. Finally, we also adopt a higher value for k.

We will start by showing the model's dynamic under both regimes in a version in which the monetary policy is absent. In the empirical model's literature, economists usually label this scenario Business as Usual (BaU), which does not include any policy intervention. The BaU is only relevant to analyze the stability of the model and to contrast the results from the policy scenarios. All the model's variables are normalized to 100 for t = 0 and we add

an exogenous shock in period t = 100 on the capital flows dynamic to mimic
a reversal (bust stage) in the GFCy cycle.

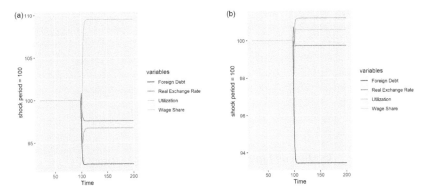

Figure 5.1   *Debt, real exchange rate, capacity utilization and distribution
under the BaU scenario*

Figure 5.1 depicts the response of the relevant variables under the BaU for
the two considered regimes. In both regimes, at t = 100, the perceived risk
rises and capital flows reverse, therefore, foreign debt stock starts to fall. The
short-run response in the two scenarios must be an initial short-lived devaluation, which pushes up prices and reduces the real interest rate. In the PDR, the
high dependence of the investment to foreign debt accumulation prevails and
impacts negatively on the utilization rate. This latter effect creates a surplus in
the current account due to lower import demand, so the nominal exchange rate
starts to progressively appreciate, and tends to raise the wage share through its
negative relation in the wage demanded by unions. The WLR behaves quite
differently. Here, the capital reversal also triggers the same short-term impacts
as before, but the dynamic evolves in a different fashion. On the one hand, the
investment demand does not rely excessively on debt accumulation, so the
lower real interest rate stimulates the economic activity. Since the activity does
not have a significant impact on imports, the exchange rate tends to stabilize
barely below the pre-shock levels. Consequently, the wage share improves, so
GDP grows even more.

Figure 5.2 presents the dynamic for the inflation rate, given the constant
nominal interest rate. In both cases there is an initial overshooting triggered
by the exchange response to the sudden stop. Nonetheless, in the PDR regime,
the variance is greater and stabilizes well below the initial value, in the same
fashion as the exchange rate.

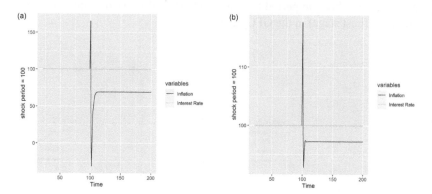

Figure 5.2   Inflation and interest rate under the BaU scenario

Now we move to the analysis of the policy scenarios in which different policy rules are used to counter the exogenous shock in the capital flows. For simplicity, we summarize the results in Tables 5.1 and 5.2, always considering the percentage difference between the BaU and the policy scenarios in the last period of the simulation, t = 200.

Table 5.1 depicts the results of the PDR regime. Starting with the price stability rule, after the shock in the financial account, the exchange rate over-reacts initially to stabilize at a lower value, followed by the same dynamic in inflation. Therefore, under this rule, the central bank is committed to stabilizing inflation, so it must reduce the interest rate to match its goal. Here, it is especially important to highlight that the monetary authority seeks to bring back inflation to the pre-shock level so that it avoids the deflationary pressures present in the BaU. As a result, the inflation and exchange rates end above the BaU level, whereas the interest rate closes below it. A lower interest rate and a higher exchange rate are associated with a lower wage share and upper output under the profit-led regime. Finally, the chartists' pressure resulting from the monetary policy pushes down the foreign debt.

In the activity rule scenario, the central bank must act to bring back the utilization rate to the pre-shock level, so that it must reduce the interest rate until such goal is met, resulting in a policy rate above the price stability rule. This response lets the exchange rate also remain above the BaU levels, but below the previous scenario so that the wage share loss is smaller. The same applies to foreign debt. Finally, the real exchange rule presents variations that are similar to the price stability rule. In consequence, under this configuration, although the central bank pursues nominal exchange rate stability, it implicitly contributes to bringing inflation back to the pre-shock level. This conclusion

Table 5.1   *Debt, real exchange rate, capacity utilization and distribution in the PDR regime under the policy scenarios (percent change with respect to the BaU)*

	BaU (t = 200)	Price stability rule	Activity rule	Real exchange rule
Capacity utilization	69%	3.7%	3.4%	3.7%
Foreign debt	87%	−2.3%	−2.1%	−2.4%
Wage share	50%	−8.7%	−7.8%	−8.7%
Exchange rate	85%	2.5%	2.2%	2.5%
Inflation	1%	44.2%	39.9%	44.4%
Interest rate	5%	−74.1%	−66.7%	−74.4%

Table 5.2   *Debt, real exchange rate, capacity utilization and distribution in the WLR regime under the policy scenarios (percent change with respect to the BaU)*

	BaU (t = 200)	Price stability rule	Activity rule	Real exchange rule
Capacity utilization	69%	3.8%	−1.2%	3.8%
Foreign debt	87%	−0.2%	0.1%	−0.2%
Wage share	50%	−0.6%	0.2%	−0.6%
Exchange rate	85%	0.3%	−0.1%	0.3%
Inflation	1%	2.9%	−0.9%	2.9%
Interest rate	5%	−25.2%	7.7%	−25.2%

seems to apply to emerging economies with high pass-through values and partial dollarization (Gopinath and Itskhoki, 2021; Reinhart et al., 2003).

Table 5.2 presents the results for the WLR regime, and the first rule analyzed is price stability. Again, the monetary authority response sets down the interest rate after the sudden change in the GFCy. Nevertheless, because the dependence of the economy on the global financial markets and imports is lower, the loose monetary policy pushes economic activity without pressing on the exchange rate. In this regime, the deflationary post-shock effect is weaker, so the interest rate reduction is also more limited. Under this more stable configuration, the central bank stabilizes the economy and pushes up utilization without provoking a massive regressive distributional shift. In this regard, the WLR resembles more to a more solid emerging economy, less exposed to the external market's volatility.

CONCLUDING REMARKS

In this chapter, we analyzed how external financial shocks conducted by the GFCy to EMDEs could be magnified or dampened out, depending on the kind of monetary policy rules followed by EMDEs' central banks under different regime configurations. To accomplish this, we evaluated the bust GFCy transmission to EMDEs through a Neo-Kaleckian model of growth, inflation, income distribution, and external debt. We calibrated and simulated the model to evaluate the effects of this phase of GFCy spread on income distribution, capacity utilization, and real exchange rates.

We treated three distinct policy rules and two regimes. We tried to emulate a profit-led regime very dependent on capital inflows to expand, and a WLR with looser ties with external financing. The model also provides some insights to think about the short-run and long-term effects of the GFCy on EMDEs. On the one hand, capital flights cause exchange rate devaluations and recession at the beginning, although the economy stabilizes into a new steady state as time goes by. Under the PDR, the post-shock scenario mixes lower output and real appreciation due to increased surplus in the current account. There, an active monetary intervention will always be effective to avoid a debt-deflation trap. Nevertheless, the inflation and real exchange rate rules seem more adequate to boost output at the cost of higher inflation, compared to the BaU. On the other hand, the output rule takes the utilization rate to the pre-shock levels and results in lower inflation in contrast to the other scenarios.

In the case of the WLR, the utilization rule looks like a less effective intervention monetary policy tool when policy makers are concerned with output maximization, but it seems to be correct if they want a lower inflation level. On the contrary, given the positive post-shock equilibria in terms of output, the price and real exchange rate rules are more adequate to restore inflation and boost output in subsequent periods.

To sum up, the use of monetary policy rules in EMDEs should consider not only the main goal of monetary authorities (inflation, capacity utilization, and external competitiveness), but also the regime that prevails in each economy, and its interaction with each monetary policy rule to dampen the negative financial spillovers related to the bust phase of the GFCy. The regulation of the financial account seems to be a key complementary policy instrument to accomplish this aim.

NOTES

1.   The usual disclaimer applies.
2.   Borio and Zhu (2008) define the risk-taking channel as the impact of changes in policy rates on either risk perceptions or risk tolerance. Rajan (2005) and Borio

and Lowe (2002) noted that the active stabilization policy from central banks may have lowered private agents' uncertainty and increased their optimism more than could be justified: higher levels of global risk aversion, all else equal, increase the likelihood of both an external crisis and a sudden stop event, confirming that global push factors matter.
3.   For a description of some of the most recognized PKAMPR, see Asensio (2012).

REFERENCES

Abeles, M., and D. Panigo (2015). "Dealing with Cost-Push Inflation in Latin America: Multi-Causality in a Context of Increased Openness and Commodity Price Volatility", *Review of Keynesian Economics* 3(4): 517–35.

Aguiar, A., B. Narayanan, and R. McDougall (2016). "An Overview of the GTAP 9 Data Base", *Journal of Global Economic Analysis* 1(1): 181–208.

Aidar, G., and J. Braga (2020). "Country-Risk Premium in the Periphery and the International Financial Cycle 1999–2019", *Investigaciones Económicas* 79(313): 78–111.

Airaudo, M., E. Buffie, and L.-F. Zanna (2016). "Inflation Targeting and Exchange Rate Management in Less Developed Countries", IMF Working Paper 16/55.

Aldasoro, I., S. Avdjiev, C. Borio, and P. Disyatat (2020). "Global and Domestic Financial Cycles: Variations on a Theme", BIS Working Papers No 864.

Asensio, A. (2012). "Between the Cup and the Lip: On Post Keynesian Interest Rate Rules and Long-Term Interest Rate Management", in L.-P. Rochon and S.Y. Olawoye (eds): *Monetary Policy and Central Banking*, 3–20. Edward Elgar Publishing.

Atesoglu, H. (2008). "Monetary Policy Rules and U.S. Monetary Policy", *Journal of Post Keynesian Economics* 30(3): 403–08.

Blecker, R. (2011). "Open Economy Models of Distribution and Growth", in E. Hein and E. Stockhammer (eds): *A Modern Guide to Keynesian Macroeconomics and Economic Policies*, 215–39. Edward Elgar Publishing.

Bofinger, T., and P. Wollmershäuser (2003). "Managed Floating as a Monetary Policy Strategy", *Economic Change and Restructuring* 36(2): 81–109.

Bonizzi, B., and A. Kaltenbrunner (2021). "A Minskyan Framework for the Analysis of Financial Flows to Emerging Economies", in B. Bonizzi, A. Kaltenbrunner, and R. Ramos (eds): *Emerging Economies and the Global Financial System Post-Keynesian Analysis*, 43–55. Routledge.

Borio, C., and P. Lowe (2002). "Asset Prices, Financial and Monetary Stability: Exploring the Nexus", BIS Working Papers No 114.

Borio, C., and H. Zhu (2008). "Capital Regulation, Risk-Taking and Monetary Policy: A Missing Link in the Transmission Mechanism?", BIS Working Papers No 268.

Bortz, P. G., G. Michelena, and F. Toledo (2018). "Foreign Debt, Conflicting Claims and Income Policies in a Kaleckian Model of Growth and Distribution", *Journal of Globalization and Development* 9(1), 1–22.

Botta, A. (2021). "Financial Liberalization, Exchange Rate Dynamics and the Financial Dutch Disease in Developing and Emerging Economies", in B. Bonizzi, A. Kaltenbrunner, and R. Ramos (eds): *Emerging Economies and the Global Financial System Post-Keynesian Analysis*, 181–96. Routledge.

Brandao-Marques, L., G. Gelos, T. Harjes, R. Sahay, and Y. Xue (2020). "Monetary Policy Transmission in Emerging Markets and Developing Economies", IMF Working Paper 20/35.

Centro de Economía Internacional (2003, April). *Cooperación Macroeconómica en El Mercosur. Un Análisis de la Interdependencia y una Propuesta de Cooperación. Estudios del CEI* No 4, Ministerio de Relaciones Exteriores, Comercio Internacional y Culto Secretaría De Comercio y Relaciones Económicas Internacionales.

Chari, A., K. Stedman, and C. Lundblad (2020). "Capital Flows in Risky Times: Risk-On/Risk-Off and Emerging Market Tail Risk", Technical Report, NBER.

Cimoli, M., G.T. Lima, and G. Porcile (2016). "The Production Structure, Exchange Rate Preferences and the Short-Run–Medium-Run Macrodynamics", *Structural Change and Economics Dynamics* 37: 13–26.

Cutler, D., J. Poterba, and L. Summers (1990). "Speculative Dynamics and the Role of Feedback Traders", *American Economic Review* 80(2): 63–8.

Damill, M., and R. Frenkel (2009). "Las Políticas Macroeconómicas en la Evolución Reciente de la Economía Argentina", *Nuevos Documentos CEDES* 65.

Fontana, G., and A. Palacio-Vera (2007). "Are Long-Run Price Stability and Short-Run Output Stabilization all that Monetary Policy Can Aim For?", *Metroeconomica* 58(2): 269–98.

Frankel, J., and K. Froot (1990). "Chartists, Fundamentalists and Trading in the Foreign Exchange Market", *American Economic Review* 80(2): 181–5.

Ghosh, A., J. Kim, M.S. Qureshi, and J. Zalduendo (2014). "Surges", *Journal of International Economics* 92(2): 266–85.

Gopinath, G., and O. Itskhoki (2021). "Dominant Currency Paradigm: A Review", NBER Working Paper 29556.

Harvey, J. (1993). "The Institution of Foreign Exchange Trading", *Journal of Economic Issues* 27(3): 679–98.

Jordà, O., M. Schularick, A. Taylor, and F. Ward (2018). "Global Financial Cycles and Risk Premiums", Federal Reserve Bank of San Francisco Working Paper 2018-05.

Kohler, K. (2021). "Post Keynesian and Structuralist Approaches to Boom–Bust Cycles in Emerging Economies", in B. Bonizzi, A. Kaltenbrunner, and R. Ramos (eds): *Emerging Economies and the Global Financial System Post-Keynesian Analysis*, 56–69. Routledge.

Langtangen, H. (2012). *A Primer on Scientific Programming with Python*. Springer.

Lavoie, M., and G. Daigle (2011). "A Behavioral Finance Model of Exchange Rate Expectations Within a Stock-Flow Consistent Framework", *Metroeconomica* 62(3): 434–58.

Miranda-Agrippino, S., and H. Rey (2021). "The Global Financial Cycle", Centre for Economic Policy Research DP16580.

Moosa, I. (2003). *International Financial Operations*. Palgrave Macmillan.

Palley, T. (2007). "Monetary Policy in an Endogenous Money Economy", in P. Arestis and M. Sawyer (eds): *A Handbook of Alternative Monetary Economics*, 242–57, Edward Elgar Publishing.

Rajan, R. (2005). "Has Financial Development Made the World Riskier?", NBER Working Paper 11728.

Reinhart, C., K. Rogoff, and M. Savastano (2003). "Addicted to Dollars", NBER Working Paper 10015.

Rey, H. (2013). "Dilemma Not Trilemma: The Global Financial Cycle and Monetary Policy Independence", Federal Reserve Bank of Kansas City Economic Policy Symposium.

Spronk, R., W. Verschoor, and R. Zwinkels (2013). "Carry Trade and Foreign Exchange Rate Puzzles", *European Economic Review* 60: 17–31.

Tadeu Lima, G., and M. Setterfield (2008). "Inflation Targeting and Macroeconomic Stability in A Post Keynesian Economy", *Journal of Post Keynesian Economics* 30(3): 435–61.

Terra, F., and P. Arestis (2017). "Monetary Policy in the Post Keynesian Theoretical Framework", *Brazilian Journal of Political Economy* 37(1): 45–64.

Tily, G. (2009). "The General Theory and Monetary Policy: Investment Versus Inflation", *European Journal of Economics and Economic Policies: Intervention* 6(1): 97–118.

Woodford, M. (2003). *Interest and Prices: Foundations of a Theory of Monetary Policy*. Princeton University Press.

Woodford, M. (2012, August 31). "Methods of Policy Accommodation at the Interest-Rate Lower Bound", presented at the Federal Reserve Bank of Kansas City Symposium on "The Changing Policy Landscape," Jackson Hole, WY.

Yilmaz, S.-D., and Godin, A. (2020). "Modelling Small Open Developing Economies in a Financialized World: A Stock-Flow Consistent Prototype Growth Model", Working Paper 5eb7e0e8-560f-4ce6-91a5-5, Agence Française de Développement.

PART III

Monetary policies and exchange rates in LACs

6. Exchange rate management in Latin America: towards the making of a policy target exchange rate

Daniel Pérez-Ruiz, Gary Dymski, and Annina Kaltenbrunner

INTRODUCTION

In recent decades, a distinctive aspect of exchange rates in developing and emerging economies (DEEs) has been their volatility and large swings, which are often caused by short-term financial flows. As a result, in these economies, political and academic debates often place the degree of "misalignment" of the exchange rate from some optimal exchange rate at the centre of the analysis (Marconi et al., 2021; Edwards, 1989; Hinkle & Montiel, 1999).

These empirical phenomena – that is, the large swings in exchange rates and values often incompatible with underlying real sector dynamics – are a challenge to neoclassical equilibrium exchange rate theorists who subscribe to the notion that the exchange rate will automatically adjust to its optimal long-term value where free-floating regimes are an optimal policy. Post-Keynesian theorists, who explain exchange rate dynamics with strong attention to the role of uncertainty and expectations, reject the notion of an equilibrium value towards which the exchange rate will adjust by market forces (i.e. Harvey, 1991; Kaltenbrunner, 2011). Nevertheless, for this approach, the challenge remains to specify an exchange rate that would be sustainable or optimum for the economy and that could act as an appropriate reference for policy formulation.

This chapter adopts the latter view and aims to set the groundwork for the Policy Target Exchange Rate (PTER) proposal consistent with post-Keynesian theory. Motivated by the emphasis on exchange rate management put forward by post-Keynesian authors, the aim of this chapter is twofold. First, it critically engages with existing equilibrium exchange rate approaches to interrogate whether they can form the basis for a policy target rate from a post-Keynesian perspective. Second, it develops the argument that an approach to the exchange rate, which identifies a sustainable or optimal exchange rate value, can be reconciled with post-Keynesian analysis if it is interpreted normatively as a target for policy rather than a value to which market forces will adjust automatically. Thus, it aims to lay a foundation for a theoretical framework to conceive an exchange rate rule such as the PTER, which is hypothetically capable of neutralising and stabilising the adverse effects of financial variables on exchange rates.

This chapter is structured as follows. The next section motivates the proposal of a PTER from a post-Keynesian perspective. The third section critically reviews existing approaches to "optimum" exchange rates and points to the Industrial Equilibrium Exchange Rate (IEER) approach as a potential candidate on which to build a coherent post-Keynesian approach to PTERs. Next, the chapter proposes two extensions to the IEER framework to take into account the importance of financial variables which, in our view, should be considered when calculating potential exchange rate targets for policymaking. The final section concludes.

WHY IS THE PTER COMPATIBLE WITH POST-KEYNESIAN THEORY?

The concept PTER draws on two main premises. First, the general use of the terms currency "undervaluation" and "overvaluation", even in post-Keynesian economics, suggests the existence of an optimum value. Academics and policymakers often debate whether a currency is "artificial", "weak", or "strong". Post-Keynesian authors are no exception to this (Moore, 2004). The notion of an optimum level of the exchange rate is necessary to assess whether markets or governments have set the exchange rate at the right level. Indeed, nominal exchange rate and real exchange rate volatility, misalignment, and the repercussions on the economy have gained increasing attention from post-Keynesian economists (Alcantara-Alencar et al., 2018; Harvey & Deprez, 1999; Harvey, 1991, 2019; Perraton, 2014). Given that an optimal value can be defined, the second premise is that active management of the exchange rate can help achieve and sustain that optimal value. These two premises underly post-Keynesian authors' support for using active macroeconomic management to achieve competitive exchange rates (Ferrari-Filho & De Paula, 2008; Guzman et al., 2018), and our own investigation here of PTER.

The notion of a PTER becomes relevant in light of the shift from an open-economy policy trilemma to an apparent dilemma (Rey, 2015). Many scholarly papers often point to the monetary policy trilemma as one of the reasons why a country needs to give up its decision to manage the exchange rate. The trilemma emphasises the idea that the exchange rate regime is key. The monetary policy trilemma suggests that a country needs to choose among three policy options: manage exchange rates, free capital mobility, and an independent monetary policy. Nowadays, motivated by the monetary policy trilemma, most countries tend to favour free capital flows and independent monetary policy. It is argued that such a combination is only possible if a country adopts a free-floating exchange rate regime, given that such a regime is thought of as one that portrays stability in the economic system.

However, the debate regarding macroeconomic management and regulated capital accounts has taken a different direction and has reduced the pessimism towards managing the exchange rate. Rey (2015) has challenged the policy trilemma and argued that there is a monetary policy dilemma. Similarly, Kaltenbrunner and Painceira (2017) suggest that combining inflation targeting and exchange rate management while operating with an open capital account can be unfeasible and detrimental. Ostry et al. (2012) suggest that, if there are two available instruments for the central bank – namely, the interest rate and foreign exchange market intervention – these need to be used together to achieve price and exchange rate objectives. In particular, using the second instrument (foreign exchange market intervention) can boost credibility in the face of volatile capital flows and large swings in exchange rates (Ostry et al., 2012).

Indeed, the emphasis on macroeconomic management – in particular, capital account regulations and exchange rate management – has characterised post-Keynesian thinking. Post-Keynesian economists have suggested managing the exchange rate given the market volatility to which DEEs are regularly exposed, arguing that these economies should target a competitive and stable real exchange rate to achieve certain policy objectives (growth and employment; Ferrari-Filho & De Paula, 2008). Furthermore, it has been argued that DEEs should aim for a rather depreciated, competitive policy rate to achieve a balanced current account to avoid boom–bust capital flow cycles (De Paula et al., 2017).

This discussion shows that identifying an optimum/equilibrium exchange rate value, and potential deviations thereof (misalignment), is a crucial issue even for post-Keynesian economists. Yet the question of which theoretical approach one should look at from this perspective remains and demands a thorough examination of the equilibrium exchange rate approaches, which will be performed in the next section.

ARE CURRENT EQUILIBRIUM APPROACHES SUITABLE FOR POST-KEYNESIAN ANALYSIS?

This section presents a brief critical review of existing equilibrium exchange rate theories with a view to interrogating whether they can form the basis for a policy target rate from a post-Keynesian perspective. These theories include the neoclassical approaches commonly used to assess exchange rate misalignment: the Purchasing Power Parity (PPP), the Fundamental Equilibrium Exchange Rate (FEER), and the Behavioural Equilibrium Exchange Rate (BEER). In addition, it reviews existing heterodox approaches to the exchange rate which envision some form of "optimum" or equilibrium values. These include the Alternative Approach to Long-Run Real Exchange Rates (AALRER) by Anwar Shaikh (1991), and the IEER proposed by New Developmentalist (ND) scholars (Bresser-Pereira, 2009, 2013; Marconi, 2012).

Three main equilibrium exchange rate theories in neoclassical economics are commonly used for policy assessment. PPP, FEER models, and BEER (Clark & MacDonald, 1998; Isard, 1995; MacDonald, 1997; Sarno & Taylor, 2003). The PPP hypothesis, for example, is used by policymakers as a rule of thumb: when "a country establishes or adjusts an exchange rate peg, it generally relies on some type of quantitative frameworks, such as the PPP formula, in order to help assess the appropriate level for the new parity" (Isard, 1995, p. 70). The International Monetary Fund's Consultative Group on Exchange Rate Issues (CGER) has extended and used these methodologies to assess exchange rate developments in DEEs. As this chapter shows, all these approaches share the assumption that, ultimately, the exchange rate will act as a market-equilibrating price. Moreover, equilibrium is reduced to a balance of payments equilibrium without considering the potentially important role of exchange rates in influencing a country's productive structure.

Equilibrium Exchange Rates in Neoclassical Theory

One of the earliest neoclassical approaches to exchange rate determination is the PPP hypothesis, which adopts a positivist stance that seeks to explain the actual behaviour of the exchange rate. The PPP hypothesis links exchange rate behaviour to the ratio of the domestic-to-foreign price level over the long run. This hypothesis is linked to the idea that prices world-wide should equalise, and exchange rate movements will equilibrate the trade balance. That is, the role of the exchange rate is to adjust if domestic prices increase, as this causes a loss of competitiveness. The nominal exchange rate needs to depreciate to ensure that the trade balance is restored. The mechanism by which this comes about is a generalisation of the law of one price (LOP; goods arbitrage) to the macroeconomic level; that is, one unit of domestic currency should have the same purchasing power to buy an identical basket of goods abroad at the prevailing exchange rate (Isard, 1995).

Formally, the absolute version of the PPP is defined as:

$$e = \frac{p}{p^*} \qquad\qquad (6.1)$$

where *e* is the nominal exchange rate measured in units of foreign currency per unit of domestic currency; *p* is the domestic price level index (for goods and services); and *p**is the foreign price level index (for goods and services). It is said that the PPP holds when the ratio of domestic and foreign price levels equals 1 (Gagnon & Hinterschweiger, 2011).

One PPP extension is the Balassa-Samuelson effect, which considers that different productivity levels and their impact on wages and goods prices lead to permanent divergence from the absolute version of the PPP (Sarno, 2008). This extension shows that, due to catching up and higher prices in the non-tradable sectors, countries might be characterised by a structural tendency to real exchange rate appreciation.

Objections to this hypothesis have taken different paths. First, the existence of transaction costs, tariffs, and taxes in trade violates one of the principles underpinning the LOP (Taylor & Taylor, 2004). Second, the calculation of price indices (consumer price indices) differs from country to country as these indices include non-tradables. In addition, the PPP assumes the real exchange rate to be a constant, an assumption that is criticised and reconsidered by BEER and FEER models, which are analysed further below. Third, the argument that the real exchange rate remains constant contrasts with the argument that, if the real exchange rate adjusts to balance the trade balance, then the real exchange rate should be determined by factors that affect both competitiveness and the demand structure for goods. The last objection led to the development of two main approaches to the real exchange rate.

Two approaches to the estimation of the real exchange rate have become particularly prominent: the BEER and FEER models. The BEER approach evaluates the behaviour and the level of the real effective exchange rate (REER) over the long run. It is a positivist approach since it displays the factors that determine the actual behaviour of the exchange rate. It is an approach in which there is an assumption of a self-equilibrating mechanism to these rates over time, as the exchange rate is assumed to be in equilibrium through time. The BEER is expressed in a general form as:

$$s_t = \beta_1' Z_{1t} + \beta_2' Z_{2t} + \tau T_t + \varepsilon_t \qquad (6.2)$$

where s_t is the BEER, Z_{1t} is a vector of macroeconomic fundamentals that influence the real exchange rate over the long term, Z_{2t} is a vector of macroeconomic fundamentals that affect the exchange rates over the medium term, T_t is a vector of transitory factors that influence the exchange rate in the short run, and ε_t is the error term (Driver & Westaway, 2004).

The BEER approach is based on the direct empirical (econometric) analysis of the relationship between the REER and its short-run and long-run fundamental determinants: the risk-adjusted interest parity condition, the terms of trade, relative prices (tradable to non-tradable), and the net foreign assets relative to gross domestic product (GDP) are among the most prominent (Clark & MacDonald, 1998). From within neoclassical economics itself, the BEER approach has been mainly criticised for its deficient links from economic theory and the lack of robustness of the reduced form equations commonly computed (Driver & Westaway, 2004; López-Villavicencio et al., 2012).

A second approach to the optimal or equilibrium real exchange rate in neoclassical economics is the FEER. Different from the two models above, the FEER adopts a normative stance, one that aims to explain the desired behaviour of exchange rates, as it is the desired level of the real exchange rate consistent with "ideal economic conditions" that guarantees the medium-term macroeconomic equilibrium (Wren-Lewis, 1992). This approach incorporates normative features but ultimately remains tied to the notion that the exchange rate will tend towards optimality over time, at least by some interpretations and empirical applications (e.g. Barisone et al., 2006; Clark & MacDonald, 1998). The FEER is a medium-run approach in which ideal macroeconomic conditions are understood as the simultaneous achievement of internal and external balance (Driver & Westaway, 2004). The internal equilibrium is given by the Non-Accelerating Inflation Rate of Unemployment (NAIRU). The external balance is characterised as the net flow of capital consistent with internal equilibrium (Williamson, 1994). Formally, the FEER is represented as follows:

$$FEER = \frac{-KA - b_0 - b_2 y_d - b_3 y_f}{b_1} \qquad (6.3)$$

where KA is the equilibrium capital account in the medium term, and y_d and y_f are the domestic and foreign output at full employment, respectively (Clark & MacDonald, 1998). Thus, the main macroeconomic fundamentals in this approach are the sustainable capital account and the domestic and foreign output, which will be the ultimate drivers of exchange rates in the medium run.

The FEER has its origins in the proposal for global macroeconomic management put forward by the Institute for International Economics which relies on the "target zone system of exchange rate management" in which some exchange rate flexibility is allowed (Krugman, 1991). Thus, it highlights the benefits of stable exchange rates, but it does so for developed countries (McKinnon, 1984; Williamson, 1986).

Several objections to the FEER approach are often made. On a theoretical level, one can raise three concerns. First, this approach is criticised because the FEER estimation does not consider real determinants of exchange rates. The main reason is that the approach focuses on the real exchange rate that equates to the current account with a sustainable capital account. Thus, it focuses on the determinants of the current account, which is then calibrated at full employment values. It is, indeed, not a complete theory of exchange rate determination but rather a normative approach of identifying an exchange rate consistent with ideal macroeconomic conditions. A second criticism is the difficulty of estimating the potential output that is associated with the concept of the NAIRU. Third, there is no theoretical explanation of how the adjustment mechanism operates, driving the real exchange rate towards equilibrium (Clark & MacDonald, 1998). Such a critique is driven by the assumption that the current real exchange rate will converge to the FEER over time (Clark & MacDonald, 1998).

Overall, neoclassical equilibrium approaches to exchange rate determination share the idea that the exchange rate's role is to act as a market-equilibrating price, which has become difficult to sustain in a world of increasing imbalances. It has been shown that the role of the exchange rate under the PPP hypothesis is limited to equilibrating the trade balance. The BEER assumes a self-equilibrating system, and the exchange rate is always tending to optimality. Perhaps the least influenced by this notion is the FEER approach because it is a normative rate, but ultimately there is some assumption of equilibrium adjustment. Exchange rates, in practice, do not automatically adjust to restore external equilibrium; rather, exchange rates have been increasingly determined by financial factors. Finally, neoclassical approaches have ignored the industrial structure of economies and instead have only paid attention to the balance of payments equilibrium and automatic adjustments towards the long-term equilibrium.

Equilibrium Exchange Rate Approaches in Heterodox Theory

Heterodox approaches to equilibrium real exchange rates are scarce and are not commonly used for exchange rate policy assessment. Among them, we find the AALRER and the IEER. Two main characteristics set them apart from the neoclassical approaches above. The first is the fact that these approaches pay key attention to the specific industrial structures of the economies. This is reflected in their consideration of the manufacturing unit labour costs as central determinants of exchange rates. The second is that these approaches acknowledge that the actual exchange rate is not around its appropriate value and, consequently, trade imbalances can persist. However, while the AALRER is concerned about the behaviour of real exchange rates, which will depend on the economies' industrial structures, and adopts a more positivist position, the IEER is concerned about promoting structural change rather than just external equilibrium and assumes a more normative position.

The AALRER models the real exchange rate's centre of gravity over the long term. The centre of gravity is a long-run equilibrium position that assumes that prices and profits are equalised. This implies that producers are employing resources in the best way, allowing them to have a uniform rate of profit (Cunningham, 1995). In the AALRER approach, the real exchange rate is a function of the relative real unit labour cost of the most efficient producers of tradable goods. Thus, the exchange rate is given by the competitive cost structures of the price-leading industries of tradable goods in two countries, adjusted by the tradable/non-tradable goods ratio (Shaikh & Antonopoulos, 2013). In addition, the model further assumes that the prices of two baskets of tradable goods are equalised after adjusting for transportation cost, tariffs, and quotas (Shaikh & Antonopoulos, 2013). The real exchange rate determination is given by the following formula:

$$s \equiv \frac{pe}{p^*} \approx \frac{v_r}{v_r^*} \frac{(\tau)}{(\tau^*)} \tag{6.4}$$

where s is the real exchange rate, e is the nominal exchange rate, p is the price of domestic tradable goods, p^* is the foreign tradable goods' price, v_r is the most efficient producer's vertically integrated unit labour cost in the domestic economy, v_r^* is the most efficient producer's vertically integrated unit labour cost in the foreign economy (both unit labour costs for tradable goods in a common currency), τ is the tradable/non-tradable adjustment ratio in the domestic economy and τ^* the tradable/non-tradable adjustment ratio in the foreign economy. It is important to note that labour productivity, technology, and tradable sectors' real wages are factors attached to v_r. Thus, a country's competitiveness is primarily driven by these factors (Martínez-Hernández, 2017).

Different implications follow the AALRER approach. First, it cannot automatically adjust itself and eliminate imbalances (Shaikh & Antonopoulos, 2013). The exchange rate is not a market-clearing price; therefore, trade imbalances can be a constant. Even by considering flexible or semi-flexible exchange rate regimes, exchange rates cannot adjust structural trade imbalances (Martínez-Hernández, 2017). Although trade imbalances, in this model, are the outcome of a country's relative competitive position (Martínez-Hernández, 2017), long-run equilibrium exchange rates are consistent with trade imbalances[1] (Antonopoulos, 1997).

Possible criticisms of these lines of reasoning can be made in terms of the relation between the trade balance and real exchange rates. The "direct" relation between trade surplus and deficits is poorly explained in this model and appears to have little notion in terms of trade elasticities. For Shaikh (1991, 2016), a fall in price will expand the market for the most efficient producer and the most efficient economy. It is clearly stated that the kind of elasticity that remains is the "Marshall–Lerner–Robinson elasticity in orthodox economics"

(Shaikh, 1991, p. 2). Overall, through real wage adjustment, a country can improve its trade balance position (Antonopoulos, 1997). Consequently, most efficient countries will tend to operate with surpluses on their trade balance since a price-cutting firm can increase its market share. However, the degree to which individuals react to price changes may not always be the same and can vary across economies because of preferences and trade patterns.

The AALRER is a well-advanced, coherent, and realistic approach to explaining real exchange rate behaviour. And even though financial factors have been considered, it does not provide the groundwork to determine exchange rate policy targets. It aims to investigate the factors determining competitiveness given its positivist nature, and its lack of normative features does not allow one to determine a value of the exchange rate that policy could target.

Unlike the AALRER approach, in the IEER approach, the equilibrium exchange rate is a desired exchange rate level; thus, it is a normative approach to exchange rate determination. It does not aim to explain real exchange rate determination, but rather seeks to determine appropriate levels of the exchange rate for macroeconomic development. In this sense, it lends itself well to be the basis for the policy target rate suggested in this chapter. Moreover, rather than assessing the exchange rate's impact on internal and external equilibrium, as in the FEER approaches, it is explicitly concerned with the exchange rate's value and countries' industrial structures. The IEER is the exchange rate that allows world-wide state-of-the-art industries to remain competitive abroad (Marconi, 2012). This value neutralises the "Dutch disease" that is considered a major structural phenomenon in DEEs, as explained below.

For the ND approach, the real exchange rate has a central role in economic development, given its impact on investment and economic growth. In addition, DEEs experience a chronic and cyclical overvaluation of the exchange rate because of the adoption of three typical policies: high interest rates, the growth cum foreign savings strategy, and the use of the exchange rate as a tool to anchor inflation (Resende & Terra, 2018). Exchange rate overvaluation reduces the profitability of manufacturer-producers (Bresser-Pereira, 2017; Frenkel & Rapetti, 2015). Two main drivers that determine such overvaluation are differentiated by their structural and cyclical nature: the Dutch disease and foreign capital inflows.

At the forefront of this approach is the Dutch disease or commodities export boom, a characteristic of countries, such as Brazil, which are endowed with abundant natural resources that possess a competitive advantage. Thus, the ND approach views the Dutch disease as a "structural" problem. As a result, large currency inflows, through higher revenues from exports, overvalue the domestic currency (Bresser-Pereira, 2006; Bresser-Pereira & Gala, 2008; Marconi, 2012). The overvaluation of the domestic currency reduces the profitability of domestic commodity exporters. However, commodity exporters still maintain a high profit rate because of their lower costs, which allows them to remain competitive in foreign markets. According to these authors, the larger issue is that such overvaluation leads to a deindustrialisation process and, therefore, lower rates of growth. In other words, the trade balance is affected by an increase in the share of exported primary goods relative to manufacturing goods in imports (Marconi, 2012).

Second, the massive speculative capital inflows are the second major driver of the exchange rate overvaluation. However, in the ND approach these capital flows are considered less important because they are a cyclical factor affecting the overvaluation of the domestic currency rather than a structural one, such as commodity dependence. For example, for Marconi (2012), it is cyclic given that capital flows respond to the difference between domestic and foreign interest rates plus the expected exchange rate. According to Carvalho (2018), two main reasons support this argument. First, this approach assumes that interest rate policies can change over time; therefore, no systemic pressures are coming from this side. Second, "autonomous changes in expectations are assumed to be random in nature so that their influence is expected to dissipate in longer stretches of time" (Carvalho, 2018, p. 117).

In this context, the ND approach devises three concepts of equilibrium exchange rates: the Current Account Equilibrium Exchange Rate (CAEER), the Foreign Debt Equilibrium Exchange Rate (FDEER), and the IEER. The CAEER is a rate that balances the current account inter-temporally, but alters the composition of the trade balance since, at such a rate, the commodities trade balance is superior to the manufacturing trade balance, leading to a loss or change in the productive capacity (Marconi, 2012). The CAEER is conceptually similar to the PPP and BEER in the sense that it is a rate that balances the current account. The FDEER is the exchange rate that allows a country to grow with foreign savings by operating with permanent current account deficits (Bresser-Pereira et al., 2014). According to Bresser-Pereira et al. (2014), a characteristic of this equilibrium exchange rate is that the net foreign inflows necessary to finance the current account deficits should be equal to the rate of growth of GDP, which guarantees that the ratio of foreign debt to GDP will remain constant. Bresser-Pereira (2019) argues that the ND approach considers this exchange rate level as a non-competitive equilibrium. For the ND approach, such a level of the exchange rate corresponds to an appreciated level compared to the IEER and the CAEER. Thus, it is a value that depresses investment and boosts consumption. He argues that this concept is Williamson's FEER, which aims to maintain the economy's internal and external equilibrium. Finally, the ND approach puts forward the IEER, which is the cornerstone of their argument; this allows manufacturers producing with "state-of-the-art" technologies to remain competitive in domestic and foreign markets with a reasonable profit margin, consistent with current account surpluses.

In the literature, there are two IEER methodologies. On the one hand, the one proposed by Marconi (2012) starts from the assumption that the price of manufactured goods is equal to that of competitors in order to be competitive in the international market. It draws on the pricing rule that manufacturing producers tend to adopt in which the main cost of production is attributed to labour. As a result, the real IEER is mainly determined by the relative unit labour costs. Formally, the IEER is given by the following equation:

$$s = \frac{ulc}{ulc*} \tag{6.5}$$

where s is the real IEER, *ulc* represents the domestic real unit labour costs, and *ulc** is the foreign real unit labour costs.

On the other hand, Oreiro et al. (2020) argue that, in DEEs, manufacturer-producers do not operate as world-wide state-of-the-art actors. They claim the existence of a technological gap that reduces the manufacturing industry's influence on real income. These authors redefine the IEER as the real exchange rate that allows a country to keep steady, across time, the manufacturing industry's effect on real income. Oreiro et al. (2020) assume that this effect is given by its previous value, the real exchange rate, the complexity index, and the real income per capita. Formally:

$$\theta_t^* = \frac{\beta_4(RCP_{t-h})^2 - [\beta_1 ICE_{t-h} + \beta_3 RCP_{t-h}]}{\beta_0} \tag{6.6}$$

where the level of the IEER is a function of RCP_{t-h}, the real per capita income, and ICE_{t-h}, which is the Hidalgo and Haussman complexity index.

In sum, with its normative character and emphasis on the relation between the exchange rate and countries' industrial structures, the ND's IEER is a potential starting point for a post-Keynesian PTER. It is a potential candidate on which to build a coherent post-Keynesian approach, given its normative nature. That is, it is an exchange rate that cannot prevail naturally, and policy is essential to achieve it. However, there are also some shortcomings. At a practical level, the level of the IEER is little explained, and the resulting equations can be easily confused with its neoclassical counterpart. Although the mechanisms and objectives are different from those of the PPP, the resulting equation shows an exchange rate that adjusts only to labour cost differentials in the same way that the PPP adjusts the exchange rate to changes in prices. An open question is whether real values are easier to target than nominal values of the exchange rate. The IEER is by nature a policy target, and as such, these types of targets should be formulated both for the real and nominal exchange rates.

More conceptually, one major drawback of the IEER approach is that trade is the "permanent source of the impulses that are durably expressed in the behaviour of the exchange rate" (Carvalho, 2018, p. 117), in which prices of manufactured goods are the main elements driving the exchange rate. In this view, the pressures arising from financial markets are only considered ephemeral, cyclical factors. Amendments to the IEER approach, such as that proposed by Oreiro et al. (2020), have failed to incorporate external factors into the exchange rate determination equation and only consider real domestic variables.

This disregards the structural pressures on exchange rates arising from financial markets. It underestimates both the pressure coming from yield-driven foreign financial flows and the stock of foreign currency denominated liabilities, which brings to the picture the relation of exchange rates and the balance of payments. It is the incorporation of these factors into the IEER to which the chapter turns in the next section.

WHAT ROLE IS THERE FOR FINANCE IN THE IEER?

To this point, this chapter has critically assessed the existing equilibrium exchange rate approaches. It has shown that neoclassical equilibrium exchange rate theory remains tied to the notion that market outcomes are optimal. On the other hand, heterodox equilibrium exchange rate theory has followed a different path. Rather than assuming market-equilibrating forces, these approaches either acknowledge permanent states of disequilibrium or highlight the links between the economies' industrial structures and exchange rates.

The concept of the PTER adopts a normative perspective. It places particular emphasis on the ND concept of the IEER. However, the IEER approach remains deeply embedded in a "real" economic analysis and does not consider the structural pressures from financial factors on the exchange rate. The current formulation relegates to a minor issue the persistent effects of financial factors over exchange rates in DEEs for Latin American economies. Moreover, the ND does not engage in methodological considerations on how to justify their approach from a conceptual/methodological level. There is an implicit assumption that the IEER is a normative approach, but the ND does not embed this normative approach in Keynes's or post-Keynesian methodology. Thus, the PTER approach aims to fill both the theoretical and the methodological gaps.[2] It emerges as a concept in which the role of financial factors is considered in the formulation of the exchange rate target.

The importance of financial factors is clear in post-Keynesian literature. More concerned about the short and the medium term, the post-Keynesian approach focuses on the major role played by uncertainty and expectations in exchange rate determination, the structure and hierarchy of the international monetary system, and the debtor–creditor relations (Miles & Davidson, 1979; Davidson, 1982; Harvey, 1991; Kaltenbrunner, 2015). In addition, the relevance of financial factors is underlined in the recent experience of several Latin American economies. A recent report by the Bank for International Settlements (2021) points out that both real and financial factors are relevant for exchange rate determination in DEEs, which suggests that the current IEER formulation can be strengthened by considering financial factors in its formulation.

Although we do not intend to go deeper to revisit the IEER formulation, we consider that there are two main empirical and theoretical issues missing in the current IEER formulation that could increase its theoretical reach to give rise to the concept of the PTER.

First is the formal consideration of *yield-driven foreign financial flows and the structurally high interest rates* in DEEs. As argued before, post-Keynesian literature points at short-term capital flows, yield differentials, and liquidity as the main drivers of exchange rates. For the currency hierarchy proponents, capital flows and, thus, exchange rates in DEEs, have become more sensitive to monetary policy in high-income countries (HICs). This formal consideration must consider the fact that DEEs normally keep their interest rates higher compared to HICs. Yield-driven foreign financial flows can be destabilising and thus constitute a challenge for DEEs as they contribute to episodes of currency appreciation. One contemporary form of yield-driven foreign financial flows that is worth bringing into the picture is the carry trade strategy (De Conti et al., 2013; Barbosa et al., 2021).

Carry trade is defined as an investment strategy in which investors borrow in low-interest-rate currencies (funding currencies) to invest in high-interest-rate currencies (investment currencies). Carry trades usually invest in short-term instruments and benefit from the excess return derived from the interest rate differential and the exchange rate appreciation as investments are unhedged. The literature on carry trade considers that carry trade gains represent compensation for providing liquidity despite the risk of considerable losses (Brunnermeier & Pedersen, 2009). However, these strategies can lead to currency crashes in the investment currencies, preventing speculators from taking long positions in the investment currencies (Brunnermeier et al., 2009).

More relevant for our purposes is the fact that carry trade strategies are profitable over the long term[3] (Monetary and Economic Department Bank for International Settlements, 2015), challenging the key tenets of the interest parity theory, particularly the idea that speculators will bring the market to a point where no profit can be made. The interest parity theory put forward by Keynes explains and predicts short-term money market flows, which are assumed as dominant in the international exchange (Carvalho, 2018).

More concretely, the PTER can make the case of an exchange rate that aims to tackle the issue of high interest rates, which in turn attract yield-driven financial flows that lead to exchange rate appreciation. The idea behind this proposition is taken from Keynes's interest rate parity; thus, it aims to create a no-profit situation for speculators without fully seeking an exchange rate that validates Keynes's parity. As a result, the exchange rate will act in such a way that it trims yield-driven gains and will therefore neutralise the effect of carry trades on exchange rates. The proposed case is one where the exchange rate remains at a competitive level and still allows the most efficient domestic producers to remain competitive in the international markets.

Second is the formal consideration of the *stock of a country's foreign-denominated liabilities* that yield-driven financial flows create. Financial crises in DEEs have manifested the importance of managing external liabilities and liquidity to prevent the foreign liabilities build-up. Large volumes of foreign liabilities, especially short-term and unhedged ones, have contributed to crises in DEEs (Hawkins & Turner, 2000). In fact, DEEs have become more vulnerable than HICs, given the currency denomination of their external debt. One explanation of the accumulation of foreign-denominated liabilities in DEEs is the so-called "original sin". The "original sin" is described as the fact that the domestic currency cannot be used to borrow abroad, thus, they need to borrow in foreign currency (Eichengreen & Hausmann, 1999) due to the lack of monetary credibility. Therefore, economies are often constrained in their supply of foreign currency and the need to generate such foreign currency for debt repayment.

The above facts highlight the necessity of bringing back Keynes's insights on the transfer problem. Indeed, Keynes's transfer problem has been little explored in post-Keynesian literature. The transfer problem is defined in general terms as the "problem of transition [in the balance of payments] which occurs when there is a change in the locality where investment takes place" (Keynes, 1930, p. 307). Such a disturbance (i.e. a sudden stop in the foreign lending or capital flows) forces monetary authorities to adjust policy variables (the interest rate and/or the exchange rate) to effect a considerable change in the trade balance through the impact they have on the labour costs and the general price level. In Keynes's transfer problem, the idea is that the exchange rate directly affects the trade balance as it can directly affect relative price levels.

Keynes's (1930) argument of forcing a favourable trade balance to drive financial accounts into the desired direction is, to a certain extent, an argument that acknowledges a successful export-led strategy implicitly, as an increase in exports does not deteriorate the balance of payments simultaneously. Moreover, it is an argument that can be thought of as generating a virtuous cycle. That is, when demand pressures reach a level close to the existing productive capacity without deteriorating the trade balance, such an increase in demand can increase the growth rate of an economy as it stimulates investment, job creation, and movement from the less efficient sectors to highly efficient ones, along with an increase in the capacity to import, as domestic resources are more productive (Thirlwall, 2011).

Thus, a second case that can be made to extend the IEER approach is to create an exchange rate that incorporates the pressures that a stock of foreign-currency-denominated liabilities generates on exchange rates. It follows the idea that a country cannot sustain endless current account deficits (López & Cruz, 2000) and the limits that capital flows impose in financing current account deficits. Therefore, the case should be one in which the exchange rate allows a country to generate current account surpluses to guide the stock of foreign-currency-denominated liabilities towards a sustainable path.

CONCLUSIONS

This chapter has motivated the idea of the PTERs, which are ultimately two possible ways the IEER approach can be extended from a post-Keynesian perspective. This chapter first underscored the relevance of developing these rates in post-Keynesian theory to inform this discussion. It then reviewed the different neoclassical and heterodox approaches to exchange rate determination that are relevant to policymaking. Finally, it was argued that the IEER approach provides a foundation on which to build a solid post-Keynesian approach to PTERs in order to tackle the challenges posed by financial flows, in particular, carry trade strategies and the stock of foreign-currency-denominated liabilities arising from foreign financial flows.

As shown above, both facts have been relevant in recent decades and of interest for Keynes and post-Keynesians. On the one hand, the incorporation of the Interest Rate Parity rationale into the IEER formulation permits that exchange rate targets to incorporate into the analysis the effect that interest rates have on exchange rates, and raises the need to influence the behaviour of yield-driven financial flows to prevent exchange rate appreciation. On the other hand, rethinking Keynes's transfer problem to inform exchange rate targets contributes to preventing the foreign liabilities build-up, thus reducing the external vulnerability in DEEs. The development of the PTERs idea is not an easy task, especially in a world of capital mobility. The challenge relies not only on the development of the theoretical models but also on the feasibility and the policy measures that would need to be in place to make this work.

Thus, it is worth mentioning two essential elements that need to be further analysed. The first corresponds to the characteristics of the exchange rate regime. Although it is evident that the approach is motivated by the post-Keynesian support for exchange rate management, the implementation of the PTERs requires further clarification. In a world of high capital mobility, it seems reasonable to argue that PTERs can be better conceived in the presence of an exchange rate band. More precisely, given the nature of the policy targets and the constraints imposed by capital flows, the monitoring band would be a regime in which PTERs can be put into practice. The monitoring band has several advantages. First, expectations are stabilising under an exchange rate band (Williamson, 1999). Second, and in the same line of thought, is the fact that allowing the exchange rate to move within the band allows the economy to avoid the possibility that the optimum exchange rate lies outside the band, which in turn could lead to speculative pressures that could be costly to sustain (Williamson, 1999). Third is the idea that monetary authorities are not committed to intervening while the exchange rate is moving within the band, allowing an economy to avoid the continuous losses of international reserves or increasing sterilisation costs.

The second element concerns capital controls that are a *sine qua non* condition to achieve the PTERs. Both permanent and cyclical capital controls (Rey, 2015) on inflows and outflows can be applied to achieve the PTERs. On the one hand, permanent capital controls can be applied to certain assets for inflows and outflows, but the selection of these subtypes of assets constitutes a challenge for the policymaker. On the other hand, cyclical capital controls can be applied to credit flows and portfolio debt at the boom of the global financial cycle. As shown in this chapter, the idea of the PTER becomes relevant in light of the policy dilemma where monetary policy is rather constrained by the global financial cycle, regardless of the exchange rate regime. In this context, capital account regulation and, as such, capital controls become a must to achieve both the PTER and an independent monetary policy.

NOTES

1.   The AALRER leads to the following conclusion: "if exchange rate variations do not reflect changes in the 'fundamentals' as determined by the economic laws of international competition, such variations can only temporarily *cover up* trade imbalances" (Antonopoulos, 1997, p.57, emphasis in original). Accordingly, the persistence of trade imbalances are part of the functioning of the economic system. Antonopoulos contrasts neoclassical and classical equilibrium conceptions, arguing that "such 'equilibrium prices' are conceivable only as accompanied by cleared markets for neoclassical economists *while they are compatible with market turbulence, and thus surpluses of shortages for classical economists*" (Antonopoulos, 1997, p.43, emphasis added).

2.   Although it is not addressed in this chapter, the idea of the Policy Target Exchange Rate argues that there is a methodological gap to fill within the New Developmentalism approach. That is, it is important to define the concept of equilibrium in the context of exchange rate economics for post-Keynesian

theory. From a post Keynesian point of view, an equilibrium rate needs to be understood as a policy target defined as a hypothetical construct, long-period position, adequate to a given context, which is an ideal state from the point of view of production (Pérez-Ruiz, 2022).

3. A point to bear in mind is that, while carry trade strategies benefit from the interest rate differential and the exchange rate appreciation, there are several alternatives that carry trades can implement (domestic assets, deliverable Foreign Exchange Swaps, non-deliverable forwards) in the context of DEEs that may change the picture from the standard investment strategy. Such empirical manifestation of yield-driven financial flows underscores the importance of bringing back the interest rate parity condition and its rationale for analysing the relationship between such strategies and the exchange rate.

REFERENCES

Alcantara-Alencar, D., Jayme, F. G., & Britto, G., 2018. Productivity, real exchange rate, and aggregate demand: An empirical exercise applied to Brazil from 1960 to 2011. *Journal of Post Keynesian Economics*, 41(3), 455–77.

Antonopoulos, R., 1997. *An Alternate Theory of Real Exchange Rate Determination for the Greek Economy*. Unpublished doctoral dissertation, New School for Social Research.

Bank for International Settlements, 2021. *Capital Flows, Exchange Rates and Monetary Policy Frameworks in Latin American and Other Economies*. Bank for International Settlements (Secretariat).

Barbosa, L., Jayme, F., & Missio, F., 2021. A Post Keynesian framework for real exchange rate determination. In: B. Bonizzi, A. Kaltenbrunner, & R. Ramos, eds. *Emerging Economies and the Global Financial System*, pp. 149–63. Routledge.

Barisone, G., Driver, R., & Wren-Lewis, S., 2006. Are our FEERs justified? *Journal of International Money and Finance*, 25(5), 741–59.

Bresser-Pereira, L. C., 2006. The New Developmentalism and conventional orthodoxy. *Économie Appliquée*, 59(3), 95–126.

Bresser-Pereira, L. C., 2009. The tendency of the exchange rate toward overvaluation. In: L. C. Bresser-Pereira, ed. *Globalization and Competition: Why Some Emergent Countries Succeed While Others Fall Behind*, pp. 125–47. Cambridge University Press.

Bresser-Pereira, L. C., 2013. The value of the exchange rate and the Dutch disease. *Brazilian Journal of Political Economy*, 33(3), 371–87.

Bresser-Pereira, L. C., 2017. La nueva teoría desarrollista: Una síntesis. *Economía UNAM*, 14(20), 48–66.

Bresser-Pereira, L. C., 2019. New Developmentalism: Development macroeconomics for middle-income countries. *Cambridge Journal of Economics*, 44(3), 629–46.

Bresser-Pereira, L. C., & Gala, P., 2008. Foreign savings, insufficiency of demand, and low growth. *Journal of Post Keynesian Economics*, 30(3), 315–34.

Bresser-Pereira, L. C., Oreiro, J. L., & Marconi, N., 2014. *Developmental Macroeconomics: New Developmentalism as a Growth Strategy*. 1st edn Routledge.

Brunnermeier, M., Nagel, S., & Pedersen, L., 2009. Carry trades and currency crashes. In: D. Acemoglu, K. Rogoff, & M. Woodford, eds. *NBER Macroeconomics Annual 2008*, pp. 313–47. National Bureau of Economic Research.

Brunnermeier, M., & Pedersen, L., 2009. Market liquidity and funding liquidity. *Review of Financial Studies*, 22(6), 2201–38.

Carvalho, F. J., 2018. Financial flows and the New Developmentalism. *Brazilian Journal of Political Economy*, 38(1), 115–24.

Clark, P., & MacDonald, R., 1998. *Exchange Rates and Economic Fundamentals: A Methodological Comparison of BEERs and FEERs.* International Monetary Fund.

Cunningham, J., 1995. *Piero Sraffa: Critical Assessments.* Routledge.

Davidson, P., 1982. *International Money and the Real World.* John Wiley and Sons.

De Conti, B., Biancarelli, A., & Rossi, P., 2013. Currency hierarchy, liquidity preference and exchange rates: A Keynesian/Minskyan approach. *Congrès de l'Association Française d'Économie Politique, Université Montesquieu Bordeaux*, Working Paper IV, 1–22.

De Paula, L. F., Fritz, B., & Prates, D. M., 2017. Keynes at the periphery: Currency hierarchy and challenges for economic policy in emerging economies. *Journal of Post Keynesian Economics*, 40(2), 183–202.

Driver, R., & Westaway, P., 2004. *Concepts of Equilibrium Exchange Rates.* Bank of England.

Edwards, S., 1989. Exchange rate misalignment in developing countries. *World Bank Research Observer*, 4(1), 3–21.

Eichengreen, B., & Hausmann, R., 1999. Exchange rates and financial fragility. *National Bureau of Economic Research*, Working Paper 7418, 1–54.

Ferrari-Filho, F., & De Paula, L. F., 2008. Exchange rate regime proposal for emerging countries: A Keynesian perspective. *Journal of Post Keynesian Economics*, 31(2), 227–48.

Frenkel, R., & Rapetti, M., 2015. The real exchange rate as a target of macroeconomic policy. In: UNCTAD, ed. *Rethinking Development Strategies after the Financial Crisis*, pp. 81–92. UNCTAD.

Gagnon, J., & Hinterschweiger, M., 2011. *Flexible Exchange Rates and the World Economy.* 1st edn. Peterson Institute for International Economics.

Guzman, M., Ocampo, J. A., & Stiglitz, J. E., 2018. Real exchange rate policies for economic development. *World Development*, 110, 51–62.

Harvey, J., 1991. A Post Keynesian view of exchange rate determination. *Journal of Post Keynesian Economics*, 14(1), 61–70.

Harvey, J., 2019. Exchange rates and the balance of payments: Reconciling an inconsistency in Post Keynesian Theory. *Journal of Post Keynesian Economics*, 42(3), 390–415.

Harvey, J., & Deprez, J., 1999. *Foundations of International Economics: A Post Keynesian Analysis.* Routledge.

Hawkins, J., & Turner, P., 2000. Managing foreign debt and liquidity risks in emerging economies: An overview. *BIS Policy Papers*, 8, 3–60.

Hinkle, L. E., & Montiel, P. J., 1999. *Exchange Rate Misalignment: Concepts and Measurement for Developing Countries.* Oxford University Press.

Isard, P., 1995. *Exchange Rate Economics.* 1st edn. Cambridge University Press.

Kaltenbrunner, A., 2011. *Currency Internationalisation and Exchange Rate Dynamics in Emerging Markets: A Post Keynesian Analysis of Brazil.* Unpublished doctoral dissertation, SOAS University of London.

Kaltenbrunner, A., 2015. A Post Keynesian framework of exchange rate determination: A Minskyan approach. *Journal of Post Keynesian Economics*, 38(3), 426–48.

Kaltenbrunner, A., & Painceira, J., 2017. The Impossible trinity: Inflation targeting, exchanger rate management and open capital accounts in emerging economies. *Development and Change*, 3(48), 452–80.

Keynes, J., 1930. *Treatise on Money*. Cambridge University Press.

Krugman, P. R., 1991. Target zones and exchange rate dynamics. *Quarterly Journal of Economics*, 106(3), 669–82.

López, G. J., & Cruz, B. A., 2000. "Thirlwall's Law" and beyond: The Latin American experience. *Journal of Post Keynesian Economics*, 22(3), 477–95.

López-Villavicencio, A., Mazier, J., & Saadaoui, J., 2012. Temporal dimension and equilibrium exchange rate: A FEER/BEER comparison. *Emerging Markets Review*, 13(1), 58–77.

MacDonald, R., 1997. *What Determines Real Exchange Rate? The Long and Short of It*. International Monetary Fund Working Papers WP/97/21.

Marconi, N., 2012. The Industrial Equilibrium Exchange Rate in Brazil: An estimation. *Brazilian Journal of Political Economy*, 32(4), 656–69.

Marconi, N., Araujo, E., Capraro-Brancher, M., & Couto-Porto, T., 2021. The relationship between exchange rate and structural change: An approach based on income elasticities of trade. *Cambridge Journal of Economics*, 45(6), 1297–1318.

Martínez-Hernández, F., 2017. The political economy of real exchange rate behavior: Theory and empirical evidence for developed and developing countries 1960–2010. *Review of Political Economy*, 29(4), 1–31.

McKinnon, R. I., 1984. *An International Standard for Monetary Stabilization*. Peterson Institute for International Economics.

Miles, M., & Davidson, P., 1979. Monetary Policy, Regulation and International Adjustment. *Economies et Societes*, 1, 1845–65.

Monetary and Economic Department Bank for International Settlements, 2015. Currency carry trades in Latin America. *BIS Papers*, 81, 1–42.

Moore, B. J., 2004. A global currency for a global economy. *Journal of Post Keynesian Economics*, 26(4), 631–53.

Oreiro, J. L., D'Agostini, L. L., & Gala, P., 2020. Deindustrialization, economic complexity and exchange rate overvaluation: The case of Brazil (1998–2017). *PSL Quarterly Review*, 73(295), 313–41.

Ostry, J., Ghosh, A., & Chamon, M., 2012. *Two Targets, Two Instruments: Monetary and Exchange Rate Policies in Emerging Market Economies*. International Monetary Fund.

Pérez-Ruiz, D. A., 2022. *Policy Target Exchange Rates for Developing and Emerging Economies: A Post Keynesian Analysis*. Unpublished doctoral thesis, University of Leeds, UK.

Perraton, J., 2014. *Economic Growth in Open Economies: Balance of Payments Constrained Growth—and Beyond?* University of Sheffield Department of Economics Working Paper.

Resende, M. F. D. C., & Terra, F. H. B., 2018. Developmental macroeconomics: A post-Keynesian assessment. *Brazilian Journal of Political Economy*, 38(1), 76–98.

Rey, H., 2015. Dilemma not trilemma: The global financial cycle and monetary policy independence. *National Bureau of Economic Research*, w21162.

Sarno, L., 2008. Purchasing power parity. In: T. Durlauf & L. Blume, eds. *The New Palgrave Dictionary of Economics*, pp. 1–19. Palgrave Macmillan.

Sarno, L., & Taylor, M. P., 2003. *The Economics of Exchange Rates*. Cambridge University Press.

Shaikh, A., 1991. *Competition and Exchange Rates: Theory and Empirical Evidence.* Working Paper No. 25, Department of Economics, New School for Social Research.

Shaikh, A., 2016. *Capitalism: Competition, Conflict, Crises.* Oxford University Press.

Shaikh, A., & Antonopoulos, R., 2013. Explaining long term exchange rate behavior in the United States and Japan. In: J. Moudud, C. Bina, & P. L. Mason, eds. *Alternative Theories of Competition*, pp. 201–28. Routledge.

Taylor, A. M., & Taylor, M. P., 2004. The purchasing power parity debate. *Journal of Economic Perspectives*, 18(4), 135–58.

Thirlwall, A. P., 2011. The balance of payments constraint as an explanation of international growth rate differences. *PSL Quarterly Review*, 64(259), 429–38.

Williamson, J., 1986. Target zones and the management of the dollar. *Brookings Papers on Economic Activity*, Working Paper 1, 165–74.

Williamson, J., 1994. Estimates of FEERs. In: J. Williamson, ed. *Estimating Equilibrium Exchange Rates*, pp. 177–243. Institute for International Economics.

Williamson, J., 1999. *Crawling Bands or Monitoring Bands: How to Manage Exchange Rates in a World of Capital Mobility*, Policy Brief 99-3. Peterson Institute for International Economics.

Wren-Lewis, S., 1992. On the analytical foundations of the Fundamental Equilibrium Exchange Rate. In: C. Hargreaves, ed. *Macroeconomic Modelling of the Long Run*, pp. 75–94. Edward Elgar Publishing.

7. Real exchange rates, growth, and inflation targeting

Nelson H. Barbosa-Filho

INTRODUCTION

Inflation targeting is the dominant paradigm of monetary policy in the world. In 2022, 19 of the 20 economies of the G20 adopted it. Saudi Arabia is the exception with a currency peg. Many other advanced and developing economies also set their domestic interest rate based on an inflation target, which theoretically lets the real exchange rate fluctuate according to the balance-of-payments constraint (BoPC) on the economy, while supply forces determine the economy's potential output growth, or so mainstream macroeconomics says.

In practice, things are more complicated than the usual New Keynesian model because the level of the real exchange rate influences economic growth through its permanent impact on productivity growth. In other words, hysteresis due to capital deepening and the impact of the trade balance on the pace of capital accumulation makes economic growth depend on the level at which the exchange rate eventually stabilizes. Evidence from Brazil (Barbosa-Filho2015) shows that economic growth is a concave-down function of the real exchange rate, meaning that either too much depreciation or too much appreciation of the domestic currency is bad for the economy.

More importantly, the result from the Brazilian experience also indicates that the impact of the real exchange rate on economic activity depends on its initial value. Appreciation from a very depreciated exchange rate is positive for growth, but as the process continues, the economy eventually reaches a tipping point where any additional real appreciation of its currency reduces its growth rate. The effect can be demonstrated through a simple one-sector model, provided we allow capital deepening to raise labor productivity, which is a standard assumption in both mainstream and heterodox macroeconomics.

The impact of the level of the real exchange rate on productivity growth makes it influence inflation as well. In other words, inflation depends on both the change and the level of the real exchange rate. The first effect is a standard issue in any Phillips curve of an open economy, but most mainstream models assume that the price impact of appreciations and depreciations ceases when the real exchange rate stabilizes at some given level. In contrast, from a heterodox post-Keynesian perspective, because the level of the real exchange rate influences productivity growth, it ends up determining the economy's equilibrium employment rate—that is, the employment rate consistent with stable inflation.

Assuming there exists some degree of substitutability between the domestic and foreign (imported) inputs to production, it is possible to show how the level of the real exchange rate can alter the economy's long-term inflation rate. In such a context, when the government adopts an inflation target, it indirectly imposes a floor and a ceiling to the real exchange rate, making monetary policy also stabilize the relative price of foreign currency. In other words, inflation targeting results in dirty floating, a disguised exchange-rate targeting where the domestic interest rate must respond to the inflationary effects of appreciations and depreciations and, by doing this, it may also determine the economy's long-term growth rate.

The objective of this chapter is to present a simple one-sector model of the mechanism described above. I will show how some sensible economic assumptions create two nonlinearities in the economy (Barbosa-Filho2010), one between the real exchange rate and growth, and the other between the real exchange rate and inflation, which then makes an exogenous inflation target set boundaries to the real exchange rate and economic growth itself.

The rest of the chapter is presented in four sections. The next section presents the link between the real exchange rate and economic growth in a one-sector economy with either a Kaldor or a Cobb–Douglas production function. Then the chapter moves to inflation and uses the cost decomposition of gross output to show how the level of the real exchange rate influences price through its permanent impact on productivity growth. Next we impose inflation targeting on the relationships presented in the preceding two sections to demonstrate how a restrictive or a lax monetary policy can create a slow-growth path for the economy. The conclusion offers a summary of the results and comments on the possible extension of the model presented in this chapter.

GROWTH AND THE REAL EXCHANGE RATE

Following Kalecki's approach instead of Lucas's critique, a model should not be more complicated than necessary to explain the question under study. For the objective of this chapter, it is sufficient to consider a one-sector open economy where gross output (Q) goes to intermediary (Q_I) and final demand, with the latter consisting of consumption (C), investment (I), and exports (X):

$$Q = C + I + X + Q_I = \left(\frac{1}{1 - B_I}\right)(C + I + X) \tag{7.1}$$

where $B_I = Q_I/Q$ is the domestic input–output coefficient.

In monetary terms, the value added (Y) is:

$$PY = PQ - PQ_I - eP_M M = P(C + I + X) - eP_M M \tag{7.2}$$

where P is the domestic price, e the nominal exchange rate (the domestic price of foreign currency), P_M the international price, and M represents imports in real terms.

Also in real terms, the gross domestic product (GDP) is:

$$Y = C + I + X - \varepsilon M \tag{7.3}$$

where $\varepsilon = eP_M/P$ is the real exchange rate from the domestic perspective, that is, the price of the foreign product in terms of the domestic product. Because we are analyzing a one-sector economy, the real exchange rate coincides with the economy's terms of trade (the price of exports divided by the price of imports).

On the supply side, suppose gross output is a function of employment:

$$Q = A_L L = A_L \lambda N \tag{7.4}$$

where L represents employment, $A_L = Q/L$ is the average labor productivity (the inverse of the labor-output coefficient $B_L = L/Q$ that we will use in the next section), N the labor force, and $\lambda = L/N$ the employment rate.

From 7.4, the growth rate of potential output Q^* is the growth rate of effective output Q when the employment rate is stable at the value compatible with stable inflation (more on this also in the next section). Formally:

$$\hat{Q}^* = \hat{A}_L + \hat{N} \tag{7.5}$$

where, to simplify notation, $\hat{Q}^*$ represents the growth rate of Q^* in continuous time, and the same logic applies to any other variable with "^" above it.

Now, based on a "Kaldorian technical progress function" (McCombie and Spreafico 2015), suppose labor productivity is a positive function of the capital–labor ratio, with a fixed elasticity. In growth terms, this means that:

$$\hat{A}_L = \alpha_0 + \alpha_1 (\hat{K} - \hat{L}) \tag{7.6}$$

where α_0 is the exogenous component of productivity growth, K is the capital stock, and α_1 is the elasticity of productivity in relation to the capital–labor ratio.

From Equations 7.5 and 7.6, when the employment rate is stable ($\hat{L} = \hat{N}$), potential output growth becomes a function of the pace of capital accumulation and population growth:

$$\hat{Q}^* = \alpha_0 + \alpha_1 \hat{K} + (1 - \alpha_1) \hat{N} \tag{7.7}$$

Before we proceed, note that, if α_1 is between zero and one, Kaldor's hypothesis becomes the usual Cobb–Douglas production function with constant returns to scale.

From the Harrod–Domar identity, the growth rate of capital in our one-sector setting is:

$$\hat{K} = (1 - c - x + \varepsilon m)u - \delta \tag{7.8}$$

where c, x and m are the ratios of C, X, and M to Y, respectively, and $u = Y/K$ is the income–capital ratio (or "capacity utilization" in some heterodox models). In terms of the heterodox literature on growth and distribution (Taylor 2004, Blecker and Setterfield 2019), Equation 7.8 adds the trade balance and the real exchange rate to capital dynamics.

Now, to show how the exchange rate can influence the long-term growth rate, suppose the trade–income ratios x and m are linear functions of the real exchange rate, say:

$$x = \frac{X}{Y} = \frac{\chi Y_F}{Y} = (\chi_0 + \chi_1 \varepsilon)\left(\frac{Y_F}{Y}\right) \tag{7.9}$$

and

$$m = \frac{M}{Y} = \frac{\mu Y}{Y} = \mu_0 - \mu_1 \varepsilon \tag{7.10}$$

where Y_F is the income in the rest of the world and χ_1 and μ_1 are positive parameters.

The logic of Equations 7.9 and 7.10 is that, given the composition of world income (Y_F/Y), the economy exports more and imports less, in relation to its GDP, at a higher real exchange rate.[1] When we substitute the two assumptions in 7.8 and 7.7, potential output growth becomes a quadratic concave-down function of the real exchange rate. Formally:

$$\widehat{Q}^* = \alpha_0 + \alpha_1 \left[-(\chi_0 + \chi_1 \varepsilon)\left(\frac{Y_F}{Y}\right) + (\mu_0 - \mu_1 \varepsilon)\varepsilon \right]$$
$$+ \alpha_1 [(1 - c)u - \delta] + (1 - \alpha_1)\widehat{N} \qquad (7.11)$$

In economic terms, given:

(i)   the parameters of the technical progress function (α_0 and α_1),
(ii)   the propensity to consume (c),
(iii) the depreciation rate (δ),
(iv)   the income–capital ratio (u),
(v)   the "catching-up" or "lagging-behind" effect (Y_F/Y), and
(vi)   the trade parameters of the economy ($\chi_0, \chi_1, \mu_0,$ and μ_1),

capital accumulation ($\widehat{K}$) and potential output ($\widehat{Q}^*$) can either accelerate or decelerate when the real exchange rate (ε) goes up.

In other words, maintaining everything else constant, the impact of ε on $\widehat{Q}^*$ depends on the initial condition of the economy. If the real exchange rate goes up from a very low level (an appreciated domestic currency), the depreciation tends to increase potential output growth. However, if the real exchange rate is already very high (a depreciated domestic currency), an increase in it tends to reduce potential output growth. Figure 7.1 shows the two cases, which I have labeled (Barbosa-Filho2010) the "Bresser" and the "Pastore" zones, based on the Brazilian debate on the topic.[2]

But will everything else remain constant as the real exchange varies? Probably not. For example, if we combine Equation 7.11 with a BoPC hypothesis, the export-led growth rate and the real exchange rate necessary to meet the financial restriction in foreign exchange determine a trade-off between the "propensity to save" $(1 - c)$ and capacity utilization (u), which is a usual result in Neo-Kaleckian models. Alternatively, from a Sraffian perspective where the income–capital ratio (u) is constant, Equation 7.11 can define the propensity to save $(1 - c)$ as a quadratic function of the real exchange rate for a given demand-led growth rate.

Suppose the depreciation rate (δ) and the growth rate of the labor force ($\widehat{N}$) are exogenous variables. In this case, Equation 7.22 defines a relationship between five variables: $\widehat{Q}^*$, u, c, Y_F/Y, and ε. We therefore need four additional

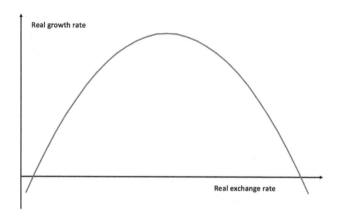

Figure 7.1   *Potential output growth as a function of the real exchange rate*

hypotheses to "close" our one-sector model. Given this chapter's objective, I will analyze how inflation targeting can determine the real exchange rate (ε) and influence the economy's potential output growth ($\widehat{Q}^*$) for a given propensity to consume (c), capacity utilization (u), and international convergence or divergence (the evolution of Y_F/Y).

INFLATION AND THE REAL EXCHANGE RATE

Continuing with the one-sector open model of the previous section, consider the cost-decomposition of gross output:

$$PQ = Profit + WL + PQ_I + eP_M Q_M \tag{7.12}$$

where "*Profit*" represents the gross non-labor income before taxes, interest, capital depreciation, and amortization, what people usually call the EBTIDA in corporate finance.

Using the input–output definitions of the previous section and letting the EBTIDA "inclusive" margin be $\rho = Profit/PQ$, Equation 7.12 can be rewritten as:

$$P = Z(WB_L + eP_M B_M) \tag{7.13}$$

where $Z = (1 - \rho - B_I)^{-1}$ is the "mark-up" multiplier over the summed labor and import unit costs, and B_L and B_M are the input–output coefficients for the labor and imported inputs, respectively.

Based on 7.13, the inflation rate is:

$$\hat{P} = \hat{Z} + \beta\left(\hat{W} - \hat{A}_L\right) + (1 - \beta)\left(\hat{e} + \hat{P}_M - \hat{A}_M\right) \tag{7.14}$$

where $\beta = WB_L/(WB_L + eP_M M)$ is the share of labor in the sum of labor and imported production costs and, to facilitate exposition, $A_L = 1/B_L$ and $A_M = 1/B_M$.

The intuitive meaning of Equation 7.14 is that inflation can come from three sources:

(i)   mark-up dynamics $(\hat{Z})$,
(ii) the excess of wage growth over labor productivity growth $(\hat{W} - \hat{A}_L)$, and
(iii) the excess of exchange-rate depreciation and imported inflation over the growth rate of the "productivity" of the imported input $(\hat{e} + \hat{P}_M - \hat{A}_M)$.

In terms of the heterodox literature on the topic, Equation 7.15 is a Structuralist-Post-Keynesian (SPK) Phillips curve (Barbosa-Filho 2014, Taylor and Barbosa-Filho 2021), where inflation depends not only on the state of the labor market, but also on imported inflation, exchange-rate dynamics, and the firms' desired rate of profit. As a result, even when nominal wages rise in line with labor productivity $(\hat{W} = \hat{A}_L)$, there can be inflationary pressures coming from an increase in the firms' mark-up $(\hat{Z} > 0)$ or from the exchange rate and foreign price shocks $(\hat{e} + \hat{P}_M > \hat{A}_M)$.

To introduce expectations formally in the analysis, and following the post-Keynesian tradition on the topic (Dalziel 1990, Palley 1996), assume firms have market power; that is, firms fix prices after knowing the nominal wage and the domestic price of imports. In such a context, workers include expected inflation $(\hat{P}_e)$ in their income claims, plus the desired growth rate of the real wage $(\hat{\omega}_d)$. Formally:

$$\hat{W} = \hat{P}_e + \hat{\omega}_d \tag{7.15}$$

Next, based on either Marx's reserve-army assumption (Foley 1986, Shaikh 2016) or a Keynesian wage curve (Blanchflower 2003), define the growth rate of the real wage as a positive function of the employment rate:

$$\hat{\omega}_d = \zeta_0 + \zeta_1 \lambda \tag{7.16}$$

Third, to facilitate exposition, define an "imported supply shock" as the difference between the change in the domestic price of the imported product and the workers' inflation expectation:

$$\hat{v}_M = \hat{e} + \hat{P}_M - \hat{P}_e \qquad (7.17)$$

Based on Equations 7.16, 7.17, and 7.18, the SPK Phillips curve is:

$$\hat{P} = \hat{Z} + \hat{P}_e + \beta\left(\hat{\omega}_d - \hat{A}_L\right) + (1 - \beta)\left(\hat{v}_M - \hat{A}_M\right) \qquad (7.18)$$

Our final step is to define an expectation hypothesis. Based on New and post-Keynesian models, let us make our life simple and use "anchored expectations" (Barbosa-Filho2014, 2022, Blanchard 2016, Rudd 2021), that is, a weighted average of current and long-term inflation expectations ($\hat{P}^*$):

$$\hat{P}_e = \theta\hat{P} + (1 - \theta)\hat{P}^* \qquad (7.19)$$

where θ is a coefficient between zero and one that represents the inertial component of inflation. Structuralist models usually allow "inertial inflation" to be endogenous to obtain alternative inflation regimes, including hyperinflation (Ros 1989, Taylor 1991). To keep things simple, I will restrict the analysis to a constant inertial coefficient θ.

The intuitive meaning of 7.19 is that workers look at current inflation and long-term inflation to form their opinions about price changes. When inflation targeting is credible, the "state of long-term expectations" about inflation coincides with the government's target.

Merging Equations 7.18 and 7.19:

$$\hat{P} = \hat{P}^* + \left(\frac{1}{1-\theta}\right)\left[\hat{Z} + \beta\left(\hat{\omega}_d - \hat{A}_L\right) + (1 - \beta)\left(\hat{v}_M - \hat{A}_M\right)\right] \qquad (7.20)$$

or simply

$$\hat{P} = \hat{P}^* + \left(\frac{1}{1-\theta}\right)\left[\hat{Z} + \beta\zeta_1(\lambda - \lambda^*) + (1 - \beta)\hat{v}_M\right] \qquad (7.21)$$

where

$$\lambda^* = \left(\frac{1}{\zeta_1}\right)\left[\hat{A}_L + \left(\frac{1-\beta}{\beta}\right)\hat{A}_M - \zeta_0\right] \qquad (7.22)$$

is the equilibrium employment rate, that is, the employment rate that does not create inflationary pressures from the demand side, what mainstream models call the "natural rate of employment." The difference between the approach of this chapter and the usual New Keynesian Phillips curve (Gordon 2011) is that, from a heterodox perspective, λ^* is a historical time-varying variable instead of natural constant parameter.

For example, because the equilibrium employment rate depends on productivity growth, and productivity growth depends on the level of the real exchange rate, the BoPC or the monetary constraint can influence the long-term state of the labor market. Be it for real or financial reasons, in both cases changes in the long-term exchange rate can alter the equilibrium employment rate.

Equation 7.22 also says that, in addition to the three sources of inflation listed earlier, changes in the state of long-term expectations about inflation can change current inflation immediately. The intuitive meaning of this result is that, even when firms are satisfied with their profit margin ($\widehat{Z} = 0$), the employment rate is non-inflationary ($\lambda = \lambda^*$) and there is no foreign price shock ($\widehat{v}_M = 0$), inflation can fluctuate due to long-term "expectational" shocks (changes in $\widehat{P}^*$). In Latin American history, the usual suspects for this kind of shock are structural breaks coming from stabilization plans (dollarization, de-dollarization, and other types of currency reform) and political shocks (elections or coups that drastically change the government's inflation target).

Still, in Equation 7.21, recall that in the previous section we followed Kaldor and assumed that labor productivity growth depends on capital deepening, which in turn depends on the level of the real exchange rate. From Equations 7.6 and 7.8, in the long run ($\widehat{L} = \widehat{N}$):

$$\widehat{A}_L = \alpha_0 + \alpha_1 [(1 - c - x + \varepsilon m)u - \delta - \widehat{N}] \tag{7.23}$$

So, if we also assume that the share of labor in unit production costs (β) is a positive function of the real exchange rate, say:

$$\beta = \beta_0 + \beta_1 \varepsilon \tag{7.24}$$

with $\beta_1 > 0$ because firms use less of the imported input when its relative price goes up, then Equation 7.22 becomes a cubic function of the level of real exchange rate, as shown in Figure 7.2.

To understand the mathematical source of Figure 7.2, suppose there are no inflationary pressures coming from either the firms' mark-up ($\widehat{Z} = 0$) or the rest of the world ($\widehat{v}_M = 0$). In this case, for any given effective employment rate (λ), Equation 7.21 becomes:

$$\widehat{P} = \widehat{P}^* + \left(\frac{1}{1-\theta}\right)\beta(\zeta_0 + \zeta_1\lambda) - \left(\frac{1}{1-\theta}\right)[\beta\widehat{A}_L + (1-\beta)\widehat{A}_M] \tag{7.25}$$

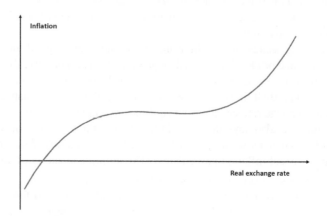

Figure 7.2   Inflation as a function of the real exchange rate

and the cubic term for the real exchange rate comes from the fact that

$$\beta \widehat{A}_L = (\beta_0 + \beta_1 \varepsilon) \left[\alpha_0 + \alpha_1 (1 - c)u - (\chi_0 + \chi_1 \varepsilon - \mu_0 \varepsilon + \mu_1 \varepsilon^2) u - \delta - \widehat{L} \right] \quad (7.26)$$

is a third-degree polynomial of ε for any given values of u and $\widehat{L}$.

In a more general setting, we can also make the growth rate of the "productivity" of the imported input $(\widehat{A}_M)$ a function of the level of the real exchange rate, and do the same for the productivity of the domestic input $(\widehat{A}_I)$, which enters in the mark-up dynamics. The result is a substitution between all three inputs, which reinforces the nonlinearity depicted in Figure 7.2.

For economic policy, the logic of Figure 7.2 is that extreme values of the real exchange rate are bad for inflation targeting. Given the employment rate and the other determinants of the price level, inflation tends to be low when the real exchange rate is low (an appreciated currency), and high when the real exchange rate is high (a depreciated currency). Between the two extremes, moderate values of the real exchange rate do not affect inflation much; that is, there can be more than one value of the real exchange rate consistent with the government's inflation target. Because of such an indeterminacy, something else must determine the real exchange rate. There are two candidates in the heterodox literature on the topic: the BoPC or an inflation constraint. The next section focuses on inflation targeting given its prevalence today.[3]

INFLATION TARGETING AS INDIRECT REAL EXCHANGE-RATE TARGETING

It is now time to combine the results of the previous sections. In the second section, we presented a model where potential growth is a concave-down function of the level of the real exchange rate. Depending on the initial condition of the economy, a depreciation of the domestic currency can either raise or lower the economy's growth rate from the supply side. In more intuitive terms, when the exchange rate is low (an appreciated domestic currency), depreciation raises economic growth. However, when the real exchange rate is high (a depreciated domestic currency), any additional depreciation would only reduce the economy's growth prospects.

In the third section, we presented a price model where inflation can come from four sources:

(i)   changes in the firms' desired mark-up margins,
(ii)   the level of economic activity (measured by the employment rate),
(iii) foreign or exchange-rate shocks to the domestic price of imported inputs, and
(iv)   changes in the state of long-term expectations about inflation.

Given the other determinants of inflation, the model of the third section also showed that inflation tends be stable for "moderate" levels of the real exchange rate, but it changes abruptly at extreme values of the foreign currency. In intuitive terms, the economy's long-term inflation rate falls when the real exchange rate is low (appreciated currency), grows when the real exchange is high (depreciated currency), and stays relatively constant for values in between the two zones.

To check the effect of inflation targeting in the above context, Figure 7.3 combines the theoretical results outlined above with a floor and a ceiling value for inflation. The result is that inflation targeting indirectly creates a fluctuation interval for the real exchange rate, which in turn limits the potential growth rate of the economy to another interval that may or may not include its maximum growth rate. In other words, inflation targeting ends up stabilizing the real exchange rate and the economy's growth rate, but the latter may not be at its optimal level.

To illustrate how inflation targeting can limit the economy's long-term growth rate, Figures 7.4 and 7.5 present two extreme cases. In Figure 7.4, a low inflation target limits the exchange rate to low (appreciated) values, which in turn may slow potential growth. In contrast, in Figure 7.5, a high inflation target limits the real exchange rate to high (depreciated) values, which may

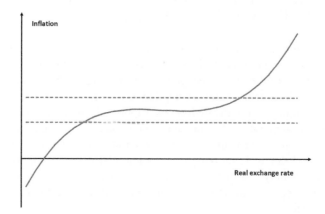

Figure 7.3   *Inflation targeting as indirect exchange-rate targeting with an inflation target that allows a wide fluctuation of the real exchange rate, moderate inflation, and fast growth*

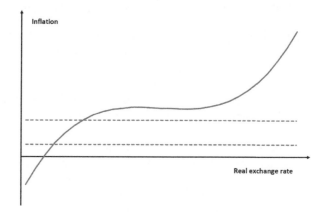

Figure 7.4   *Inflation targeting as indirect exchange-rate targeting, with an inflation target that allows a narrow fluctuation of the real exchange rate, low inflation, and slow growth*

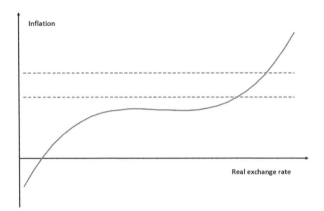

Figure 7.5   *Inflation targeting as indirect exchange-rate targeting, with an inflation target that allows a narrow fluctuation of the real exchange rate, high inflation, and slow growth*

also decelerate potential output. The difference between the two cases is the long-term inflation rate: low in Figure 7.4 and high in Figure 7.5.

The main conclusion from the logical exercise of this section is that infla-tion targeting creates an indirect exchange-rate targeting in which monetary policy limits the fluctuation of the real exchange rate to the interval consistent with the government's inflation target. In this process, the real exchange rate influences the economy's investment rate and, therefore, its long-term growth rate. Ambitious inflation targeting tends to reduce the economy's growth rate for a long period of time, while lax inflation targeting can also do the same, with the extra risk of exploding indexation. To avoid the two dangers, it is important to define the inflation targets in a way that does not depress pro-ductivity growth in the short run, and to combine demand management with structural policies that raise productivity growth from sources other than the real exchange rate.

CONCLUSION

The real exchange rate is a crucial variable for macroeconomic dynamics. The previous sections showed that, even in the very simplified setting of a one-sector economy, the level of the real exchange rate can influence the economy's long-term growth rate through its impact on the investment–income ratio. To obtain such a result, we just had to assume that labor pro-ductivity is a positive function of the capital–labor ratio, which is a common hypothesis in both heterodox (Kaldor's production function) and mainstream (Cobb–Douglas production function) models. Whatever the reader's theoretical choice, when capital deepening raises labor productivity, potential output growth becomes a concave-down function of the real exchange rate, meaning too much currency appreciation or depreciation is bad for long-term growth.

Things get more interesting when we add inflation to the picture. Based on a simple cost decomposition of price in terms of the firms' mark-up and three input prices (labor, the domestic product, and imports), the economy's long-term inflation rate also becomes a function of the real exchange rate. Assuming there exists some degree of substitution between the imported input and labor in the long run, inflation becomes a cubic function of the real exchange rate, and this ends up making inflation targeting a disguised form of exchange-rate targeting, with possible permanent repercussions for growth and welfare.

NOTES

1.   In a more detailed model (Barbosa-Filho 2021), the balance-of-payments constraint can be represented by a trade-off between the real exchange rate and the weight of the domestic income in the world income, with interest-rate arbitrage (carry trade) determining the domestic interest rate.
2.   Since the 1990s, Luiz Carlos Bresser-Pereira, a former Brazilian Finance Minister, has been arguing that competitive (depreciated) exchange rate is crucial for economic growth. In contrast and in the same period, Afonso Celso Pastore, a former Governor of the Brazilian Central Bank, often replied that an appreciated currency could boost growth through the reduction in the relative price of investment.
3.   For alternative BoPC models, see McCombie and Thirlwall (2004).

REFERENCES

Barbosa-Filho, N.H. (2010) "Duas não linearidades e uma assimetria: taxa de câmbio e metas de inflação no Brasil." Paper presented at the 7th Economic Forum of the Getulio Vargas Foundation, São Paulo.
Barbosa-Filho, N.H. (2014) "A Structuralist Inflation Curve," *Metroeconomica*, 65, 349–76.
Barbosa-Filho, N.H. (2015) "Monetary Policy with a Volatile Exchange Rate: The Case of Brazil since 1999," *Comparative Economic Studies*, 57, 401–25.
Barbosa-Filho, N.H. (2021) "Carry Trade, Exchange Rates, and the Balance-of-Payments," *Journal of Globalization and Development*, 12(1), 103–16.
Barbosa-Filho, N.H. (2022) "Hysteresis and the New Consensus Three-Equation Model: A Post-Keynesian Amendment," *Review of Keynesian Economics*, 10, 109–22.
Blanchard, O. (2016), "The Phillips Curve: Back to the '60s?," *American Economic Review*, 106(5), 31–4.
Blanchflower, D. (2003) *The Wage Curve*, Cambridge, MA: MIT Press.

Blecker, R.A., and M. Setterfield (2019), *Heterodox Macroeconomics: Models of Demand, Distribution and Growth*, Cheltenham, UK, and Northampton, MA: Edward Elgar Publishing.

Dalziel, P.C. (1990) "Market Power, Inflation, and Incomes Policy," *Journal of Post Keynesian Economics*, 12, 424–38.

Foley, D. (1986) *Understanding Capital: Marx's Economic Theory*, Cambridge, MA: Harvard University Press.

Gordon, R.J. (2011) "The History of the Phillips Curve: Consensus and Bifurcation," *Economica*, 78(309), 10–50.

McCombie, J., and A.P. Thirlwall (2004) *Essays on Balance of Payments Constrained Growth: Theory and Evidence*, London: Routledge.

McCombie, J.S.L., and M.R.M. Spreafico (2015) "Kaldor's 'Technical Progress Function' and Verdoorn's Law Revisited," *Cambridge Journal of Economics*, 40(4), 1117–36.

Palley, T. (1996) *Post Keynesian Economics: Debt, Distribution and the Macroeconomy*, New York: Palgrave Macmillan.

Ros, J. (1989) "On Inertia, Social Conflict, and the Structuralist Analysis of Inflation," Working Paper 128, Kellogg Institute.

Rudd, J.B. (2021) "Why Do We Think That Inflation Expectations Matter for Inflation? (And Should We?)," *Review of Keynesian Economics*, 10, 25–45.

Shaikh, A. (2016) *Capitalism: Competition, Conflict, Crises*, Oxford: Oxford University Press.

Taylor, L. (1991) *Income Distribution, Inflation and Growth*, Cambridge, MA: MIT Press.

Taylor, L. (2004) *Reconstructing Macroeconomics: Structuralist Proposals and Critiques of the Mainstream*, Cambridge, MA: Harvard University Press.

Taylor, L., and N.H. Barbosa-Filho (2021) "Inflation? It's Import Prices and the Labor Share!" *International Journal of Political Economy*, 50, 116–42.

8. When are devaluations more contractionary? A quantile VAR estimation for Argentina

Gabriel Montes-Rojas and Nicolás Bertholet

INTRODUCTION

The coefficient or elasticity of exchange rate pass-through (ERPT) to domestic prices, *pass-through* for short, is the effect of a change in the exchange rate on prices within an economy.[1] For Argentina, a high-inflation economy where the US dollar is the main currency of reference (a dollarized or bimonetary economy), the study of the magnitude and persistence of pass-through plays a central role in macroeconomic analysis. Other than prices, the ERPT is also important for its impact on output. Periods of growth generate a high demand for foreign currency (for imports or savings in foreign currency-denominated assets), which determines a binding external constraint, a process known as *stop-and-go*.

This chapter studies ERPT on prices, output, and wages after an initial shock to the exchange rate. Standard models, such as vector autoregressive (VAR) and panel data models, cannot appropriately account for the presence of asymmetric and heterogeneous dynamic responses, which are common in ERPT analysis.[2] Using a novel econometric technique known as VAR models with directional quantiles (VARQ) developed in Montes-Rojas (2017, 2019a), we study the effects of devaluations and provide a characterization of when these have contractionary effects. The results show large heterogeneity in output effects, with both contractionary and expansionary values. Our empirical findings show that the negative effect on output occurs when the real wage deteriorates, suggesting a specific mechanism on the effect of devaluations on output.

This chapter is organized as follows. The second section presents a succinct literature review on the ERPT effects on output. Then, we describe the econometric model. The fourth section presents the data used for estimation, and the fifth section depicts the empirical results. The final section concludes.

LITERATURE REVIEW

Theoretical Literature

The traditional approach points out that devaluations are expansive in both the short and long run due to the increase in competitiveness (see Laursen and Metzler, 1950; Harberger, 1950; Alexander, 1959). The main effect comes from switching foreign and domestic demand toward home goods, which produces an output expansion.

The literature on contractive devaluations formalized different mechanisms through which devaluations can affect the demand and the supply side (see, among others, Lizondo and Montiel, 1989; Agénor, 1991). One of the main mechanisms is the redistributive effect (Díaz-Alejandro, 1963, 1965; Ferrer, 1963; Krugman and Taylor, 1978). If money wages lag behind, prices increase, and if the marginal propensity to save from profits is higher than from wages, *ex ante* national savings go up and the demand for goods decreases, as do production and employment (Krugman and Taylor, 1978).

Several authors proposed additional considerations on the demand side. The contractionary effects of a devaluation can occur even if the redistributive effect does not operate, and workers and capitalists have a similar propensity to consume. The first case is when the trade balance is initially in deficit (Hirschman, 1949; Cooper, 1971; Krugman and Taylor, 1978). Moreover, if there are taxes on exports and imports, then a devaluation redistributes income from the private sector to the government, which has a saving propensity of one in the short run (Krugman and Taylor, 1978).

Other scholars provided different explanations on the channels that affect aggregate supply. Buffie (1986a, 1986b) incorporates investment goods as outputs of a composite good produced by combining domestic and imported components in fixed proportions, and concludes that the Marshall–Lerner condition is neither necessary nor sufficient for an expansionary outcome; furthermore, under simple and plausible conditions, a devaluation may worsen the balance of payments. Due to the nature of imports, devaluations would be contractionary in developing countries. Other contributions have also examined the imported intermediate input channels (Shea, 1976; Findlay and Rodríguez, 1977).

Chang and Lai (1989) and Lai (1990) explored the role of income taxes and efficiency wages on aggregate supply: a devaluation increases costs and therefore leads to an output contraction. Larraín and Sachs (1986) extended the basic model to incorporate wages and export dynamics to show that the effects that produce contractionary devaluations in the short run can damage long-term growth.

Van Wijnbergen (1983, 1986) explored three channels through which a devaluation has a contractionary effect on the aggregate supply side: local currency costs of intermediate imports, wage indexing in the presence of food imports, and reduced volume of real credit to firms. The author showed that contractionary effects via the supply side are more damaging than Krugman–Taylor effects. The wage indexation channel is also analyzed by other studies (see also Solimano, 1986).

In recent decades, new studies have emerged that focus on the balance sheet effect of devaluations. Céspedes et al. (2004) show that, because liabilities are dollarized, a real devaluation has detrimental effects on entrepreneurial net worth, which in turn constrains investment due to financial frictions. These authors developed a simple IS-LM-BP model with balance sheet effects and capital market imperfections and show similar conclusions (Céspedes et al., 2003). Using a similar approach, Tovar (2005) estimates a dynamic stochastic general equilibrium (DSGE) model that incorporates the balance sheet effect.

Recently, a new body of theorical and empirical studies has emerged based on dominant currency pricing (Gopinath et al., 2010, 2020; Boz et al., 2018; Adler, G. et al., 2020). Under this approach, firms set export prices in a dominant currency (most often the dollar) and face strategic complementarities in pricing. These models have also incorporated imported inputs in production.

This paradigm has important implications in terms of ERPT, as pointed out by Gopinath et al. (2020). First, at both short and medium horizons, the terms of trade should be insensitive to exchange rate fluctuations. Second, for non-US countries, ERPT into import prices (in home currency) should be high and driven by the dollar exchange rate as opposed to the bilateral exchange rate. For the United States, on the contrary, pass-through into import prices should be low. Third, for non-US countries, import quantities should be driven by the dollar exchange rate as opposed to the bilateral exchange rate. In addition, US import quantities should be less responsive to dollar exchange rate movements as compared to non-US countries. Fourth, when the dollar appreciates uniformly against all other currencies, it should lead to a decline in trade between countries in the rest of the world (Gopinath et al., 2020: 678).

Empirical Literature

The literature on contractionary devaluation has focused primarily on developing countries (see Edwards, 1986; Solimano, 1986; Agénor, 1991; Bahmani-Oskooee and Rhee, 1997; Kamin and Klau, 1997; Kamin and Rogers, 2000; Acar, 2000). These studies found mixed evidence depending on the time horizon analyzed, econometric specification, and the estimation period. Bebczuk et al. (2006) found that devaluations are contractive in highly dollarized economies, but otherwise expansive, while other studies suggest that devaluations are contractive in the short term, but expansive or "neutral" in the long run (Edwards, 1986; Killick et al., 1992; Kamin and Klau, 1997).

There has been a large empirical literature framed using panel data. One of the first papers was by Edwards (1986), who estimated a fixed-effects model using a panel of 12 developing countries over the period 1965–84 and showed that devaluations have negative effects on output in the short run, but after the first year, they have expansionary effects. In the long run, devaluations have no effect on the product. Agénor (1991) provided a different approach by distinguishing between expected and unexpected devaluations. Using a panel of 23 developing countries for the period 1978–87, he found that an anticipated depreciation of the real exchange rate has negative effects on economic activity, while an unanticipated depreciation has a positive impact. The contractionary effects of early depreciations remain after the first year.

Morley (1992) examined 28 devaluations in developing countries, controlling for terms of trade, export and import growth, money supply, and fiscal balance, and found that real exchange rate depreciations tended to reduce output over two years. Christopolous (2004) analyzed 11 Asian economies using cointegrated panel techniques and showed that depreciations are contractive in the long term in at least five of them, and expansive in three. Moreno (1999) noted that real depreciation slowed economic activity in a panel of East Asian countries. Using a Lucas-type supply function, Sheehey (1986) set up a panel with 16 Latin American countries and the results strongly supported the contractionary impact of the devaluation in Latin America.

On the other hand, Bahmani-Oskooee (1998), using quarterly data on output and the real and nominal effective exchange rate for 23 developing countries over the period 1973–88, estimated the long-term relationship between output and exchange rate and noted that devaluations did not have a long-term effect on production in developing countries.

Kamin and Klau (1997) examined the impact of devaluation on 27 countries for the 1970–96 period, using different methodologies with panel data (fixed effects, two-stage least squares) and time-series data (vector error-correction, VEC) and found no evidence that devaluations are contractionary in the long run. Controlling for sources of spurious correlation and reverse causality, the effect of devaluation in the short run is reduced, although evidence that this effect exists remains even after these controls are introduced. They found no evidence of significant differences among the regions, and none showing that this effect is stronger in developing countries than in industrialized countries.

The short-run contractionary devaluation hypothesis has also received considerable empirical support in time-series studies, mainly in Latin American countries. The few exceptions are studies on Asian countries. Bahmani-Oskooee and Rhee (1997) analyzed the effects of depreciation in South Korea using quarterly data from 1971 to 1994 and found that real depreciation is expansive in the short run. Bahmani-Oskooee et al. (2002) estimated a VEC model for Asian countries and concluded that there are long-term relationships between output, real exchange rate, and other policy variables, using quarterly data from 1976 to 1999. They found that, while real depreciation is contractionary in the long run for Indonesia and Malaysia, it is expansive for the Philippines and Thailand. For South Korea, output growth does not respond significantly to a change in the level of the real exchange rate.

Kim and Ying (2007) developed a six-variable VAR model (capital inflows, real income, relative price, real money supply, current account balance, and nominal exchange rate) for seven East Asian countries using the pre-1997 crisis data and the trade-weighted exchange rate, and found no evidence of contractionary devaluation. In fact, currency devaluation appears strongly expansionary in several countries. This is contrasted to the case of Chile and Mexico where the evidence of devaluation is persistent.

Nevertheless, the evidence in Latin America is mostly favorable to the hypothesis of contractionary devaluations. Rogers and Wang (1995) estimated a structural VAR model for Mexico using monthly data from January 1977 to June 1990, and suggested that output is influenced primarily by real shocks, but exchange rate shocks are also significant.

Santaella and Vela (1996) estimated a two-variable VAR model for Mexico and found that a reduction in exchange rate depreciation increased output initially, but it was later reversed. By using a VAR model to study Uruguay, Hoffmaister and Végh (1996) found that a permanent reduction in the exchange rate depreciation leads to a long-lasting increase in output. Kamin and Rogers (2000) estimated quarterly VAR for Mexico for 1981–95 and concluded that, even after sources of spurious correlation and reverse causation are controlled for, real devaluation has led to high inflation and economic contraction in Mexico.

Ahmed (2003) estimated an annual VAR model for Argentina, Brazil, Chile, Colombia, and Mexico over 1983–99, taking the real exchange rate, output, inflation and terms of trade, world output, and the US interest rate as endogenous variables, and reported that devaluations have contractionary effects in the short term. Amman and Baer (2003), who analyzed the impact of the devaluation of Brazil in 1999, also found evidence of contractionary effects on output.

An et al. (2014) examined 16 countries and found that, unlike Asian and non-G3 developed nations, output generally decreases after real devaluations in Latin American countries. Campos and Rapetti (2018), using Bayesian VAR for Argentina over the period 1854–2017, found that devaluations were mostly contractionary. Montané et al. (2021) examined monthly data for Brazil, Chile, Colombia, Mexico, Argentina, and Peru during the 2000s and demonstrated that devaluations seem to be contractionary in Brazil and

Mexico. Bertholet (2021) estimated an annual VAR model for Argentina, Chile, and Colombia over 1960–2010 and found that devaluations in all countries have contractionary effects in the short run, but this is reversed, at least partially, in the medium run.

To summarize, most empirical studies show that devaluations have short-run contractionary effects that can be expansionary or neutral when the period of analysis is long enough. Furthermore, the evidence in favor of the short-run contractionary devaluation hypothesis is even more favorable when using VAR methods and focusing on Latin American countries.

ECONOMETRIC MODEL

VARQ Model

This chapter uses an extension of the linear VAR model to multivariate quantile regression. In particular, we follow the implementation of Montes-Rojas (2019a) that builds on the directional quantile models used by Hallin et al. (2010), Paindaveine and Šiman (2011, 2012), Carlier et al. (2016), and Montes-Rojas (2017). These models will be defined as VARQ.

Consider a multivariate process of m variables, $Y_t = (Y_{1t}, ..., Y_{mt})' \in \mathbb{R}^m$ and a $k \times 1$ vector of control variables X_t. Consider also the sigma-field generated by $\{Y_s : s < t\}$ containing all the information available at t. For the case of VARQ of order p, $X_{t-1} = (Y_{t-1}, ..., Y_{t-p})$ with $k = mp$. VARQ models are indexed by the number of lags, VARQ(p).

Let $\tau = (\tau_1, ..., \tau_m)$ be a vector of quantile indexes $(0,1)$, where each index corresponds to a given endogenous variable. Then, the VARQ(1) evaluated at τ is:

$$Q_{Y_t}(\tau | x_{t-1} = X_{t-1}) = B(\tau) x_{t-1} + A(\tau) \tag{8.1}$$

where Q is an $m \times 1$ vector corresponding to the conditional quantiles of the m endogenous variables; $B(\tau) = (B_1(\tau), ..., B_m(\tau))$ is an $m \times k$ matrix of coefficients $B_j(\tau)$ for each $j = 1, ..., m$, vectors of dimension $k \times 1$ with coefficients of each j variable in Y; and $A(\tau)$ is an $m \times 1$ vector. Thus, Q maps the quantile index vector and lags into the domain of the endogenous variables. Model 8.1 can be estimated using univariate quantile regressions for each $j = 1, 2, ..., m$ endogenous variables with respect to all other $-j$ variables and all lagged values, each using the corresponding component in τ.

Conditional quantile models in time-series equations can be interpreted in terms of the business cycle of each variable (see Koenker et al., 2006; Galvao et al., 2013). For instance, a low quantile of output, conditional on the lagged values of all variables, can be interpreted as a low performance of output with respect to the expected response, given those lagged values. That is, a low quantile means that the variable has a response that is in the low part of the conditional distribution. In contrast, a high quantile means that output is in the upper part of the conditional distribution of conditional outcomes. In model 8.1, the same applies to each of the m endogenous variables.

Shocks and Impulse Response Functions

Ramey (2016: 52–5) defines shocks as exogenous primitive forces that are not correlated with each other and that are economically meaningful. Shocks should satisfy the following characteristics: (1) they should be exogenous with respect to the other endogenous variables and lags; (2) they should not be correlated with other shocks; and (3) they should represent unanticipated changes (for a literature review, see Ramey, 2016, and Stock and Watson, 2016).

For multivariate quantiles, we consider a shock as the counterfactual effect $\delta \in \mathbb{R}^m$. Thus, we compare the conditional models on $x_t^\delta = (y_t + \delta, y_{t-1}, \ldots, y_{t-p})$ with $x_t = (y_t, y_{t-1}, \ldots, y_{t-p})$.

Define the impulse-response function at τ_1 in $t + 1$ for a given shock in t, δ, as:

$$IRFQ_1\left(\tau_1, \delta | x_t\right) = Q_1\left(\tau_1 | x_t^\delta\right) - Q_1\left(\tau_1 | x_t\right) \tag{8.2}$$

where Q_1 is the one-period-ahead prediction using τ_1.

Consider now the prediction at $t + 2$, using quantiles τ_2. Note that this response depends on that used in $t + 1$ with τ_1. That is, the effect at $t + 2$ should be evaluated at (τ_1, τ_2), defined as a *quantile path*. Then,

$$IRFQ_2\left((\tau_1, \tau_2), \delta | x_t\right) = Q_2\left((\tau_1, \tau_2) | x_t^\delta\right) - Q_2\left((\tau_1, \tau_2) | x_t\right) \tag{8.3}$$

where Q_2 is the two-periods-ahead prediction using quantile path (τ_1, τ_2).

This procedure can generalize for h periods $(\tau_1, \tau_2, \ldots, \tau_h)$, thus defining:

$$IRFQ_h\left((\tau_1, \tau_2, \ldots, \tau_h), \delta | x_t\right) = Q_h\left((\tau_1, \tau_2, \ldots, \tau_h) | x_t^\delta\right) - Q_h\left((\tau_1, \tau_2, \ldots, \tau_h) | x_t\right) \tag{8.4}$$

As is common with time-series data, we are interested in the accumulated effects, which will be defined as aIRFQ. This is the sum of all effects evaluated at the quantile path $(\tau_1, \tau_2, \ldots, \tau_h)$.

Finally, the distribution of potential accumulated effects can be simulated using uniform random variables, where the indexes $(\tau_1, \tau_2, \ldots, \tau_h)$ are replaced by independent $U(0,1)$ random variables.

DATA AND SIMULATION OF AN IRFQ

The empirical model has four macroeconomic variables on a monthly basis: nominal official exchange rate (ER, in first-differences of logarithms),[3] consumer price index (inflation, in first-differences of logarithms),[4] economic activity (output, in logs, seasonally adjusted and using the cyclical Hodrick–Prescott component),[5] and nominal wages (wages, in first-differences of logarithms, seasonally adjusted)[6] for the period January 2004–December 2018.

The main effect of interest is a unit shock in the nominal ER. This can be interpreted as doubling the exchange rate (i.e., a 100 percent increase in the rate of devaluation shock). Note that, since the model is linear (and uses ordinary least squares [OLS] regression), the shocks will be interpreted in terms of elasticities, independent of the size of the shock; therefore, we will consider a 1 percent shock and evaluate the percentage response on all other variables. The effect on the variables will be called pass-through.

Shock identification is based on a standard Cholesky decomposition. We will assume that the exchange rate adjusts first and is contemporaneously affected by all other variables. Then, prices adjust based on output and wages, but not the exchange rate; then output; and finally wages. Both Akaike and Bayesian information criteria suggest using one lag, thus the model is a VARQ(1) with m = 4. For a given shock, we will consider 1000 simulated quantile paths for h = 1, 2, ..., 12 horizons of this VARQ(1) model.

EMPIRICAL RESULTS

Univariate Effects

From the quantile paths we can evaluate the dynamics of pass-through by studying the distributions of accumulated impulse-response functions effects (aIRF hereafter).

Figures 8.1–8.4 plot the kernel density estimation for the aIRF for single variables and for different horizons, h = 3, 6, 9, 12 . These graphs allow us to evaluate the heterogeneity in the short- and medium-run effects, up to 12 months.

Prices pass-through (Figure 8.2) has an increasing effect across h. It has an h = 12 effect with an average of 0.29 and a 95 percent confidence interval (CI95) of [0.15, 0.45]. Wages pass-through (Figure 8.3) has an h = 12 effect with an average of 0.062 and a CI95 of [0, 0.13]. Taking both effects together we observe that an exchange rate shock of 1 percent produces a real wage fall of 0.23 percent with a CI95 that lies entirely on the negative domain, [−0.33%,

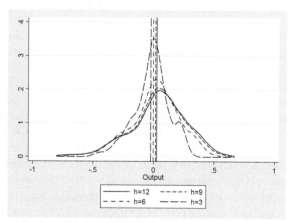

Notes: Kernel density estimation of aIFRQ effects for h = 3, 6, 9, 12 months ahead; vertical
lines correspond to the VAR-OLS effect.
Source: Authors' calculations.

Figure 8.1   *Output pass-through*

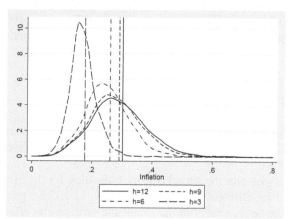

Notes: Kernel density estimation of aIFRQ effects for h = 3, 6, 9, 12 months ahead; vertical
lines correspond to the VAR-OLS effect.
Source: Authors' calculations.

Figure 8.2   *Prices pass-through*

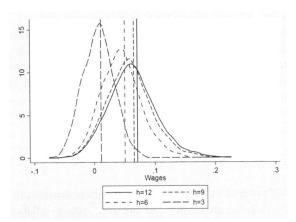

Notes: Kernel density estimation of aIFRQ effects for h = 3, 6, 9, 12 months ahead; vertical lines correspond to the VAR-OLS effect.
Source: Authors' calculations.

Figure 8.3 *Wages pass-through*

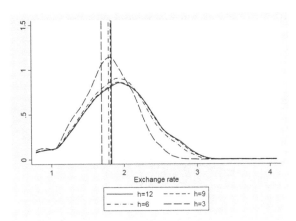

Notes: Kernel density estimation of aIFRQ effects for h = 3, 6, 9, 12 months ahead; vertical lines correspond to the VAR-OLS effect.
Source: Authors' calculations.

Figure 8.4 *Exchange rate pass-through*

−0.12%]. For the latter, the real wage effect is calculated by taking the difference of the wage and price effects for the same quantile path.

Output pass-through (Figure 8.1) has no clear sign effect, containing both positive and negative effects. This is compatible with the bimodal effect found in Montes-Rojas (2019b), where expansionary and contractionary devaluations were equally probable. Overall, it has an average effect of 0.045 with a CI95 of [−0.37, 0.41].

Finally, the exchange rate shock also generates some persistence, producing an overall effect of double the initial shock (Figure 8.1).

Joint Effects

Figures 8.5–8.7 produce kernel estimates of bivariate densities using different pairs of aIRF variables at the h = 12 horizon: output–inflation, inflation–wages, and output–wages. This analysis lets us study the association between different types of effects.

Figure 8.5 shows the joint distribution of the output and price effects. Overall, this shows that a higher price pass-through is positively correlated with a higher output pass-through, although this is a weak effect ($R^2 = 0.055$). This association suggests a price rigidity hypothesis where the positive (or less negative) effects of a devaluation require prices to accommodate the new exchange rate.

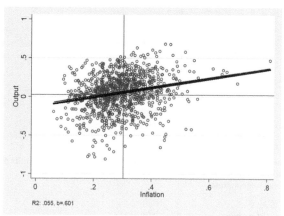

Note: Bivariate model of IRFQ for 1000 quantile paths; mean (solid) and median (thin) regression lines are imposed.
Source: Authors' calculations.

Figure 8.5   *aIRFQ on output and inflation*

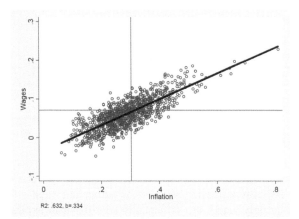

Note: Bivariate model of IRFQ for 1000 quantile paths; mean (solid) and median (thin) regression lines are imposed.
Source: Authors' calculations.

Figure 8.6   *aIRFQ on nominal wages (dif. log) and inflation*

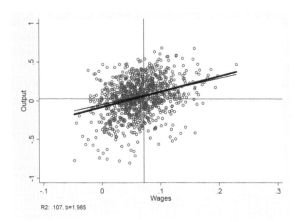

Note: Bivariate model of IRFQ for 1000 quantile paths; mean (solid) and median (thin) regression lines are imposed.
Source: Authors' calculations.

Figure 8.7   *aIRFQ on nominal wages (dif. log) and output*

Figure 8.6 shows a positive relation between price and wage effects (R^2 = 0.632). Note that, as analyzed in the univariate density estimates, these prices are always above wages, producing a negative effect on real wages. The results show that, after a 1 percent increment in inflation that follows an exchange rate shock, wages increase only ⅓ percent.

Table 8.1   *OLS regression estimates using aIRF*

Output	=	Wages	+	Inflation	+	Const
		2.31**		−0.172		−0.050*
R² = 0.1089		(0.299)		(0.126)		(0.026)

Notes: ** significant at 1 percent; * significant at 5 percent; Standard errors in parentheses.
Source: Authors' calculations.

Finally, Figure 8.7 produces the output and wages joint effects distributions ($R^2 = 0.107$). A linear regression between the output and wage and price aIRFs determined that only wages are statistically significant in explaining output. These results suggest that, after a 1 percent real wage reduction that follows an exchange rate shock, output reduces by 2.3 percent (Table 8.1). How can this result be interpreted? Exchange rate devaluations are followed by relative price changes and distributive conflicts (Montes-Rojas and Toledo, 2022; Bastian and Setterfield, 2020). Salaried workers with non-indexed nominal wages are probably the ones that suffer the most and the ones whose wage adjustment takes the longest. Real wage reductions may affect output performance, which seems to be the channel producing the main effect. The main result is, then, that devaluations are more contractionary when they are followed by a greater real wage adjustment.

Consider now a principal component analysis of the aIRF estimates using the four endogenous variables (Table 8.2). The analysis reports only one factor

Table 8.2   *Principal component factor analysis of aIRF estimates*

Factor	Eigenvalue	Difference	Proportion
Factor 1	2.33287	1.91045	0.8467
Factor 2	0.42242	0.42242	0.1533
Factor 3	0.00019	0.00039	0.0001
Factor 4	−0.00020		
	Factor 1	Factor 2	
Output	0.2545	0.3223	
Inflation	1.0039	−0.0611	
Wages	0.8147	0.3724	
ER	0.7723	−0.4197	

Notes: Iterated principal component analysis, retaining two factors.
Source: Authors' calculations.

with an eigenvalue greater than 1 that explains 85 percent of the variance, followed by a second factor with an eigenvalue of 0.422 and explaining the remaining 15 percent. The first factor corresponds mostly to a price channel, explained first by inflation, next wages, and then the exchange rate, but output appears with a much lower factor loading. The second factor, however, is the one that has output and wages on the same footing, also exchange rate persistence. The main object of this chapter, then, corresponds to this second factor. In other words, there is a distinctive effect of devaluations with a characteristic negative association between output growth and wage rate variations.

CONCLUSION

This chapter proposes a characterization of ERPT effects and contractionary devaluations. The negative output effect of a devaluation is larger when it has a negative impact on real wages. The estimates suggest that, after a shock on the exchange rate, a 1 percent real wage reduction reduces output by 2.3 percent.

These results can be extended in several directions. First, further characterization of exchange rate shocks may illustrate the different channels through which output is affected by external imbalances. We use here a Cholesky decomposition that is common in the empirical literature. However, different exchange rate shock identifications can be implemented. Second, changes in domestic demand components can be studied separately to identify specific pass-through effects. The wage effect is only one component of a multivariate array to characterize distributional effects.

The results in this chapter have important implications for economic policy. Currency devaluations are common in emerging economies with balance of payments crises and have considerable negative social effects. The empirical results for Argentina highlight that devaluations that are not associated with distributive conflicts are, in general, less contractionary. As such, the exchange rate policy followed by a central bank should avoid exchange rate devaluations that are produced to resolve or trigger distributive conflicts.

NOTES

1. The authors would like to thank the following colleagues for their constructive comments: Daniel Aromí, Ariel Dvoskin, Hernán Herrera, Emiliano Libman, Fernando Toledo, and Iván Werning. All opinions and errors are our own responsibility.
2. See Menon (1995), Aron et al. (2014), Caselli and Roitman (2016), and Jašová et al. (2016) for a comprehensive literature review and empirical applications.
3. Monthly average official exchange rate, US dollar/pesos, source: BCRA (https://www.bcra.gob.ar/PublicacionesEstadisticas/Tipos_de_cambios.asp).

4. Several sources were used here. The official INDEC (Instituto Nacional de Estadísticas y Censos) series has been discredited for the period 2007–15. We thus use the INDEC series for January 2004–December 2006, then the City of Buenos Aires index for January 2007–May 2016, and then the INDEC again.
5. Estimador Mensual de Actividad Económica (EMAE).
6. Registered formal salaried wages (SIPA).

REFERENCES

Acar, M. (2000). Devaluation in developing countries: Expansionary or contractionary? *Journal of Economic and Social Research*, 2 (1), 59–83.

Adler, G., Casas, C., Cubeddu, L., Gopinath, G., Li, N., Meleshchuk, S., Osorio Buitron, C., Puy, D., & Timmer, Y. (2020). Dominant Currencies andExternal Adjustment. Staff Discussion Notes, 20(05). https://doi.org/10.5089/9781513512150.006

Agénor, P.-R. (1991). Output, devaluation and the real exchange rate in developing countries. Review of World Economics, 127(1), 18–41. https://doi.org/10.1007/BF02707309

Ahmed, S. (2003). Sources of economic fluctuations in Latin America and implications for choice of exchange rate regimes. *Journal of Development Economics*, 72 (1), 181–202.

Alexander, S.S. (1959). Effects of a devaluation: A simplified synthesis of elasticities and absorption approaches. *American Economic Review*, 49(1), 22–42.

Amman, E., & Baer, W. (2003). Anchors away: The costs and benefits of Brazil's devaluation. *World Development*, 6 (31), 1033–46.

An, L., Kim, G., & Ren, X. (2014). Is devaluation expansionary or contractionary: Evidence based on vector autoregression with sign restrictions. *Journal of Asian Economics*, 34, 27–41. https://doi.org/10.1016/j.asieco.2014.03.003

Aron, J., Macdonald, R., & Muellbauer, J. (2014). Exchange rate pass-through in developing and emerging markets: A survey of conceptual, methodological and policy issues, and selected empirical findings. *Journal of Development Studies*, 50 (1), 101–43.

Bahmani-Oskooee, M. (1998). Are devaluations contractionary in LDCs? *Journal of Economic Development*, 23 (1), 131–45.

Bahmani-Oskooee, M., Chomsisengphet, S., & Kandil, M. (2002). Are devaluations contractionary in Asia? *Journal of Post Keynesian Economics*, 25 (1), 69–81.

Bahmani-Oskooee, M., & Rhee, H.-J. (1997). Response of domestic production to depreciation in South Korea: An application of Johansen's cointegration methodology. *International Economic Journal*, 11 (4), 103–12.

Bastian, E., & Setterfield, M. (2020). Nominal exchange rate shocks and inflation in an open economy: towards a structuralist inflation targeting agenda. *Cambridge Journal of Economics*, 44 (6), 1271–99.

Bebczuk, R., Galindo, J., & Panizza, U. (2006). An evaluation of the contractionary devaluation hypothesis. IDB Working Paper No 486.

Bertholet, N. (2021). *Contractionary devaluation in Latin America. The case of Argentina, Brazil and Chile* (1950–2010). Mimeo.

Boz, E., Gopinath, G., & Plagborg-Møller, M. (2018). *Global Trade and the Dollar*, Harvard University Press, Cambridge, MA.

Buffie, E. (1986a). Devaluation and imported inputs: The large economy case. *International Economic Review*, 27 (1), 123–40.

Buffie, E. (1986b). Devaluation, investment and growth in LDCs. *Journal of Development Economics*, 20(2), 361–79. https://doi.org/10.1016/0304-3878(86)90030-1

Campos, L., & Rapetti, M. (2018). *Short and long-run effects of devaluations. Evidence from Argentina 1854–2017*. Mimeo.

Carlier, G., Chernozhukov, V., & Galichon, A. (2016). Vector quantile regression. *Annals of Statistics*, 44(3), 1165–92.

Caselli, F.G., & Roitman, A. (2016). Non-linear exchange rate pass-through in emerging markets. IMF Working Paper No. 16/1.

Céspedes, L., Chang, R., & Velasco, A. (2003). IS-LM-BP in the Pampas. *IMF Staff Papers*, 50 (1), 143–56

Céspedes, L., Chang, R., & Velasco, A. (2004). Balance sheets and exchange rate policy. *American Economic Review*, 94 (4), 1183–93.

Chang, W., & Lai, C. (1989). Income taxes, supply-side effects and currency devaluation. *Journal of Macroeconomics*, 11 (2), 281–95.

Christopolous, D. (2004). Currency devaluation and output growth: New evidence from panel data analysis. *Applied Economic Letters*, 11(13), 809–13.

Cooper, R. (1971). *Currency Devaluation in Developing Countries*, Princeton University Press, Princeton, NJ.

Díaz-Alejandro, C. (1963). A note on the impact of devaluation and the redistributive effect. *Journal of Political Economy*, 71(6), 577–580. https://doi.org/10.1086/258816

Díaz-Alejandro, C. (1965). *Exchange Rate Devaluation in a Semi-Industrialized Country*, MIT Press, Cambridge, MA.

Edwards, S. (1986). Are devaluations contractionary? *Review of Economics and Statistics*, 68 (3), 501–08.

Ferrer, A. (1963). Devaluación, redistribución del ingreso y el proceso de desarticulación industrial en la Argentina. *Desarrollo Económico*, 2 (4), 5–18.

Findlay, R., & Rodríguez, C. (1977). Intermediate imports and macroeconomic policy under flexible exchange rates. *Canadian Journal of Economics*, 10 (2), 208–17.

Galvao, A., Montes-Rojas, G., & Park, S.-Y. (2013). Quantile autoregressive distributed lag model with an application to house price returns. *Oxford Bulletin of Economics and Statistics*, 75 (2), 307–321.

Gopinath, G., Boz, E., Casas, C., Díez, F.J., Gourinchas, P.-O., & Plagborg-Møller, M. (2020). Dominant currency paradigm. *American Economic Review*, 110 (3), 677–719.

Gopinath, G., Itskhoki, O., & Rigobon, R. (2010). Currency choice and exchange rate pass-through. *American Economic Review*, 100 (1), 304–36.

Hallin, M., Paindaveine, D., & Šiman, M. (2010). Multivariate quantiles and multiple-output regression quantiles: From L1 optimization to halfspace depth. *Annals of Statistics*, 38 (2), 635–69.

Harberger, A.C. (1950). Currency depreciation, income and the balance of trade. *Journal of Political Economy*, 58(1), 47–60. http://www.jstor.org/stable/1826198

Hirschman, A. (1949). Devaluation and the trade balance. A note. *Review of Economics and Statistics*, 31 (1), 50–53.

Hoffmaister, A. W., & Vegh, C. A. (1996). Disinflation and The Recession-Now-versus-Recession-Later Hypothesis: Evidence from Uruguay. *Staff Papers - International Monetary Fund*, 43(2), 355–394. https://doi.org/10.2307/3867401

Jašová, M., Moessner, R., & Takáts, E. (2016). Exchange rate pass-through: What has changed since the crisis? BIS Working Paper 583, Bank for International Settlements.

Kamin, S., & Klau, M. (1997). Some multi-country evidence on the effects of real exchange rates on output. BIS Working Paper 48, Bank for International Settlements.

Kamin, S.B., & Rogers, J. H. (2000). Output and the real exchange rate in developing countries: An application to Mexico. *Journal of Development Economics*, 61 (1), 85–109.

Killick, T., Malik, M., & Manuel, M. (1992). What can we know about the effects of IMF programmes? *World Economy*, 15 (5), 575–98.

Kim, Y., & Ying, Y.H. (2007). An empirical assessment of currency devaluation in East Asian countries. *Journal of International Money and Finance*, 26(2), 0–283. doi:10.1016/j.jimonfin.2006.11.004

Koenker, R., Xiao, Z., Fan, J., Fan, Y., Knight, M., Hallin, M., Werker, B.J.M., Hafner, C.M., Linton, O.B., & P. M. Robinson (2006). Quantile autoregression. [with Comments, Rejoinder]. *Journal of the American Statistical Association*, 101(475), 980–1006. doi:10.2307/27590777

Krugman, P., & Taylor, L. (1978). Contractionary effects of devaluation. *Journal of International Economics*, 8(3), 0–456. doi:10.1016/0022-1996(78)90007-7

Lai, C. (1990). Efficiency wages and currency devaluation. *Economic Letters*, 33 (4), 353–7.

Larraín, F., & Sachs, J. (1986). Contractionary devaluation and dynamic adjustment of exports and wages. NBER Working Paper No. 2078.

Laursen, S., & Metzler, L. (1950). Flexible exchange rate and the theory of employment. *Review of Economics and Statistics*, 32(4), 281. https://doi.org/10.2307/1925577.

Lizondo, S., & Montiel, P. (1989). Contractionary devaluation in developing countries: An analytical overview. *IMF Staff Papers*, 36 (1), 182–227.

Menon, J. (1995). Exchange rate pass-through. *Journal of Economic Surveys*, 9, 197–231.

Montané, M., Libman, E., & Zack, G. (2021). Contractionary depreciations in Latin America during the 2000s. *Brazilian Journal of Political Economy*, 41 (4), 723–44.

Montes-Rojas, G. (2017). Reduced form vector directional quantiles. *Journal of Multivariate Analysis*, 158 (C), 20–30.

Montes-Rojas, G. (2019a). Multivariate quantile impulse response functions. *Journal of Time-series Analysis*, 40 (5), 739–52.

Montes-Rojas, G. (2019b). Una evaluación del pass-through en la Argentina usando funciones impulse respuesta de cuantiles multivariados. *Estudios Económicos*, 36 (73), 145–89.

Montes-Rojas, G., & Toledo, T. (2022). External shocks and inflationary pressures in Argentina: A post-Keynesian-structuralist empirical approach. *Review of Political Economy*, 34 (4), 789–806. https://doi.org/10.1080/09538259.2021.1993001

Moreno, R. (1999). Depreciation and recessions in East Asia, *Economic Review*, 27–40. https://EconPapers.repec.org/RePEc:fip:fedfer:y:1999:p:27-40:n:3.

Morley, S. A. (1992). On the Effect of Devaluation During Stabilization Programs in LDCs. *The Review of Economics and Statistics*, 74(1), 21. https://doi.org/10.2307/2109538

Paindaveine, D., & Šiman, M. (2011). On directional multiple-output quantile regression. *Journal of Multivariate Analysis*, 102(2), 193–212. doi:10.1016/j.jmva.2010.08.004

Paindaveine, D., & Šiman, M. (2012). Computing multiple-output regression quantile regions. *Computational Statistics and Data Analysis*, 56(4), 840–853. doi:10.1016/j.csda.2010.11.014

Ramey, V. A. (2016). Macroeconomic Shocks and Their Propagation. In *Handbook of Macroeconomics* (Vol. 2, pp. 71–162). Elsevier. https://doi.org/10.1016/bs.hesmac .2016.03.003

Rogers, J., & Wang, P. (1995). Output, inflation and stabilization in a small open economy: Evidence from Mexico. *Journal of Development Economics*, 46 (2), 271–93.

Santaella, J., & Vela, A. (1996). The 1987 Mexican disinflation program: An exchange-rate-based stabilization? IMF Working Paper No. 96/24.

Shea, K.-L. (1976) Imported inputs, devaluation, and the balance of payments: A Keynesian macro-approach. *Southern Economic Journal*, 43(2), 1106–1111. doi:10.2307/1057335

Sheehey, E. (1986). Unanticipated inflation, devaluation and output in Latin America. *World Development*, 14 (5), 665–71.

Solimano, A. (1986). Contractionary devaluation in the southern cone. The case of Chile. *Journal of Development Economics*, 23 (1), 135–51.

Stock, J. H., & Watson, M. W. (2016). Dynamic Factor Models, Factor-Augmented Vector Autoregressions, and Structural Vector Autoregressions in Macroeconomics. In *Handbook of Macroeconomics* (Vol. 2, pp. 415–525). Elsevier. https://doi.org/10 .1016/bs.hesmac.2016.04.002

Tovar, C. (2005). *The mechanics of devaluations and the output response in a DSGE model: How relevant is the balance sheet effect?* BIS Working Paper No. 192.

Van Wijnbergen, S. (1983). Credit policy, inflation and growth in a financially repressed economy. *Journal of Development Economics*, 13 (1), 45–65.

Van Wijnbergen, S. (1986). Exchange rate management and stabilization policies in developing countries. *Journal of Development Economics*, 23 (2), 227–47.

PART IV

Monetary policies, international reserves, and sustainable finance in LACs

9. Latin American Reserve Fund: Latin America's alternative to the IMF?

William N. Kring

INTRODUCTION

As the global economy faces increasing challenges related to the COVID-19 pandemic and interest rates continue to rapidly rise in the United States and across the Global North, emerging markets and developing economies are facing a perfect storm of high inflation, increased borrowing costs, and surging debt levels. What is often underappreciated is that a key component of the Global Financial Safety Net (GFSN) is Latin America's own Fondo Latinoamericano de Reservas (the Latin American Reserve Fund, or FLAR, which has been in existence for nearly 50 years).

Originally founded in 1978 as the Andean Reserve Fund (FAR) before being renamed, the FLAR is a multilateral reserve pooling arrangement and the second of its kind in the history of the international financial system. While initially an Andean-region initiative to promote subregional economic integration, membership was expanded in 1989 to all Latin America; Costa Rica, Uruguay, Paraguay, and Chile joined in 2000, 2009, 2015, and 2022, respectively. FLAR's primary objective is to support member countries' balance-of-payments conditions in times of need. Through a variety of instruments, FLAR provides loans, or guarantees third-party loans, to member countries through the utilization of its approximately US$4 billion in paid-in capital from member countries (FLAR n.d.) and recapitalized profits.

While FLAR went largely unnoticed for much of its 20th-century existence, it has evolved considerably during its more than four decades in operation. It began as a small reserve pooling arrangement for Andean countries and now occupies a vital role as the only liquidity mechanism in the region. The FLAR has become so important to regional financial stability that it has even out-lent the International Monetary Fund (IMF) to its member countries during key periods in its history. While this book explores the multiplicity of challenges that Latin American countries face, such as financial instability, exchange rate volatility, and debt sustainability, this chapter highlights the unique and important role that FLAR plays in advising member countries on macroeconomic stability efforts and in responding to balance-of-payments and liquidity challenges. The chapter explains how adaptability is one of the FLAR's keys to success over its history and demonstrates how members broadened FLAR's scope and bolstered the mechanism's lending capacity to US$6.8 billion in response to the COVID-19 crisis. The chapter concludes with a brief discussion of how further efforts toward regional integration and the expansion of existing efforts, such as FLAR, could help to continue to foster financial stability in the region.

PRIMER: THE FLAR AND ITS KEY FUNCTIONS

The FLAR is a regional liquidity facility that provides balance of payment and liquidity support to member countries (Table 9.1). As of October 2020, FLAR's paid-in capital totals US$2.92 billion, and its lending capacity is US$3.93 billion, which it leverages to provide a variety of loans for liquidity and balance-of-payments needs for member countries.[1] Despite the relatively small size of FLAR's capitalization as compared to other liquidity funds, the FLAR has lent more than the IMF to member countries for much of its history. Most notably, the FLAR has significantly out-lent the IMF *to* FLAR member countries from 1998 to 2017. During this period, FLAR loan disbursements totaled US$4.47 billion, as compared to US$660.26 million in IMF disbursements. Thus, the primary focus of the FLAR since its founding has been to provide liquidity support through loans to member countries, as it is a successful "regional reserve pooling arrangement that acts largely as a credit cooperative" (Grabel 2013, 9).

Table 9.1   FLAR membership through the years

	Countries
Founding members of the Andean Reserve Fund, 1978–91	Bolivarian Republic of Venezuela (1988), Colombia, Ecuador (1988), Plurinational State of Bolivia (1988), Peru (1988)
New members of the FLAR, 1991–present	Costa Rica (1999), Uruguay (2009), Paraguay (2015), Chile (2022)

In terms of its mission, the FLAR is tasked with executing three main objectives as articulated in Chapter 1 of its Constitutive Agreement, "1. To provide support to member countries … during balance-of-payments crises. 2. To improve the investment conditions of international reserves of member countries. 3. To facilitate harmonization of the exchange, monetary and financial policies of member countries" (FLAR 1976, 6). In addition to crisis financing, the scope of the institution also includes working to help member countries improve the investment conditions of foreign exchange reserves, which it has accomplished by helping "to manage the reserve portfolios of member countries and other public sector institutions" (Ocampo 2015, 160). Additionally, the third objective has facilitated dialogue between member countries. While harmonization is unlikely, as the policy regimes of member countries vary – for example, Ecuador is dollarized, while Colombia and Costa Rica use inflation targeting – the FLAR can continue to serve as a forum for dialogue.

Requests by members for loans from FLAR are first discussed with headquarters informally. Then the requesting member country submits a formal proposal to the Executive Director, who forwards the request to the Division of Economic Studies (DES). The economic team then evaluates the viability of the country's proposed economic recovery and debt sustainability. The analysis by the DES is then submitted to the Executive President's office. For liquidity and contingency loans, the centralization of authority is absolute, and the Executive President can approve the request for a loan. However, in instances of requests for balance of payment and debt restructuring loans, the process is more decentralized, as the non-resident Board of Directors, comprised of the central bank governors of the member countries, votes on the loan. Nevertheless, the FLAR has significant flexibility to quickly disburse and approve funds, with loans typically originating in fewer than 30 days.

The governance structure that controls the FLAR is comprised of a Representative Assembly made up of the finance ministers from each member country, a Board of Directors including the central bank governors of each member country, and an Executive President. However, FLAR's governance differs from that of other international institutions. First, each member country's vote is weighted equally, regardless of its financial contribution. This is reflected in the Representative Assembly and Board of Directors, where each country has one seat, thus one seat/one vote, regardless of its capital contribution.

Further, FLAR strives for consensus in its decision-making. For a proposal to be approved, a minimum of 75 percent of the directors and governors must be present to deliberate, and 75 percent of those present must vote in favor of a decision to pass it. Certain decisions, such as modifying credit limits, altering the terms of the FLAR's charter, or increasing capital, require a supermajority of 80 percent of members. Finally, some loan packages do not require the approval of the Board of Directors, allowing for rapid disbursement of funds.

FLAR is designed to be flexible and adaptable, as the moment may warrant. For example, the Board of Directors is tasked, when necessary, with proposing special purpose funds "with resources contributed by one or more of the member countries, by third countries or by international negotiations." In addition, adaptive changes, such as increasing the credit limits of member countries, fall on the shoulders of the Representative Assembly.

Despite lending activity that has replaced the typical role of the IMF for its member countries over certain periods, the FLAR does not present itself as an IMF alternative. The FLAR initially emerged as part of the regional integration process in the Andean region. The founding members identified a "need for a cooperative institution of its own that would complement the action of global mechanisms in addressing issues regarding access to external liquidity" (Carrasquilla 2015, 13). As part of the Andean Subregional Integration Agreement, or the Cartagena Agreement, the founders of FLAR envisioned it as a regional financial institution designed "to address the problems resulting from imbalances in the external sector of their economics and to facilitate the regional integration process" (FLAR 2022). Of course, this was in part due to frustration with the IMF, though FAR or FLAR never publicly acknowledged this motivating factor. Now, before exploring the historical usage and evolution to FLAR, let us turn to a more substantive discussion of its emergence.

CREATING THE ANDEAN RESERVE FUND

The roots of Andean subregional institutions, such as the Andean Development Corporation (CAF) and the FAR, can be found in Latin America's historical pursuit of regional integration. Some of the earliest roots lie in the Treaty of Montevideo, to which Argentina, Brazil, Chile, Mexico, Paraguay, Peru, and Uruguay were signatories. This treaty gave rise to the Latin American Free Trade Association (LAFTA), which sought to eliminate "barriers to trade among the countries" (Ffrench-Davis 1977, 138) by establishing a common market. This initiative sputtered for a variety of reasons, including "the legal instrument with which the association was founded and ... the lack of political will on the part of member countries to accelerate the integration process" (Ffrench-Davis 1977, 138).

In response to the failures of the LAFTA effort, the Andean subregional bloc of countries pursued an integration effort that would account for some of LAFTA's shortcomings. On May 26, 1969, the Andean nations of Bolivia, Chile, Colombia, Ecuador, Peru, and Venezuela signed the Cartagena Agreement, concluding negotiations that began with the Declaration of Bogotá.[2] Signatories aimed to create "an integration and cooperation system that [would] lead to the balanced, harmonious, and shared economic development of their countries" (Andean Subregional Integration Agreement (Cartagena Agreement) 1969). Such aims led to the creation of a system and institutions to "promote the process of Andean subregion integration" (Cartagena Agreement 1969). One of the institutions that would emerge from the agreement in 1976 was the FAR.

While Latin America's vulnerability to sudden shifts in the global economy frequently leads one to think of the Latin American Debt Crisis, the history of regional vulnerabilities dates to the 19th century.[3] While the FLAR cannot be linked to a particular episode, Ocampo and Titelman (2012) note FAR was founded following regional efforts in the 1950s and 1960s to achieve stronger regional integration. In addition, the FAR was created as "the foreign reserves branch of the Andean Community of nations" (Rosero 2014, 63), intended to reduce cyclical volatility in the region and vulnerability "to boom–bust cycles in external financing and other external shocks" (Ocampo and Titelman 2012, 17). The ability to quickly provide liquidity support in times of crisis was a key to the successful promotion of intraregional trade.

FAR's founding members had experienced periods in which external financing was scarce, and thus sought to create their own regional solution. FAR was designed to be a cooperative reserve pooling arrangement that "could complement and in some cases replace the [IMF] at a time when external imbalances created barriers to economic growth" (Urrutia 2015, 197). Further, when countries did go to the IMF, as all Andean countries borrowed from the IMF at some point during the 1950s and 1960s, they found "the macroeconomic adjustments required by the IMF ... unsuitable for the specific conditions of the countries, and furthermore that they were very costly politically" (Urrutia 2015, 197).

One of the legacies of the Western international financial order, apart from the conditionality of IMF loans, was the "pattern of financial dependence that Washington and the multilateral banks used as policy leverage" (Kofas 2001, 51) over certain Latin American countries. As Colombia struggled with a financial crisis in the early 1960s and its budget deficit grew, the IMF and US Treasury pressed for Colombia "to devalue the currency and undertake a series of austerity measures as a prelude to a new round of foreign loans" (Kofas 2002, 54). Upon self-reflection, IMF staff documents on the Colombia loan package "concluded that it was not too strong to say that the Colombian case tends to support many of the recent criticisms of the Fund" (Hibben 2006, 49). Similarly, in Ecuador and other Andean countries, "the fiscal, monetary, and foreign investment policy advice of the IMF, the World Bank, and Washington fostered" (Kofas 2001, 52) high levels of external indebtedness fueled by dependence on private loans.

According to a former Venezuelan official familiar with the negotiations of the FAR, the legacy of the IMF and Washington's influence in the region in the 1950s and 1960s was a key contributing factor to the creation of the FAR. Regional integration was also a genuine goal of officials and, "if the IMF were to become less necessary or irrelevant, so be it" (former member of the Central Bank of Venezuela, personal interview, July 14, 2017). While the proposed FAR represented a genuine Southern-led attempt to create a regional liquidity fund, for a number of years it seemed destined for the same fate as many other failed Latin American regional and subregional governance initiatives, such as the New Economic International Order. Despite common concerns about the IMF among the signatory countries to the Cartagena Agreement, there was a nearly seven-year delay in negotiating the charter of the FAR and a nine-year delay in getting the fund operational.

The 1969 Cartagena Agreement established the FAR for the Andean Group, but an agreement still had to be reached on the institution itself. At first, the delay was the result of a series of economic struggles that Colombia faced beginning in the 1960s. From 1959 through 1973, with only two exceptions, Colombia had an annual IMF stand-by arrangement for "financial consolidation and import liberalization" ("Colombia – Request for Stand-by Arrangement" 1971). Despite the seeming need for such a mechanism in light of Colombia's repeated trips to the Fund, Colombia's central bank initially blocked the ratification of the FAR (former Colombian official) At the time, the Colombia Central Bank pointed to IMF stand-by arrangements the country had received and struggled to conceive of a situation in which Colombia would require the assistance of FAR. The central bank's line of thinking was "Colombia is one of the largest countries in the group" (former Colombian official, personal interview, February 2018) and therefore will never have a need for the small loans the FAR could offer (former Colombian official, personal interview, February 2018).

In response, Minister of Finance Botero, in consultation with some trusted economists, launched a campaign to convince the central bank to support the FAR. Former government economists and officials familiar with the effort note that two lines of thinking were advanced to convince the central bank. First, the Minister of Finance argued that one never can predict when "a little loan or the amount of time it can buy can be useful, especially if you do not want to go to the IMF or want to negotiate on your terms" (former Minister of Finance in Colombia, personal interview, February 2018). While the central bank was arguing that "Colombia will not need the FAR. We are one of the largest countries in the group" (former Colombian official, personal interview, February 2018), it did begin to recognize that the FAR could provide key support to Andean member countries and, thus, indirectly benefit Colombia. During these negotiations, debt levels in the region were quickly rising and the Colombian central bank was concerned about the debt levels of other Andean member countries.

Second, Botero emphasized that the FAR would provide support for intraregional trade. Colombia relies heavily on trade with Ecuador and Venezuela, and he emphasized that, "if either Ecuador or Venezuela has a crisis and shuts off trade because they have no other option, we could have a problem" (former Colombian official, personal interview, February 2018). To assuage concerns of the central bank and other members, an explicit conditionality for *all* FAR loans was written into the agreement:

> The loans referred to in this clause shall require the commitment of the applicant country that should it adopt restrictive measures to resolve its balance-of-payments deficit,[4] these shall not affect imports from the subregion, even if said measures are adopted in accordance with the application of the safeguard clauses. (Pate 1979, 1194)

With protections for trade between members, the Bank of the Republic of Colombia was finally convinced of the benefits of the FAR and agreed to move forward with its development. The FAR launched in 1976 with limited conditionality, a regionally exclusive membership, and no formal linkage to the IMF. While the FAR was clearly designed as an alternative to the IMF from a governance perspective, its initial capitalization and limited scope meant that it could only help one member country at a time. In contrast to the rival design, the framing of the FAR was not proactively rival to the role of the IMF. Member countries were aware of the limitations of the capacity and resources of the FAR and saw the institution as a "first line of defense" (former FLAR official, personal interview, March 2019). That said, the agreement framed FAR as an international entity *distinct* from all other countries and, importantly, any other international organizations.[5] According to one prominent Venezuelan official, the IMF had "won the position of enemy number one in Latin America, and the FAR had a mission of no conditionality" (former FLAR official, personal interview, March 2019) that represented a clear response to the historic role of the IMF in the region.

When Japan proposed the Asian Monetary Fund in the aftermath of the 1997 Asian Financial Crisis, the response from the US Treasury and the IMF was swift in criticizing the proposal and moving to block it. In contrast, the FAR was created without much fanfare or objection from the United States. This is likely because the small size of the FAR allowed the institution, which was designed as an alternative to the IMF with virtually conditionality-free loans, to fly under the radar, a pattern that continued until the G20 and other multilateral bodies recognized the importance of changes unfolding in the GFSN following the 2007–08 financial crisis.

FLAR'S EVOLUTION

While FLAR did not emerge in response to a particular financial crisis, the Latin American Debt Crisis was key to "locking in" the success of the institution. Upon the FAR's official launch in 1982, the institution was quickly hamstrung by its first loan to Peru in 1978. This led member states to gradually increase the capital of the Fund. Meeting minutes from the Board of Directors and General Assembly at the FAR show that members quickly grew concerned about the capacity of the fund, and accordingly, the General Assembly agreed to increase the subscribed capital by 148 percent from its original US$250 million. Increases in the subscribed capital, and the corresponding increases in paid-in capital from member states, strengthened the position of FAR and enabled it to lend money to member countries in increasingly large amounts and with increasing frequency in the 1980s. Bolivia, Colombia, Ecuador, and Peru frequently used the FAR throughout the 1980s due to increasing pressure from the external debt crisis in Latin America. The experience of the crisis and the IMF response, coupled with the success of the FAR as a regional liquidity lender, motivated member countries to strengthen the FAR and expand the fund region-wide.

FAR's Initial Success

During the Latin American Debt Crisis, every member country of the FAR borrowed from the mechanism via either the balance of payment or the liquidity credit facilities (Morón 2015, 216). In addition to Peru, Bolivia and Ecuador borrowed three times each from the mechanism, while Colombia and Venezuela each borrowed one time from the FAR during the 1980s. The demand was so strong for FAR funding during this period that an additional short-term liquidity line was created that provided more than US$1.5 billion in loans. However, some countries' needs exceeded the FLAR's funding. Countries like Bolivia and Peru turned to the IMF for additional funding and saw IMF conditionality and lending policies exacerbate their crises.

The experiences of Bolivia, Peru, and Colombia in borrowing from the FAR and/or the IMF during the Latin American Debt Crisis provide key insights into the lessons policymakers took from the decade. The nature of the IMF's response and the conditionality associated with IMF programs reinforced the stigma of the IMF in the region and highlighted the comparative advantage of FAR as a conditionality-free lender. The success of the FAR during this period vindicated the efforts of the Andean countries and emboldened the members to expand the mechanism.

During the Latin American Debt Crisis, Bolivia saw its borrowing costs on international capital markets increase exponentially. It devalued its currency and "appealed to the IMF and received a stand-by loan" (Morales 2015, 224) to finance the macroeconomic adjustment that would accompany devaluation. However, the IMF canceled the loan "before the last disbursement due to a lack of compliance with the terms of the letter of intent" (Morales 2015, 226). Bolivia then turned to the FAR for a loan of US$39.4 million in 1980 and US$13.1 million in 1981 (Morales 2015, 227). When Bolivia approached the

IMF later in the 1980s, Bolivian authorities realized that "the IMF's resources were insufficient, being limited by the small quota Bolivia had in this institution" (Morales 2015, 227). Bolivia also did not like the slow nature of the IMF lending process and the conditionality that accompanied the loans. Further complicating the negotiation between the Bolivian authorities and IMF was the status of Bolivia's arrears with international creditors (Boughton 2001).

So, Bolivia returned to FAR repeatedly during its challenges in the 1980s and benefited from its conditionality-free loans. These loans were repaid in full and "helped Bolivia pay for essential imports" (Morales 2015, 227) and later to implement a stabilization program negotiated with the IMF. Bolivia became adept at first negotiating loan packages with the IMF and then supplementing the IMF resources available with loans from FAR. Juan Antonio Morales, former president of the Central Bank of Bolivia, asserts that Bolivia went to the IMF before the FAR for "political economy considerations: the programs with the IMF reinforced the credibility of its economic policy, especially stabilization, which opened the door to the financing" (Morales 2015, 229) through other channels.

During the 1980s, FAR not only aided countries in mitigating the effects of the Latin American Debt Crisis, but also helped countries such as Peru, Ecuador, and Bolivia navigate periods of hyperinflation that followed. What is more, FAR helped Colombia avoid going to the IMF in 1984 through a series of lending instruments. The experience of the FAR in helping member countries navigate the Latin American Debt Crisis reinforced the relevance and regional need for an IMF alternative.

From FAR to FLAR

Many member countries of the FAR had long expressed discontent with the IMF. In an impassioned speech before the General Assembly of the United Nations, Peruvian President Alan García once warned that, "if the IMF does not adopt reforms in the monetary system and the distribution of world liquidity at its next meeting, his country will reconsider membership" (El País Agencies 1985). To draw attention to the dominant role the US plays in controlling the IMF, García declared that "we are not interested in belonging to an organization that services the benefit of a single country" (El País Agencies 1985).

While the discontent was deep-seated and emerged over a period of decades, the Latin American Debt Crisis created an opening for member countries to challenge the role of the IMF more directly. Pleased with the FAR's performance throughout the crisis, FAR members sought to strengthen and expand the FAR (former FLAR official, personal interview, March 2019). They recognized that "more resources were needed, more capacity was needed, and that the FAR had to transform itself into a robust lender of first resort" (Director of National Taxes and Ministry of Finance in Colombia, personal interview, February 2018). While its available capital was one constraint, former FAR/ FLAR officials note that "increasing the number of members helps with lending capacity. But including countries from across Latin America fortifies FLAR through diversification [of membership]. The same logic was behind the expansion of FAR" (former and current FLAR officials, personal interview, February 9, 2018). Hence, the decision was made to diversify the FAR by making it a Latin American-wide fund.

On January 15, 1988, at an assembly meeting in Venezuela, the members of FAR negotiated substantive changes to the institution that would "represent an answer given by Latin America to the [IMF], since future loans will be granted without the conditionality or adjustment recipes imposed by the IMF" (Vinogradoff 1988). The assembly meeting resulted in an agreement to modify the FAR to allow more Latin American countries to join, pending FAR member country government ratification. At the close of the meeting, the assembly released a statement noting that "the modification will permit the incorporation of other Latin American countries to [FLAR] under the same conditions as the current members" (Vinogradoff 1988) and thus allows them to receive balance-of-payments support when necessary. The statement also emphasized that the FAR "offered more credits to the Andean nations than the IMF ... without imposing virtually interventionist economic programs" (Johnson 1988).

While the FLAR's initial subscribed capital would equal the level of the FAR, US$500 million, its framing was now rival. The statement stressed the differences with the IMF, such as members being able to borrow money *without* IMF conditionality. However, it is important to note that, if not for the debt crisis, it is unlikely the FAR would have been further developed and/ or tested. The fact that it was successfully used by *all* member countries and fully repaid during the crisis created institutional "lock-in," which emboldened member countries to go further.

Apart from the very public effort to criticize the IMF and highlight the FAR's historic ability to help its member countries, the creation of the FLAR also had practical and substantive objectives. First, the FAR wanted to increase its membership base and, in doing so, diversify the types of member economies. Second, the FAR wanted to increase its capital and, thus, its lending capacity. The FAR was "truly conceived of as a capable lender of first resort. But to kick the IMF out of Latin America permanently, the institution would need a major player, such as Mexico or Brazil to join" (former FLAR Executive President, personal interview, July 14, 2017). Finally, expanding the FAR to be a Latin America-wide institution was intended to signal member countries' frustration with the IMF.

Despite the high hopes and lofty rhetoric that accompanied the FLAR, the membership base remained the same for more than a decade after expansion. Although the size of the FLAR was gradually increased through both increases in paid-in and subscribed capital, no additional members were added until Costa Rica joined in 2000. Further, the FLAR continued to act, to varying degrees, as a bridge to the IMF throughout the 1990s. That said, the FLAR adapted to the needs of member countries primarily through the creation of new financing instruments, such as the "central bank external public debt restructuring" and the "contingent credit line."[6] It is this adaptiveness and flexibility to market developments that are part of the reason member countries sought to bolster FAR in the first place.

Today's FLAR

Since the turn of the 21st century, FLAR has undergone some of the boldest reforms in its history. Member countries have significantly increased their capital contributions; FLAR leadership established and has maintained the highest credit rating throughout Latin America; the economic studies division has continued to develop its capacity in surveillance; and the FLAR has consistently demonstrated that it is an alternative to the IMF, despite the non-rival public framing of the institution (Table 9.2). Over the course of the last two decades, this has often been the result of executive leadership and their vision for the institution. Because the FLAR's governance structure is "one country, one vote," the smallest member has the same weighted vote as the largest. This contributes to solidarity between members, but also gives the Executive Director "the ability to set the agenda and drive the direction, if [they] can convince the board" (former FLAR Executive President, personal interview, July 14, 2017).

In the last two decades, the FLAR has seen its capital base increase significantly to nearly US$4 billion. This has been accompanied by the addition of four new members: Costa Rica, Uruguay, Paraguay, and Chile. To help further expand its membership base, after nearly ten years of negotiations, FLAR convinced the IMF to count the paid-in capital of member countries as reserved assets. Finally, in 2015, "the IMF Statistics Department declared that the Convertible Capital met the requirements to be classified as reserve assets" (FLAR n.d.). This marked a major victory for FLAR with the IMF; clearly, paid-in capital to the FLAR should be counted as reserves, as FLAR enjoys the highest credit rating in Latin America.

Table 9.2   *Loans by FLAR vs IMF*

	FLAR loans (1984–95), USD (in millions)	IMF loans disbursed (1984–95), SDR (in millions)	FLAR loans (1996–2006), USD (in millions)	IMF loans disbursed (1996–2006), USD (in millions)	FLAR loans (2007–17), USD (in millions)	IMF loans disbursed (2007–17), SDR (in millions)
Bolivia	698	357	181	242	0	0
Colombia	614	0	500	0	0	0
Costa Rica*	–	–	156	0	1000	0
Ecuador	909	452	927	287	2407	262
Paraguay***	–	–	–	–	0	0
Peru	922	747	0	161	0	0
Uruguay**	–	–	–	–	0	0
Venezuela	294	2349	0	350	967	0
Total	3436	3095	1764	1040	4374	262

Notes: Special drawing rights (SDR); * Costa Rica joined FLAR in 1999; ** Uruguay joined FLAR in 2009; *** Paraguay joined FLAR in 2015.
Source: FLAR data and IMF Transaction Detail.

FLAR'S OPERATIONS

While FLAR does not have a formal surveillance entity, like the Chiang Mai Initiative Multilateralizations (CMIM) ASEAN+3 Macroeconomic Research Office (AMRO), FLAR has its economic surveillance, monitoring, and consultations conducted with member countries. It also maintains regular remote video conference check-ins with member countries and confidentially shares data with member countries. In contrast to the very public Article IV consultation process, FLAR conducts its consultations in a more informal and confidential manner. Officials from the FLAR visit member countries and generate internal reports on the state of the economy, foreign exchange reserves, exchange rate, and fiscal and monetary policies. They also evaluate the likelihood of the member country's need for credit soon. There is an agreement between member countries and the FLAR not to publish this information, but to keep it private between the central banks, the Representative Assembly, and the Board of Directors.

Although the FLAR's surveillance is not public, nor as extensive as the IMF, it does frequently provide technical advisory services to central banks and other regional institutions. In addition, it has been working on bolstering its policy guidance and research capacity, as evidenced by the strategic alliance it maintains with the Bank for International Settlements and, as of 2016, with AMRO. These organizations maintain a dialogue and share their respective experiences with surveillance and research. These relationships also guide the FLAR in strategically planning the further development of its surveillance process and macroeconomic policy guidance. This is an important goal, as regional mechanisms like the FLAR may be better equipped than the IMF to address "region-specific problems and risks, given that they possess an abundance of local knowledge" (Eichengreen 2015, 137).

Finally, since FLAR resources are paid-in capital, the organization is responsible for their investment and security. FLAR prides itself on its ortho-dox approach to such investment that seeks to minimize risk and safeguard member capital contributions. And it strives for significant liquidity and security by investing in AA- and AAA-rated securities. However, as seen in the most recent global financial crisis(2008–9), this does not always prevent losses: the FLAR suffered losses on investments in highly rated assets that lost money, such as mortgage-backed securities. Indeed, it is worth noting that the FLAR would have suffered net losses in 2009 and 2010 had it not earned interest on its loans to Ecuador.

Lending Instruments

The FLAR contingency, liquidity, and balance-of-payments credit facilities are designed to address similar issues as the IMF's short-term mechanisms, including stand-by arrangements (SBAs), the Stand-by Credit Facility, the Rapid Credit Facility (RCF), and the Rapid Financing Instrument. The maximum duration of the IMF facilities, such as the RCF, can range from one year to as many as ten years. The interest rate of loans in the form of special drawing rights (SDRs) is currently 1.050 percent and the IMF has seniority as a creditor, a fact that is recognized by markets. These loans are often accompa-nied by the requirement that a member country signs an agreement to commit to a variety of conditions, such as privatization or austerity measures.

In contrast, FLAR has shorter-term mechanisms that have a maximum dura-tion of three years. Interest rates are calculated using an internal formula, and are steeper than those of the IMF, typically around the three-month London Inter-Bank Offered Rate plus 300–400 basis points. However, these rates are significantly lower than the rates at which the member countries could typically borrow in private capital markets, provided the country has access to private capital at all. The FLAR enjoys de facto seniority status as a creditor because "the degree of involvement and a sense of belonging of its members [has] guaranteed the total and timely reimbursement of loans" (Corvalan 2015, 273).

The FLAR does not attach conditionality to its loans to the same degree as the IMF. That said, there is very limited explicit conditionality associated with FLAR loans. A major conditionality explicitly stated in its covenant is that member countries must not impede trade by instituting trade barriers. Nonetheless, such conditions are substantially less burdensome than those imposed by the IMF.

When a country seeks a loan, it contacts the FLAR's economic team and the Executive President, leading to discussions about the country's macroeconomic conditions, its plans to address the issues, and its credit needs. While these discussions progress, the member country submits a formal request for credit and a detailed macroeconomic plan to the DES, which is responsible for reviewing the macroeconomic conditions of member countries. This division assesses the extent to which the stated goals are attainable and conducive to the country's economic recovery and its ability to repay its debt obligations. This analysis is then submitted to the Executive President who can either approve or refuse the request for the loan (for liquidity and contingency loans) or present the plan to the Board of Directors for a vote (for balance-of-payments and debt restructuring loans).

The amount of capital available to member countries varies in proportion to a country's paid-in capital. Depending on the circumstances, these loans can be disbursed within as short a period as one week for liquidity support purposes. Debt refinancing can take as long as four to eight weeks. The interest charged on the different mechanisms listed in Table 9.2 and the spread is determined by the FLAR's Asset and Liability Committee, which evaluates external financing conditions in international markets. While IMF officials may visit countries where there are ongoing IMF loan programs as often as quarterly for monitoring, FLAR officials visit member countries with FLAR loans approximately twice a year to monitor progress toward economic stability. Officials also hold monthly phone conferences with the officials in the borrowing country.

A comparison of project governance between the FLAR and the IMF shows that the FLAR is significantly more agile and, in the experience of those interviewed, faster in responding to member countries' requests for funds. In addition, it imposes significantly fewer conditions on member countries and has never denied a loan request by a member country. However, the interest rate is higher than that of the IMF, which suggests that FLAR members attach greater value to its flexibility and lack of conditionality. Overall, the approach of the FLAR is deeply embedded in the creditor–debtor dynamics of the institution. Member countries feel a sense of shared ownership and responsibility, which leads them not only to support each other but also to repay the loans extended by this mechanism.

FLAR's Response to COVID-19

While the FLAR does not publish reports on macroeconomic oversight, unlike the IMF with its Article IV consultations, or CMIM-AMRO, FLAR officials have suggested that press releases can be a powerful tool for deterring speculators or assuring creditors. Specifically, FLAR staff noted that they signal, through public confirmation, a member country's access to certain amounts of credit facilities at the FLAR or that member countries have drawn from the mechanisms. This was evidenced at the onset of the COVID-19 pandemic when FLAR took the unprecedented step of announcing its available resources to help member countries.

In a video posted in April 2020, FLAR's president, José Darío Uribe, points to the importance of international cooperation and institutions like the FLAR. After reiterating the key importance of the FLAR and its role, Uribe emphasized that FLAR can provide agile and flexible disbursements using its US$2.25 billion in resources and "has the potential to mobilize larger amounts" (FLAR 2020a). In an unprecedented move, Uribe also announced that FLAR was working on new measures to help member countries and bolster its lending capacity.

Following a meeting of its Board of Directors on May 25, 2020, FLAR approved a debt program to expand its lending capacity and strengthen its credit capacity. Shortly thereafter, it advertised these developments in a prominent press release. Under this program, FLAR increased its lending resources for member countries to US$6.8 billion, "which represents a 60 percent increase in the Fund's financing possibilities before the decision" (FLAR 2020b). In the same press release, FLAR announced a more flexible and longer tenure "exceptional credit line" with a three-year grace period to rapidly disburse funds to member countries.

FLAR also made it easier to join the institution in the wake of the COVID-19 pandemic. In July 2021, the Representative Assembly of FLAR voted to approve "the creation of a complementary membership mechanism to join FLAR, creating a new member category called 'associated central bank'" (FLAR 2021). While countries can continue to become full-fledged members in which they adhere to the Constitutive Agreement of the institution, the new mechanism represents a new "modality of associated central banks, by means of a relationship agreement approved by the Board of Directors and the Assembly of the Latin American Reserve Fund" (FLAR 2021).

CONCLUSION

While regional financial arrangements are clearly linked, or "nested," in the GFSN and directly associated with the IMF, like CMIM, the FLAR represents an outlier. With nearly five decades of successful lending and a virtually perfect repayment history by member countries, the institution with conditionality-free loans and a "one country, one vote" philosophy provides many valuable lessons for multilateral institutions in general. That said, while the

FLAR certainly continues to provide a viable alternative for its member countries as compared to the IMF in the region, Latin America as a whole is yet to
have a region-wide alternative that can completely displace the IMF or allow
Latin America to leave the nest of the traditional multilateral lending institutions (Kring and Grimes 2019, 72). The challenges and regional responses
to COVID-19 are certain to strengthen the FLAR, much like the region's
response to the Latin American Debt Crisis.

NOTES

1. Historically, in decreasing order of usage, member countries have received loans
    for balance of payments support, liquidity credits, contingency financing credit
    lines, and central bank external public debt restructuring.
2. Chile resigned in 1976.
3. Roberto Junguito highlights how Latin America faced its first debt crisis in
    1825–26 because of over-indebtedness incurred through the financing of wars
    for independence. In *The First Latin American Debt Crisis: The City of London
    and the 1822–25 Loan Bubble* (1990), Frank Dawson terms this the "First Great
    Bubble of Latin America." Later in the century, Latin America proved unable
    to meet its obligation to bondholders. As a result of these episodes, "the main
    episode learned by Latin American countries … was that public indebtedness
    leads to an inability to meet external obligation" (Junguito 2015, 66). Latin
    America learned in the 20th century that it was incredibly vulnerable to "fluctu-
    ations in the global economy" (Junguito 2015, 70).
4. Thus, while FAR, and later FLAR, loans are essentially conditionality-free when
    issued, there is superseding conditionality as per the constitutive agreement of
    the fund that prohibits member countries from impeding trade among member
    countries.
5. The agreement states that the Executive President "shall act exclusively in the
    function of the interests of the subregion and shall not solicit or accept instruc-
    tions from any government or national or international entity." (Pate 1979, 1198).
6. Upon the creation of the FLAR in 1988, the fund had three primary credit
    instruments: balance of payments, liquidity credit lines, and short-term liquidity.
    However, on February 20, 1995, the Board of Directors agreed to the creation of
    a "central bank external public debt restructuring" credit line. The justification
    used was "that the restructuring of the public external debt of member countries
    contributes positively to the alleviation of balance of payments, and conse-
    quently, to preventing their deterioration" (FLAR Board Agreement, 180). The
    credit facility would have a two-year tenure, a six-month grace period, and either
    be for 1.5 or 2.2 times paid-in capital. The Board of Directors also created the
    contingent credit line in March 1998. Amid volatile international capital flows
    and the AFC, the Board sought to develop a short-term credit facility for when
    member countries face "contingencies of external or internal origin over the
    short-term capital flows that could lead to negative exchange-rate expectations
    and pressure in foreign exchange markets" (FLAR Board Agreement, 121). The
    credit facility would be for a six-month period, renewable only once, for no more
    than two times paid-in capital. The timing of the creation of these new credit lines
    were pivotal, as Ecuador used the external public debt restructuring mechanisms

in 1995 and Colombia used the contingency line in 1999. For more information, see Eduardo Morón (2015).

REFERENCES

Andean Subregional Integration Agreement (Cartagena Agreement). 1969, May 26. *WIPO TRT/ASIACA/001.* www.wipo.int/wipolex/en/other_treaties/text.jsp?file_id= 220450 (accessed 28 November, 2022)

Boughton, James M. 2001. *Silent Revolution: The International Monetary Fund, 1979–89.* International Monetary Fund.

Carrasquilla, Ana Maria. 2015. "Presentation: 35 years of the Latin American Reserve Fund, FLAR." In G. Perry (Ed.), *Building a Latin American Reserve Fund: 35 Years of FLAR,* 13–15. Pan-American Formas e Impresos SA.

"Colombia—Request for Stand-By Arrangement." 1971, March 23. *IMF Archives EBS/71/69.*

Corvalan, J. 2015. "Paraguay in the FLAR." In G. Perry (Ed.), *Building a Latin American Reserve Fund: 35 Years of FLAR,* 265–278. Pan-American Formas e Impresos SA.

Dawson, Frank. 1990. *The First Latin American Debt Crisis: The City of London and the 1822–25 Loan Bubble.* Yale University Press.

Eichengreen, Barry. 2015. "Regional Financial Arrangements and the IMF." In G. Perry (Ed.), *Building a Latin American Reserve Fund: 35 Years of FLAR,* 133–142. Pan-American Formas e Impresos SA.

El País Agencies. 1985, September 23. "Alan García dice que reconsiderará la pertenencia de su país al FMI." *EL PAÍS.* https://elpais.com/diario/1985/09/24/ internacional/496360821_850215.html (accessed 18 November, 2023)

Ffrench-Davis, Ricardo. 1977. "The Andean Pact: A Model of Economic Integration for Developing Countries." *World Development* 5(1–2): 137–53.

Grabel, Ilene. 2013. "Global Financial Governance and Development Finance in the Wake of the 2008 Financial Crisis." *Feminist Economics* 19(3): 32–54.

Hibben, Mark. 2006. *Poor States, Power and the Politics of IMF Reform: Drivers of Change in the Post-Washington Consensus.* Palgrave Macmillan.

International Monetary Fund (IMF) Financial Data Query Tool. (2022)

Johnson, Tim. 1988, June 10. "Five Latin American Countries Create Regional Lending Bank." *United Press International.* www.upi.com/Archives/1988/06/10/Five-Latin -American-countries-create-regional-lending-bank/2500581918400/ (accessed 18 November, 2023)

Junguito, Roberto. 2015. "Lessons from the Financial Crisis After Independence." In G. Perry (Ed.), *Building a Latin American Reserve Fund: 35 Years of FLAR,* 65–80. Pan-American Formas e Impresos SA.

Kofas, Jon V. 2001. "The IMF, the World Bank, and US Foreign Policy in Ecuador, 1956–1966." *Latin American Perspectives* 28(5): 50–83.

Kofas, Jon V. 2002. *The Sword of Damocles: U.S. Financial Hegemony in Colombia and Chile, 1950–1970.* Praeger.

Kring, William N., and William W. Grimes. 2019. "Leaving the Nest: The Rise of Regional Financial Arrangements and the Future of Global Governance." *Development and Change* 50(1): 72–95.

Latin American Reserve Fund (FLAR). 1976. "FLAR Constitutive Agreement." www.flar.net/uploads/default/projects/0e341bbcf9d8effc176f77a97cc53767.pdf (accessed 18 November, 2023)

Latin American Reserve Fund (FLAR). 2020a. "FLAR Ante Crisis COVID-19." https://flar.com/2020/04/21/jose-dario-uribe-presidente-ejecutivo-del-fondo-latinoamericano-de-reservas-habla-del-flar-ante-la-crisis-del-covid-19/

Latin American Reserve Fund (FLAR). 2020b. Latin American Reserve Fund: Management Report 2004–2017. https://flar.com/index.php/en/news/flar-strengthens-itself-support-its-member-countries-covid-19-crisis (accessed 10 November, 2022)

Latin American Reserve Fund (FLAR). 2021. "FLAR Approves Complementary Membership Mechanism." https://flar.com/en/flar-approves-complementary-membership-mechanism

Latin American Reserve Fund (FLAR). 2022. "History and Evolution." https://flar.com/history-and-evolution/

Latin American Reserve Fund (FLAR). n.d. "Capital Structure." https://flar.com/index.php/en/about-flar/capital-structure

Morales, Juan Antonio. 2015. "Bolivia in the history of FLAR." In G. Perry (Ed.), *Building a Latin American Reserve Fund: 35 Years of FLAR*, 224–33. Pan-American Formas e Impresos SA.

Morón, Eduardo. 2015. "FLAR as a tool for the macroeconomic stability of the region." In G. Perry (Ed.), *Building a Latin American Reserve Fund: 35 Years of FLAR*, 216–22. Pan-American Formas e Impresos SA.

Ocampo, José Antonio. 2015. "FLAR and Its Role in the Regional and International Financial Architecture." In G. Perry (Ed.), *Building a Latin American Reserve Fund: 35 Years of FLAR*, 155–74. Pan-American Formas e Impresos SA.

Ocampo, José Antonio, and Titelman, Daniel. 2012. "Regional Monetary Cooperation in Latin America." *ABDI Working Paper Series* 373: 17.

Pate, John R. (trans.). 1979. "Andean Group: Treaty for the Creation of the Andean Reserve Fund." *International Legal Materials* 18(5): 1191–1202. https://doi.org/10.1017/S0020782900040183

Rosero, Luis D. 2014. "Regional Pooling of International Reserves: The Latin American Reserve Fund in Perspective." *Latin American Policy* 5(1): 62–86.

Urrutia, Miguel. 2015. "Brief History of FLAR." In G. Perry (Ed.), *Building a Latin American Reserve Fund: 35 Years of FLAR*, 197. Pan-American Formas e Impresos SA.

Vinogradoff, Ludmila. 1988, January 16. "Creación del Fondo Latinoamericano de Reservas como una alternativa al FMI." *EL PAÍS*.

10. Climate change, monetary policy, and green finance in Latin America: the open economy dimension

Pablo G. Bortz and Nicole Toftum

INTRODUCTION

Climate change (CC) has been defined as an existential threat to human life.[1] Though it is difficult to make forecasts, there is consensus that the effects of CC will have a substantial impact on standards of living and productive capacity. The Intergovernmental Panel on Climate Change (IPCC 2018: 264) states that "The mean net present value of the costs of damages from warming in 2100 for 1.5°C and 2°C (including costs associated with climate change-induced market and non-market impacts, impacts due to sea level rise, and impacts associated with large-scale discontinuities) are \$54 and \$69 trillion, respectively, relative to 1961–1990." Fighting, mitigating, and adapting to these challenges requires substantial amounts of investment. Emerging Market Economies (EMEs), including Latin American economies (LAEs), face a double task in this regard. The economic impact of CC will be stronger in warmer countries, of which the majority are either an EME or a low-income country (International Monetary Fund IMF) 2017). Countries in Central America and the Caribbean, for instance, are among the economies that are most exposed to the effects of CC (IMF 2021). Furthermore, on top of (and to some extent, overlapping with) climate-change-related investment (CCRI), EMEs face the task of achieving the Sustainable Development Goals (SDGs), which also requires important investment. This has raised questions about the capabilities to mobilize resources and funding, given the limited domestic capital and financial market that characterizes EMEs in general and LAEs in particular (with some notable exceptions).

LAEs face what Ocampo (2016) called "balance-of-payments dominance," that is, a situation in which the short-term macroeconomic dynamics are heavily influenced by external shocks beyond the implications of familiar concepts such as the external gap or the Dutch disease (Ocampo 2016: 211).

The implications of CC also materialize through this channel, which has been scarcely reviewed in the literature. A recent exception is Löscher and Kaltenbrunner (2022), on which this chapter draws and expands.

CC can have an impact on the production and trading profile of LAEs via both physical and transition risks. The emissions of greenhouse gases (GHG) in the region is broadly in line with its global share of population and gross domestic product (GDP), but it faces both physical and transition risks that will influence the performance of LAEs' balance of payments (IMF 2021: 3). For instance, the region is characterized by a high level of emissions from the agricultural sector and change in land use and forestry (IMF 2021: 3), a sector that generates substantial foreign exchange (FX) revenues in countries like Argentina, Uruguay, Paraguay, and Brazil. The agricultural sector is exposed to more frequent droughts, floods, and temperature change, as well as transition risks arising from carbon taxes and transport costs, for instance. In turn, there are many countries that have (or are planning to develop) an important fossil fuel sector, which also contributes (or is expected to contribute) as a generator of FX revenues through exports.

Adding to balance-of-trade considerations, the impacts and challenges transmitted through the financial account will be considerable. As the literature on currency hierarchy has shown, EMEs are forced to pay a liquidity premium on their external borrowing, and this feature may be aggravated by CC. The underdevelopment of financial systems may call for larger external flows. But since these flows are mainly governed by external factors such as the Global Financial Cycle, the availability and stability of foreign inflows may pose a challenge to monetary policy and other macroeconomic variables (Bortz et al. 2018). Furthermore, the channels and conditions by which these flows enter (and exit) EMEs is not neutral in terms of balance sheet exposure, for instance, because of currency denomination, Environmental, Social, and Governance (ESG) labeling, and the borrowing sector (Carnevali et al. 2021).

The implications of CC for monetary policy in EMEs in general, and in LAEs in particular, have multiple angles, ranging from inflation control to financial stability (Network for Greening the Financial System NGFS) 2019; McKibbin et al. 2020; Cantelmo et al. 2022). However, the open economy dimension has been generally neglected. This chapter tries to remedy this fault. Its structure is as follows. The second section will revise the financial needs for CC and SDGs as estimated by different international bodies, as well as the current trends in green finance in the region. Next, we examine the risks and opportunities of CC for export performance of LAEs, while the fourth section focuses on the impact of CC on the financial account of the balance of payments, and the dangers of international financial integration dedicated to CC-related investment. The final section elaborates on the general implications for the design and implementation of monetary policy in LAEs.

INVESTMENT NEEDS AND SUSTAINABLE FINANCE

Given the uncertain bases on which to estimate the investment required to fight, mitigate, and adapt to the different scenarios envisioned by CC, there are multiple estimations of how much is needed, depending on the projected increase in temperature and the investment gaps that keep accumulating. In 2013, the World Economic Forum estimated US$5.7 trillion investment per year until 2030 to secure future growth in a 2°C-higher scenario. The New Climate Economy Report (Global Commission on the Economy and Climate 2014) estimated US$90 trillion in 15 years, or around US$6 trillion per year. The Organisation for Economic Co-operation and Development (OECD 2017: 28) increased those estimations to US$6.9 trillion until 2030 to provide for a climate-resilient, low-carbon economy consistent with a 2°C-higher scenario (with 66 percent probability). In its 2018 1.5° Report, the IPCC stated that "1.5°C-consistent climate policies would require a marked upscaling of *energy system supply-side investments* (resource extraction, power generation, fuel conversion, pipelines/transmission, and energy storage) between now and mid-century, reaching levels of between US$1.6–3.8 trillion globally on average over the 2016–2050 time frame" (IPCC 2018: 154, emphasis added). More recent updates still disagree about the approximate requirements. In 2021, the International Energy Agency (IEA 2021: 30) estimated that investment needs required for a Net-Zero Emissions scenario reached US$4 trillion per year until 2030, triple the current investment. McKinsey (2022), in turn, suggested a figure of US$9 trillion per year (more than double the estimations of the IEA) for global investment needs between 2021 and 2050.

Investment for CC mitigation and adaptation is not disconnected, however, from the commitments required to achieve the SDGs, within the United Nations (UN) 2030 Agenda for Sustainable Development. In fact, SDG 13 refers explicitly to the urgency of addressing CC. IPCC (2018) states that CC has non-neutral effects on poverty and income distribution. The UN estimated US$5–7 trillion globally per year to achieve the SDGs (United Nations Framework Convention on Climate Change 2015; UN Environment Programme 2017, 2018). Estimated needs for developing Asia reach US$200 billion per year (Sachs et al. 2019), while Latin America needs to invest US$175 billion considering only mitigation and adaptation expenditures related to CC (Abramskiehn et al. 2017: 2). A more recent estimation by Galindo et al. (2022: 4) affirms that "the infrastructure and social spending needed to meet climate change goals in the region is between 7 percent and 19 percent of GDP by 2030 (US$470 billion to US$1300 billion in 2030) depending on initial conditions and proposed economic and social targets."

The OECD (2019), the World Bank (2018), and other multilateral institutions claim that the magnitude of funding required is far superior to the financial capabilities of the public sector, and it also dwarfs the resources of development banks. In addition, the introduction of Basel III regulations discourages lending by banks to enterprises and activities with little to no prior record on which to assess riskiness. Also, financial stability concerns are raised against prioritizing bank credit as a finance channel. Therefore, these institutions encourage the tapping of private financial markets as a means to fund CC-related "green" investment. And ever since the European Investment Bank issued the first labeled "green bond" in 2007, there have been developments in the field of "green finance" that are not devoid of fluctuations and volatility.

Green bonds and other debt instruments labeled within the "sustainable finance" category reached US$1.1 trillion in 2021, an increment of 46 percent relative to the sums issued in 2020 (Climate Bond Initiative (CBI) 2022: 5). Half of total issuance in 2021 corresponded to green bonds, which grew 75 percent with respect to the previous year (CBI 2022: 5). This growth more than compensates for the decrease in the issuance of social bonds in 2021, a fall of 13 percent from 2020 (CBI 2022: 5). The market continues to be concentrated in issuances by advanced economies, capturing 73 percent of all green finance volume issued in 2021. EMEs increased their share, from 17 percent in 2020 to 21 percent in 2021 (CBI 2022: 8). However, these figures hide heterogeneous behavior across regions. While bonds issuance in the Asia-Pacific region grew by 129 percent, the volumes for Latin America fell from 2020 to 2021. The numbers for sovereign bond issuance in the region are particularly striking: they fell from US$3.8 billion in 2020 to only US$1.2 billion (a 68 percent decline), with only one country entering the market (Chile; CBI 2022: 8). As for the currency of denomination (a major topic developed below), the euro, the US dollar, and the Chinese RMB concentrate 81 percent of gross issuance (CBI 2022: 11).

When looking at climate finance flows for *new projects*, total climate finance reached US$630 billion in 2019–20, an increase of 10 percent compared to 2017–18 (Climate Policy Initiative (CPI) 2021: 2). Growth in climate financing decelerated in relation to the previous period (CPI 2021: 2). Data by CPI are not necessarily compatible with green bond issuance data because the proceeds of the latter are not always devoted to *new primary investment* (*repeated* issuers captured 63 percent of the volume green bonds issued), while the quality of reporting needs improvement (CBI 2022: 3). With those caveats, the average of climate flows for the years 2019 and 2020 shows that public financing sources indeed represent 51 percent of the funding, and market-rate debt comprises 49 percent of the instruments (CPI 2021: 3). Public finance is also mainly conducted through Development Financial Institutions (DFIs). Most of the funding indeed is directed toward the domestic economy

(75 percent, according to CPI 2021). In terms of destinations, three-quarters of global climate investment were concentrated in East Asia and the Pacific, Western Europe, and North America, with East Asia taking 46 percent of all climate finance flows (CPI 2021: 29). Latin America barely captured 5.5 percent of total climate finance in the period 2019–20 (CPI 2021: 30).

As mentioned above, the green bond market increased substantially in 2021. However, the data show a marked volatility, with years of stagnation in bond issuance (CBI 2022), such as 2016 and 2018. It is likely as well that, in 2022, we observe another decrease in bond issuance. This volatility reveals one of the vulnerabilities of climate-related investment: its exposure to global financial conditions independent of the awareness about the urgency of such a type of investment. The tightening of financial markets in years such as 2018, and likely in 2022 as well, provides a warning about the reliance in private funding for such purposes. The restrictions are not limited to bond markets: supranational entities and DFIs also funded substantial shares of their long-term investment in the bond market, and are therefore affected by spillovers. The "greenium" of green bond markets (the price premium investors pay for green bonds compared to conventional bonds) is very small, on average, ranging between 1 and 20 basis points (Larcker and Watts 2020; Löffler et al. 2021; Lau et al. 2022), and depends on perceptions about the risk of greenwashing in specific bonds (Intonti et al. 2022; Lau et al. 2022; Wu 2022).

CLIMATE CHANGE, EXPORTS, AND MONETARY POLICY

The threats of CC to financial stability and monetary policy have been broadly classified into two groups (NGFS 2019; Bank for International Settlements (BIS) 2021).[2] On the one hand, there are physical risks related to damages from meteorological events such as floods, droughts, fire, rising temperatures, rising sea levels, damage to ecosystems and the services they provide, and so on. In that sense, these risks can be of an acute nature (such as floods) or of a chronic nature (such as changes in rain patterns, or rising temperatures). On the other hand, there are transition risks. These refer to policy, regulatory, and technological changes as part of adaptation and mitigation strategies to cope with CC. Among these risks, one can mention the impacts of carbon taxes, the need to decrease the reliance on fossil fuels, technological advances that may render current technologies obsolete, and so on. Transition risks also include changes in consumers' preferences, which may influence demand in several sectors.

There is a growing literature on the macroeconomic and financial impacts of CC (e.g., Kahn et al. 2019; BIS 2021; Ciccarelli and Marotta 2021; for a focus on EMEs, see Espagne et al. 2021). Commodity-dependent EMEs are among the countries that are most vulnerable to the effects of CC (United Nations

Conference on Trade and Development 2019). Some of these vulnerabilities arise through the impact on export performance.

The literature on the effects of CC on the balance of payments, however, is still limited, with some notable exceptions (Brenton and Chemutai 2021; Löscher and Kaltenbrunner 2022). Dellink et al. (2017) use a dynamic stochastic general equilibrium model developed by the OECD to provide a qualitative and regional assessment of the direct and indirect effects of CC on trade, distinguishing between physical and transition risks. CC is already affecting crops and livestock and will have a negative impact on the export performance of EMEs (Food and Agriculture Organization 2018; Barua and Valenzuela 2018; Dallmann 2019; Coulibaly et al. 2020; Osberghaus 2019; Brenton and Chemutai 2021). In one of the few studies addressing the impact for monetary policy objectives, Bortz and Toftum (2022) analyze the effects of changing rain patterns on FX reserve accumulation in Argentina. They find that decreasing rain in the most important months for agricultural production has a negative impact on reserve accumulation, instrumented through the exports of the main agricultural complexes (soya, wheat, corn, and sunflower). This effect is robust to several specifications and control variables.

The effects of CC, however, will be asymmetrical across countries (Bolton et al. 2020; Volz et al. 2021). Dellink et al. (2017) find that physical risks will affect air, land, river, and sea-based transport. The influence on inland river-based transport systems (either through lower depth levels, or through floods and rising water levels in delta and port areas) will increase transportation costs, production networks, and grain transport, among others (Curtis 2009). The melting of the Arctic Sea, however, would reduce time and transport costs by opening new routes and redirecting existing ones. On the other hand, this may lead to a further concentration of trade between advanced Northern economies at the disadvantage of developing countries, but also Southern and Eastern European countries. An obvious remark relates to the severe impact of increased trade in the Arctic ecosystem. Temperate and cold regions, such as Canada and Northern Europe, will increase their land productivity. Crops such as wheat will suffer less auspicious conditions in most of the world, but will increase their productivity in Northern America and Europe.

But transition risks will also have a bearing on global trade. The transition to a net-zero economy will disproportionally affect EMEs, which are major exporters of fossil fuels like coal, oil, and gas (IEA 2021; Volz et al. 2021). For that goal to be achieved, fossil fuel reserves and the capital equipment related to that industry will have to be registered at a loss and simply remain unexploited (McGlade and Ekins 2015; Caldecott 2018). In that sense, they will be "stranded assets." This will reduce exports of several EMEs (including in Latin America) (Mercure et al. 2018; Espagne et al. 2021). Carbon taxes will disproportionally affect EMEs' exports, directly and indirectly, for instance, through carbon border adjustment policies fostered by the European Union (Brenton and Chemutai 2021: 68). Regulatory policies like banning fossil-fueled cars and discouraging short-flights (and favoring train transportation) will also drive down oil demand.

Furthermore, the development of new technologies, particularly related to the expansion of the renewable energy sector, may impact energy exporters *twice*, if they do not participate in the production network (Volz et al. 2021). Not only will their main export product be negatively affected by the low-carbon transition, but they will also need to import new products and technologies. However, the effects are not homogeneously negative for all countries. EMEs exporting minerals will see growing demand and rising prices for their main staples.

Finally, there is the use of the link between exchange rates and commodity prices. Exchange rates in commodity-exporting countries tend to move with the prices of their main export product. However, the presence of transition risks (for instance, regarding fossil fuel policies) weakens the links between commodity prices and exchange rates, as found by Kapfhammer et al. (2020).

There is, of course, a high degree of uncertainty in these projections. Regulatory policies and feedback effects will influence the dynamics of the adjustments. Copyright and patent issues, and lock-in effects may deter the access of EMEs (and low-income economies) to new, environmentally efficient technology (Brown et al. 2008).

CLIMATE CHANGE AND THE FINANCIAL ACCOUNT OF THE BALANCE OF PAYMENTS

The impacts of CC will also be felt in the financial account of the balance of payments, through real and financial investment, debt, and equity markets (Löscher and Kaltenbrunner 2022). To some extent, changes in trade patterns will also affect foreign direct investment (FDI) flows, particularly toward commodity-exporting countries. Stranded assets themselves (such as coal and oil reserves) are a major concern for both FDI *stocks* and *flows*, on top of the eventual impact on domestic investment, employment, fiscal revenues, and financial stability (Volz et al. 2021: 20). But the impacts on FDI flows exceed transition risks. The literature on the topic, however, is scarce.

Li and Gallagher (2022) point out that CC-related natural disasters have already affected FDI *stock*. However, their findings suggest that, within countries, there are no significant differences between the exposure of FDI and local investment to physical climate risks. These results change from sector to sector, with agriculture and mining having the highest aggregate climate risk (Li and Gallagher 2022: 2). Barua et al. (2020), in turn, find that temperature and precipitation changes have an effect on FDI flows, which is uneven across regions. Furthermore, increments in temperature are associated with lower FDI inflows to developing countries, but larger FDI inflows to developed countries (Barua et al. 2020), in line with the mentioned asymmetrical impacts of CC on agricultural production. Finally, Drabo (2021) shows that climate shocks decrease the positive effects of FDI (as well as Official Development Assistance and remittances) on economic growth in low- and middle-income countries.

However, given the investment needs for adaptation and mitigation mentioned above and the development of new financial instruments (such as bonds of different "labels"), international debt flows are very relevant. Around 75 percent of the funds for *new projects* is directed toward the domestic economy (CPI 2021). However, the gap between current outlays and investment needs surveyed in the second section of this chapter called for an engagement with external sources of funding. This call is compounded by the smaller size of financial markets in most EMEs. An additional constraint is the global turn toward market-based funding rather than bank-based. EMEs' financial systems are generally oriented precisely toward bank-based finance. Basel III rules discriminate against loans considered "risky," and the field of renewable energy fits that criterion. This does not imply that there have been no advances in the sphere of "green loans" in EMEs. Standards for green loans were established in Asian and Latin American countries, a useful step for the development of that market. However, Basel III allows for different banking risks models generated by the institutions themselves. But the orientation fostered by multilateral organizations is toward the integration of international capital markets in the provision of funds for CC-related investment.

However, this integration is not devoid of risks and costs. Some of these are not exclusively related to "green finance." The rhythm and pace of financial flows responds to the monetary and financial conditions in advanced markets (notably, the US) more than the state of "fundamentals" in recipient countries. In this sense, the supply of finance for climate-related projects is tied to the evolution of the Global Financial Cycle (Miranda-Agrippino and Rey 2020). As mentioned above, the gaps in funding cumulate at an exponential rate. The damage is larger because of specific characteristics of renewable energy projects (Ghisetti et al. 2017; Natural Resources Defense Council (NRDC) 2016).

The fact that the green bond market is mainly denominated in "hard" currencies is also a well-known factor of risk for EMEs as it creates a currency mismatch problem; in particular, benefited projects do not lead to an improvement in the current account balance (Avdjiev et al. 2019; Obstfeld and Zhou 2022). This danger is not merely restricted to fully market-based finance. The involvement of National Development Banks (NDBs) and other types of public finance under the strategy of blended finance, as sponsored by the OECD (2019), for instance, also relies on the NDBs and the public sector to take over risks that the private sector refuses to take, thus carrying in its balance sheet a possible currency mismatch, among other burdens. Public–Private Partnerships (PPPs) also present a potential currency and fiscal burden for the public sector (Gabor 2021). However, the involvement of NDBs, Multilateral Development Banks (MDBs), and other financial institutions has advantages that will be mentioned further below.

Mispricing of risk and credit rationing or misallocation is further compounded by the identification of environmentally sustainable projects, the eventual destination of the funding. One of the most disseminated criteria for assessing investment is the ESG classification, which will label a growing share of the portfolio of global funds (Nelson 2018; Gabor et al. 2019). The certification of green bonds is carried by an increasing number of rating agencies, both public and private (Ehlers and Packer 2017). The rating of these bonds and, generally, ESG assets is not highly correlated across agencies for the same companies (Berg et al. 2022). In this sense, the ESG label has turned into a speculative valuation practice (Leins 2020), creating risks for "greenwashing." This creates another channel for mispricing of climate-related risks and misallocation of investment (Simpson et al. 2021). Capital market lending for EME projects is not excluded from this risk.

This feature is a particular manifestation of a more general theme: the type of investor matters for the type of project to be financed, and the general direction of innovation, for instance, in renewable energy (Mazzucato and Semieniuk 2018). Environmental innovation has additional risks compared to traditional innovation, such as longer maturity, capital intensity, lock-in effects, and path dependency (Aghion et al. 2014), so that financial restrictions and misallocations can have a lasting impact (Ghisetti et al. 2017). Different actors have different portfolios in terms of technologies and risk. The involvement of MDBs also helps to improve the access to credit for riskier debtors and provides a signaling function (Gurara et al. 2020).

One further aspect of the impact of CC on the financial side of the balance of payments refers to the ability of EMEs' governments to access international capital markets. There are two sides to the issue: the effects of natural disasters on sovereign risks, and the longer-term implications of both physical and transition risks. On the first topic, Mallucci (2022) finds that natural disasters, such as hurricanes, depress governments' abilities to issue debt. Klomp (2015) found that natural disasters increase bond premia in EMEs, both in the short and in the long run. On the second issue, Beirne et al. (2021) show that, in a sample of advanced and developing countries, vulnerability to CC is a significant determinant of sovereign risk. Furthermore, the impact on bond premia becomes permanent, and the more so in highly vulnerable economies. Boehm (2020) identifies a negative impact of rising temperatures in sovereign bond yields of EMEs. Shah (2020) finds an impact not merely on bond yields but also on bond maturities, though with significant heterogeneity across countries. These results are congruent with those of Cevik and Jalles (2020).

CLIMATE CHANGE, BALANCE OF PAYMENTS, AND MONETARY POLICY IN LATIN AMERICA

The implications of CC for the design and implementation of monetary policy are numerous, and it is beyond the scope of this chapter to review an already enormous and still growing literature (among many others, see Dikau and Volz 2018; Dafermos et al. 2018; D'Orazio and Popoyan 2019; Krogstrup and Oman 2019; Batten et al. 2019; Bolton et al. 2020; Hansen 2022; IMF 2022). Dees et al. (2022) provide a brief summary of the transmission channels of CC for the design and implementation of monetary policy. Physical risks may increase the impact of non-demand-driven factors on inflation, while transition risks may affect risk premia, with both factors hampering the transmission of interest rates to economic activity. They may also endanger financial stability through their impact on borrowers (lower net worth, decrease in collateral) and lenders (increasing non-performing loans and hampering banks' funding). Capital destruction due to natural disasters and stranded assets may affect asset prices. Monetary policy would be less predictable and less credible.

The consensus in the literature, however, is that central banks can con- tribute to the efforts for adaptation and mitigation of CC, by increasing the "resilience" of their financial sector and the economy in general (Dikau and Ryan-Collins 2017; Dafermos et al. 2018; NGFS 2019; Beirne et al. 2021; IMF 2022). The two main channels to achieve that objective are enhancing financial stability and fostering investment in renewable energies and in low-carbon sectors. If successful, these policies will have material benefits from a balance-of-payments perspective by reducing sovereign risk premia and facilitating access to international capital markets, particularly in the case of emerging economies (Arndt et al. 2020; Boehm 2020; Cevik and Jalles 2020).

Monetary and financial authorities in Latin America have already started to adopt policies in this regard (Frisari et al. 2020). While writing this chapter, there are 13 central bank and financial supervisory authorities from Latin America that are members of the Network for Greening the Financial System (NGFS), a global group of central bankers who aim to strengthen the resil- ience of their financial system to CC and to mobilize sustainable finance. Furthermore, many central banks and supervisory authorities (of the banking sector, of capital markets, of the insurance sector) have implemented specific policies. The Central Bank of Brazil, for instance, has implemented climate stress tests for banking institutions, and has mandated that banks incorpo- rate environmental and social risks in their capital requirements (Dikau and

Ryan-Collins 2017). Banco de Mexico has also adopted a strategy in line with the different financial supervisors to develop disclosure guidelines, climate stress tests, and forward-looking scenarios (Banxico 2020).

At the time of writing (October 2022), several central banks and financial supervisors in the region have implemented, or are in the process of implementing (Frisari et al. 2020), consultations and surveys of their financial sectors about their exposures to climate risks and risk management practices, in a variety of financial institutions (banks, pension funds, asset managers, insurance companies, etc.). They have also issued guidelines to stimulate and scale private sustainable lending through capital markets, as in Argentina, Chile, Brazil, Colombia, Peru, and others. All these countries have already observed domestic green issuance, and some of them even issued green-labeled bonds in international markets (CBI 2020). However, as mentioned above, recourse to international sustainable capital markets has been volatile, and it is unlikely to resurge in the context of rising global interest rates observed since 2021.

It is a well-known feature of most financial systems in EMEs in general, and Latin America in particular, that they are predominantly bank-based and with a lower level of development and depth than advanced economies (Bortz 2022). The exception in the region is probably Chile, and to an extent Brazil. Precisely with the aim of developing capital markets, multilateral organizations such as the IMF, the World Bank, and the Inter-American Development Bank (among others) have fostered policies to catalyze private lending for sustainable investment in developing countries. Their preferred policy is to design mechanisms and instruments that minimize the risk for private lenders to improve the risk–return profile of green and sustainable projects (World Bank 2020; Prasad et al. 2022). However, these initiatives risk burdening the public sector with contingent claims that have a high likelihood of materializing, while the outcomes are in doubt (Gabor 2021).

In our opinion, monetary policy remains an important tool to promote sustainable investment across the region, not merely because of its role in promoting macroeconomic stability and addressing financial instability concerns. However, the objectives would be better served if authorities adopt a pro-active green finance policy (as argued and exemplified by Dikau and Ryan-Collins 2017) through public institutions, specialized banks, and development banks (Mazzucato and Semieniuk 2018) that are relatively isolated from market fluctuations, at least until the private banking and financial sector finds it profitable and less risky to expand credit to them.

NOTES

1.   We are grateful for the comments and suggestions of Yannis Dafermos, Daniela Gabor, Annina Kaltenbrunner, Maria Nikolaidi, Servaas Storm, and Fernando

Toledo. We also acknowledge the financial support of the Higher Education Links Grant of the British Council. All errors and mistakes are our own responsibility.
2.   This section draws on Bortz and Toftum (2022).

REFERENCES

Abramskiehn, D., Hallmeyer, K.,Trabacchi, C., Escalante, D., Netto, M., Cabrera, M., and Vasa, A. (2017). "Supporting National Development Banks to drive investment in the nationally determined contributions of Brazil, Mexico, and Chile," Inter-American Development Bank.
Aghion, P., Hepburn, C., Teytelboym, A., and Zenghelis, D. (2014). "Path-dependency, innovation and the economics of climate change." Supporting paper for the new climate economy. Grantham Research Institute on Climate Change and the Environment, London School of Economics and Political Science.
Arndt, C., Loewald, C., and Makrelov, K. (2020). "Climate change and its implications for central banks in emerging and developing economies," Working Paper WP/20/04, South African Reserve Bank.
Avdjiev, S., Bruno, V., Koch, C., and Shin, H.S. (2019). "The dollar exchange rate as a global risk factor: Evidence from investment," *IMF Economic Review* 67 (1): 151–73.
Bank for International Settlements (BIS) (2021). "Climate-related risk drivers and their transmission mechanisms," Basel Committee on Banking Supervision.
Banxico (2020). "Climate and environmental risks and opportunities in Mexico's financial System. From diagnosis to action," Banco de Mexico.
Barua, S., Colombage, S., and Valenzuela, E. (2020). "Climate change impact on foreign direct investment inflows: A dynamic assessment at the global, regional and economic level." Working Paper https://ssrn.com/abstract=3674777
Barua, S., and Valenzuela, E. 2018. "Climate change impacts on global agricultural trade patterns: Evidence from the past 50 years." Proceedings of the Sixth International Conference on Sustainable Development 2018, Columbia University, New York, September 26–28. https://ssrn.com/abstract=3281550
Batten, S., Sowerbutts, R., and Tanaka, M. (2019). "Climate change: Macroeconomic impact and implications for monetary policy," in T. Walker, D. Gramlich, M. Bitar, and P. Fardnia (eds): *Ecological, Societal, and Technological Risks and the Financial Sector*, 13–38, Palgrave Macmillan.
Beirne, J., Renzhi, N., and Volz, U. (2021). "Feeling the heat: Climate risks and the costs of sovereign borrowing," *International Review of Economics and Finance* 76 (C): 920–36.
Berg, F., Koelbel, J., and Rigobon, R. (2022). "Aggregate confusion: The divergence of ESG ratings," *Review of Finance* 26(6): 1315–44.
Boehm, H. (2020). "Physical climate change risks and the sovereign creditworthiness of emerging economies," IWH Discussion Papers No. 8/2020, Halle Institute for Economic Research.
Bolton, P., Despres, M., Pereira Da Silva, L., Samama, P., and Svaartzman, R. (2020). "The Green Swan", Bank for International Settlements, Basel.
Bortz, P.G. (2022). "Macroprudential policies in Latin America," in E. Perez Caldentey (ed): *Financial openness, financial fragility and policies for economic stability*, 257–304, CEPAL and UNCTAD.

Bortz, P.G., Michelena, G., and Toledo, F. (2018). "Foreign debt, conflicting claims and income policies in a Kaleckian model of growth and distribution," *Journal of Globalization and Development* 9 (1): 1–22.

Bortz, P.G., and Toftum, B.N. (2022). "Changes in rainfall, agricultural exports and reserves: Macroeconomic impacts of climate change in Argentina," Documentos de Investigación No. 22, Escuela Interdisciplinaria de Altos Estudios Sociales – Universidad Nacional de San Martín.

Brenton, P., and Chemutai, V. (2021). "The Trade and Climate Change Nexus," World Bank Group.

Brown, M., Chandler, J., Lapsa, M., and Sovacool, B. (2008). "Carbon lock-in: Barriers to deploying climate-change mitigation technologies," Oak-Ridge National Laboratory.

Caldecott, B. (2018). *Stranded Assets and the Environment: Risk, Resilience and Opportunity*, Routledge.

Cantelmo, A., Fatouros, N., Melina, G., and Papageorgiou, C. (2022). "Monetary policy in disaster-prone developing countries," IMF Working Paper WP/22/67.

Carnevali, E., Deleidi, M., Pariboni, R., and Veronese Passarella, M. (2021). "Cross-border financial flows and global warming in a two-area ecological SFC model," *Socio-Economic Planning Sciences*, 75 (C): 100819.

Cevik, S., and J. Jalles (2020). "This changes everything: Climate shocks and sovereign bonds," IMF Working Paper WP/20/79.

Ciccarelli, M., and Marotta, F. (2021). "Demand or supply? An empirical exploration of the effects of climate change on the macroeconomy," European Central Bank Working Paper No. 2608.

Climate Bond Initiative (CBI) (2020). "2019 Green bond market summary."

Climate Bond Initiative (CBI) (2022). "Sustainable debt. Global state of the market 2021."

Climate Policy Initiative (CBI) (2021). "Global Landscape of Climate Finance 2021." https://climatepolicyinitiative.org/publication/ global-climate-finance-2021/ (last accessed 10 October, 2022)

Coulibaly, T., Islam, M., and Managi, S. (2020). "The impacts of climate change and natural disasters on agriculture in African countries," *Economics of Disasters and Climate Change*, 4 (2): 347–64.

Curtis, F. (2009). "Peak globalization: Climate change, oil depletion and global trade," *Ecological Economics* 69 (2): 427–34.

Dafermos, Y., Nikolaidi, M., and Galanis, G. (2018). "Climate change, financial stability and monetary policy," *Ecological Economics*, 152 (C): 219–34.

Dallmann, I. (2019) "Weather variations and international trade," *Environmental and Resource Economics* 72 (1): 155–206.

Dees, S., Ouvrard, J.F., and Weber, P.F. (2022). "Climate change and implications for the conduct of monetary policy," Eco Notepad Post 265, Banque de France. https://blocnotesdeleco.banque-france.fr/en/blog-entry/climate-change-and-implications -conduct-monetary-policy (last accessed 25 October, 2022)

Dellink, R., Hwang, H., Lanzi, E., and Chateau, J. (2017). "International trade consequences of climate change," OECD Trade and Environment Working Paper 2017/01.

Dikau, S., and Ryan-Collins, J. (2017). "Green central banking in emerging market and developing country economies," New Economics Foundation.

Dikau, S., and Volz, U. (2018). "Central banking, climate change, and green finance," in J. Sachs, W.T. Woo, N. Yoshino, and F. Taghizade-Hesari (eds): *Handbook of Green Finance*, 81–102, Springer and Asian Development Bank Institute.

D'Orazio, P., and Popoyan, L. (2019). "Fostering green investments and tackling climate-related financial risks: Which role for macroprudential policies?" *Ecological Economics*, 160 (C): 25–37.

Drabo, A. (2021). "How do climate shocks affect the impact of FDI, ODA and remittances on economic growth?" IMF Working Paper WP/21/193.

Ehlers, T., and Packer, F. (2017). "Green bond finance and certification," *BIS Quarterly Review* (September): 89–104.

Espagne, E., Godin, A., Magacho, G., Mantes, A., and Yilmaz, D. (2021). "Developing countries' macroeconomic exposure to the low-carbon transition," Research Paper No. 220, Agence Française de Développement.

Food and Agriculture Organization (2018). "The state of agricultural commodity markets 2018." http://dx.doi.org/10.18235/0002046

Frisari, G., Gallardo, M., Nakano, C., Cárdenas, V., and Monnin, P. (2020). "Sistemas financieros y riesgos climáticos," Technical note No. IDB-TN-01823, Inter-American Development Bank.

Gabor, D. (2021). "The Wall Street consensus," *Development and Change* 52 (3): 429–59.

Gabor, D., Dafermos, Y. Nikolaidi, N., Rice, P., van Lerven, F., Kerslake, R., Pettifor, A., and Jacobs, M. (2019). "Finance and climate change. A progressive green finance strategy for the UK," Report of the independent panel commissioned by Shadow Chancellor of the Exchequer John McDonnell MP, Labour Party.

Galindo, L.M., Hoffman, B., and Vogt-Schilb, A. (2022). "How much will it cost to achieve the climate goals in Latin America and the Caribbean?" IDB Working Paper Series No. IDB-WP-01310, Inter-American Development Bank.

Ghisetti, C., Mancinelli, S., Mazzanti, M., and Zoli, M. (2017). "Financial barriers and environmental innovations: Evidence from EU manufacturing firms," *Climate Policy* 17 (1): S131–47.

Global Commission on the Economy and Climate (2014). "Better growth, better climate. The New Climate Economy Report." http://dx.doi.org/10.1080/14693062.2016.1242057

Gurara, D., Presbitero, A., and Sarmiento, M. (2020). "Borrowing costs and the role of multilateral development banks: Evidence from a cross-border syndicated lending bank lending," *Journal of International Money and Finance* 100 (February): 1–18.

Hansen, L.C. (2022). "Central banking challenges posed by uncertain climate change and natural disasters," *Journal of Monetary Economics* 125 (C): 1–15.

International Energy Agency (2021). *World Energy Outlook.*

Intergovernmental Panel on Climate Change (2018). *Global Warming of 1.5°C IPCC Special Report* (V. Masson Delmotte et al., eds).

International Monetary Fund (IMF) (2017). *World Economic Outlook*, October.

International Monetary Fund (IMF) (2021). *Regional Economic Outlook for Latin America and the Caribbean*, October.

International Monetary Fund (IMF) (2022). *World Economic Outlook*, October.

Intonti, M., Serlenga, L., Ferri, G., and De Leonardis, M. (2022). "The green bond premium: A comparative analysis," CERBE Working Paper No. 40, LUMSA Universita.

Kahn, M., Mohaddes, K., Ng, R., Pesaran, H., Raissi, M., and Yand, J.C. (2019). "Long-term macroeconomic effects of climate change: A cross-country analysis," IMF Working Paper WP/19/215.

Kapfhammer, F., Larsen, V., and Thorsrud, L. (2020). "Climate risk and commodity currencies," Center for Economic Studies and Ifo Institute Working Paper No. 8788.

Klomp, J. (2015). "Sovereign risk and natural disasters in emerging markets," *Emerging Markets Finance and Trade* 51 (6): 1326–41.

Krogstrup, S., and Oman, W. (2019). "Macroeconomic and financial policies for climate change mitigation: A review of the literature," IMF Working Paper WP/19/185.

Larcker, D., and Watts, E. (2020). "Where is the greenium?" *Journal of Accounting and Economics* 69 (2–3): 101312.

Lau, P., Sze, A., Wan, W., and Wong, A. (2022). "The economics of the greenium: How much is the world willing to pay to save the Earth?" *Environmental & Resource Economics* 81 (2): 379–408.

Leins, S. (2020). "'Responsible investment': ESG and the post-crisis ethical order," *Economy and Society* 49 (1): 71–91.

Li, X., and Gallagher, K. (2022). "Assessing the climate change exposure of foreign direct investment," *Nature Communications* 13 (1): 1–9

Löffler, K., Petreski, A., and Stephan, A. (2021). "Drivers of green bond issuance and new evidence on the 'greenium,'" *Eurasian Economic Review* 11 (1): 1–24.

Löscher, A., and Kaltenbrunner, A. (2022). "Climate change and macroeconomic policy space in developing and emerging economies," *Journal of Post Keynesian Economics*, 46 (1): 113–41. https://doi.org/10.1080/01603477.2022.2084630

Mallucci, E. (2022). "Natural disasters, climate change and sovereign risks," *Journal of International Economics*, 139 (November): 103672.

Mazzucato, M., and Semieniuk, G. (2018). "Financing renewable energy: Who is financing and why it matters," *Technological Forecasting and Social Change* 127 (February): 8–22.

McGlade, C., and Ekins, P. (2015). "The geographical distribution of fossil fuels unused when limiting global warming to 2C," *Nature* 517 (7533): 187–90.

McKibbin, W., Morris, A., Wilcoxen, P., and Panton, A. (2020). "Climate change and monetary policy: Issues for policy design and modelling," *Oxford Review of Economic Policy* 36 (3): 579–603.

McKinsey (2022). *The Net Zero Transition: What it Would Cost, What it Would Bring.* McKinsey Global Institute.

Mercure, J.F, Pollit, H., Viñuales, J.E., Edwards, N., Holden, P., Chewpreecha, U., Salas, P., Sognnaes, I., Lam, A., and Knobloch, F. (2018). "Macroeconomic impact of stranded fossil fuel assets," *Nature Climate Change* 8 (7): 588–96.

Miranda-Agrippino, S., and Rey, H. (2020). "US monetary policy and the Global Financial Cycle," *Review of Economic Studies* 87 (6): 2754–76.

Natural Resources Defense Council (2016). "Green and Resilient Banks."

Nelson, E. (2018). "When will 'socially responsible investing' become just 'investing'?" *Quartz*, July 9.

Network for Greening the Financial System (2019). "A call for action. Climate change as a source of financial risk," Banque de France.

Obstfeld, M., and Zhou, H. (2022). "The global dollar cycle," presented at the Brookings Papers Economic on Economic Activity Conference, September 8–9, Washington, D.C.

Ocampo, J.A. (2016). "Balance-of-payments dominance: Implications for macroeconomic policy," in M. Damill, M. Rapetti, and G. Rozenwurcel (eds): *Macroeconomics and Development*, 211–28, Columbia University Press.

Organisation for Economic Co-operation and Development (OECD) (2017). "Investing in Climate, Investing in Growth." https://doi.org/10.1787/9789264273528-en

Organisation for Economic Co-operation and Development (OECD) (2019). "Scaling-up climate-compatible infrastructure," OECD Environment Policy Paper No. 18.

Osberghaus, D. (2019). "The effects of natural disasters and weather variations on international trade and financial flows: A literature review," *Economics of Disasters and Climate Change*, 3 (3): 305–25.

Prasad, A., Loukoianova, E., Feng, A., and Oman, W. (2022). "Mobilizing private climate financing in emerging market and developing economies," IMF Staff Climate Note 2022/007.

Sachs, J., Woo, W.T., Yoshino, N., and Taghizade-Hesari, F. (2019). "Importance of green finance for achieving Sustainable Development Goals and energy security," in J. Sachs, W.T. Woo, N. Yoshino, and F. Taghizade-Hesari (eds): *Handbook of Green Finance*, 3–12, Springer and Asian Development Bank Institute.

Shah, B. (2020). "How climate transition risk may impact sovereign bond yields," Research Insights, MSCI.

Simpson, C., Rathi, A., and Kishan, S. (2021). "The ESG mirage," *Bloomberg Business Week*, December 9.

United Nations Conference on Trade and Development (2019). "Trade and Development Report 2019."

United Nations Environment Programme (UNEP) (2017). "UNEP 2016 Annual Report – Empowering people to protect the planet."

United Nations Environment Programme (UNEP) (2018). "Rethinking impact to finance the SDGs," UNEP Finance Initiative.

United Nations Framework Convention on Climate Change (2015). "Adoption of the Paris Agreement," 21st Conference of the Parties.

Volz, U., Campiglio, E., Espagne, E., Mercure, J.F., Oman, W., Pollitt, H., Semieniuk, G., and Svartzman, R. (2021). "Transboundary climate-related risks: Analysing the impacts of a decarbonisation of the global economy on international trade, finance, and money," presented at the 9th IMF Statistical Forum, November 17–18, Washington, D.C.

World Bank (2018). "Strategic use of climate finance to maximize climate action: a guiding framework." https://doi.org/10.1596/30475

World Bank (2020). "Transformative Climate Finance: A New Approach for Climate Finance to Achieve Low-Carbon Resilient Development in Developing Countries."

World Economic Forum (2013). "The Green Investment Report: The Ways and Means to Unlock Private Finance for Green Growth."

Wu, Y. (2022). "Are green bonds priced lower than their conventional peers?" *Emerging Markets Review* 52 (September): 100909.

PART V

Monetary policies, central banks, income inequality, and fiscal policies in LACs

11. Fiscal responses to income inequality surges. A panel estimation for Emerging Market and Developing Economies

Jorge Carrera, Pablo de la Vega, and Fernando Toledo

INTRODUCTION

Standard measures of within-country income inequality, such as the Gini coefficient or the share of income accruing to the top 10 percent of earners, have trended up globally since the 1980s (Bank for International Settlements, 2021: 41). Regarding the Organisation for Economic Co-operation and Development (OECD) Economic Outlook (2021), the World Bank Global Economic Prospects (2021), and the International Monetary Fund (IMF) Outlook for Latin America and the Caribbean (2021), income inequality is expected to grow from an already high level before the COVID-19 crisis. According to the IMF's projections for different regions, these tendencies will be greater in Latin American countries (LACs) than in other Emerging Markets and Developing Economies (EMDEs).

In the present chapter, we assess the different fiscal policy responses of EMDE governments to unexpected shocks that increase income inequality. Fiscal policy reactions are limited to choosing among a set of options. To lessen income inequality, EMDEs must decide on a constrained fiscal policy mix. We particularly focus on the relationships between income inequality and (1) public expenditure, (2) progressive taxation, and (3) public debt.

Public expenditure is an effective tool to reduce income disparities, mainly when it is focused on social and infrastructure items, and there exist incentives to use government spending before elections to increase the probability of political permanency. Meanwhile, progressive taxation negatively correlates with income inequality, both in advanced and developing economies. Most of the time it is difficult to implement this alternative because of resistance from high-income taxpayers. Moreover, it can have negative effects on elections. Finally, economic and political motivations exist for using public debt to reduce income inequality through the financing of greater fiscal needs

We find that, for EMDEs, the interaction between the political cycle—proxied by the remaining time to complete the mandate—and income inequality is significant and positively related only to public debt. The marginal effect of inequality on the public debt increases with the share of the executive term completed, and it becomes statistically significant after completing 85 percent of the corresponding term. Our empirical approach takes some arguments from political economy contributions to prove that policymakers frequently opt for using public debt to face unexpected shocks that increase income inequality and maximize their chances of being re-elected. The interaction term is not statistically significant for the other three fiscal policy alternatives (government consumption, progressive taxation, and the primary balance), which suggests that the relationships between income inequality and these variables are not mediated by the political cycle. However, there is a statistically significant and negative (positive) linear effect of income inequality on government consumption (primary balance).

According to our robustness checks, the marginal effect of the top 1 percent on the public debt increases with the share of the executive term completed, and it becomes statistically significant after completing around 15 percent of the corresponding term. The marginal effect of the unemployment rate on the public debt also increases with the share of the executive term completed, and it becomes statistically significant after completing around 20 percent of the term.

Regarding the existence of heterogeneous effects, the political-cycle-mediated effect that we have seen in the baseline estimates takes place when the external position of the whole country is increasingly negative. However, at higher levels of Net Foreign Assets (NFAs), the marginal effect of income inequality on the public debt, although statistically significant, does not depend on the political cycle. The effect on the public debt that we have seen in the baseline estimates is evidenced for LACs, whereas it is not significant for non-LACs. We also tested if this effect is more pronounced in the case of the Public External Debt (PED). We identified a positive effect of inequality on the PED, but it is not mediated by the political cycle.

The remainder of the chapter proceeds as follows. The next section presents the theoretical framework, explaining the motivation and providing a review of the literature on income inequality and different fiscal policy responses. The third section describes the empirical strategy and shows our main empirical findings. Next, we test the sensibility of these empirical findings with different robustness checks. The fifth section examines some empirical heterogeneous effects of income inequality, the political cycle, and our constrained fiscal policy mix, with an emphasis on the degree of openness in the financial account and LACs. The final section concludes the chapter.

THEORETICAL FRAMEWORK

Motivation

To fully appreciate our problem, we assume that an initial unexpected shock increases income inequality in a "non-Ricardian" government with a relatively high intertemporal discount rate.[1] In such a case, the growing social conflict will negatively affect the government's probability of re-election. From a macroeconomic point of view, consumption will fall due to the higher marginal propensities to consume of lowest deciles vis-á-vis the highest ones. Under certain conditions, savings and investment will increase, but never in a sufficient way to compensate for the fall in aggregate consumption. The decrease in consumption will reduce tax collection. If there is not an adjustment of fiscal expenditure, the fiscal deficit will most likely rise.

Thus, policymakers will face a trade-off of falling tax revenues and increasing social demands for higher public expenditures. If they focus on their political permanency, they will be tempted to expand public expenditures. If governments use greater progressive taxation, this alternative could negatively affect their electoral base, given that high-income groups will face greater tax pressures and eventually decide to vote for political alternatives.

Recent evidence suggests that public debt and income inequality have risen with financial globalization. Henceforth, governments can choose higher levels of public debt when domestic financial markets become deeper and, particularly, when the country becomes internationally integrated and income inequality increases. International tax arbitrage issues linked to greater financial openness restrict the ability to tax top incomes.[2] In addition, the effectiveness of progressive taxation in reducing inequality in EMDEs is limited by several factors, such as the low average tax revenue as a percentage of gross domestic product (GDP), the relatively high contribution of indirect taxes, the inability to tax top incomes, the elevated labor market informality, and the limited institutional capacity.

Based on the previous discussion, and although we empirically consider the different governments' responses according to our constrained fiscal policy mix, we focus particularly on the strategic use of public debt to finance greater public expenditure targeted to lessen the negative effects of increases in income inequality. We contribute to the literature by empirically showing that, in EMDEs, governments prefer this option when considering that preserving social and political stability enhances their chances of permanency in office.

Related Literature

The association between income inequality and public expenditure has been analyzed by Brender and Drazen (2008), Shi and Svensson (2006), Tabellini and Alesina (1990), Aghion and Bolton (1989), and Persson and Svensson (1989). These contributions confirm that governments have incentives to increase public expenditures before the elections to raise their re-election probabilities. This result applies in the presence of fiscal illusion or naïve voters' expectations (Nordhaus, 1975, 1989), or in the context of the rational expectations of voters who face informational asymmetries about the incumbent government's skills (Brender and Drazen, 2008; Shi and Svensson, 2006; Persson and Tabellini, 2000; Rogoff, 1990; Rogoff and Sibert, 1988).

Using newly assembled data on spending composition for 83 countries across all income groups, Doumbia and Kinda (2019) provide empirical support that reallocating spending toward social protection and public infrastructure is associated with income inequality drops. A recent survey by Anderson et al. (2017) identifies 84 studies containing over 900 estimations. This meta-analysis shows some evidence of a moderate negative relationship between government spending and income inequality, which is stronger for social welfare and other social spending. Muinello-Gallo and Roca-Sagalés (2011) study the impact of public expenditure and investment on income inequality in 43 middle- and high-income economies from 1972 to 2006. Their analysis uncovers equalizing effects of both government expenditure and public investment.

The link between income inequality and progressive taxation has been studied by Alesina and Passalacqua (2016), Hager (2016), Röhrs and Winter (2014), and Meltzer and Richard (1981). These contributions show that income inequality decreases: (1) with the progressivity of the income tax structure (Alesina and Passalacqua, 2016; Hager, 2016); and (2) when policymakers reduce the negative effects of borrowing constraints on the private sector, improving the progressiveness of tax systems (Röhrs and Winter, 2014). They also demonstrate that tax progressivity increases when the distance between the median voter and the rest of the voters declines (Meltzer and Richard, 1981).

Martorano (2016) confirms that, for the 2000s, the increasing contribution of direct taxes in LACs concerning indirect taxes supported the progressivity of the tax system and contributed to the reduction of income inequality. Muinello-Gallo and Roca-Sagalés (2013) estimate unbalanced panel data of 21 high-income OECD countries during the period 1972–2006 to reveal that direct taxes generate sizable reductions in income inequality. Using several unique measures of progressivity over the 1981–2005 period for a large panel of countries, Duncan and Peter (2012) also find that tax progressivity reduces income disparities. Hollar and Cubero (2010) surveyed the available evidence on the structure of taxes by income quintiles in Central American countries and found that the distributional effect of taxation is regressive but small.

Last but not least, the relationship between income inequality and public debt has been examined by Carrera and de la Vega (2021), Yared (2018), Alesina and Passalacqua (2016), Hager (2016), Azzimonti et al. (2014), Röhrs and Winter (2014), and Persson and Tabellini (2000: 345), who indicate that: "an incumbent government can also use the debt level to enhance its re-election probability." Furthermore,

> The party deciding on public policy in the current period is aware that with some probability it will not hold office in the next period. This may induce too much borrowing because the costs in terms of future spending cuts are not fully internalized. An incumbent government may also want to choose debt issues strategically for another reason, however—namely, to influence its likelihood of re-election, which relates to a key empirical stylized fact: greater political instability should be associated with a more volatile public debt policy. (Persson and Tabellini, 2000: 356)

Aksman (2017) investigates the hypothesis that countries with the highest levels of income inequality are the most indebted because they have higher social spending to face this problem. He finds that income inequality is not a statistically significant predictor of the public debt-to-GDP ratio. Davtyan (2014) points out that economic recessions accompanied by greater inequality can generate political pressures, which induce large discretionary public expenditures. Azzimonti et al. (2014) show that governments choose higher levels of public debt if financial markets are internationally integrated and income inequality increases. Arawatari and Onoz (2015) illustrates that when the elasticity of intertemporal substitution is less than one, a country with low inequality pursues a strict fiscal policy with a small increase in public debt, while a country with high inequality experiences a policy fiscal lax with a large public debt. Jabłoński (2013) reports that an increase in income inequality led to an increase in public debt in OECD countries in the period 1995–2010. Larch (2012) shows that countries with greater inequality have large deficits and tend to accumulate large public debt. Song et al. (2012) present a two-period overlapping-generations model with small open countries that differ in their public goods preferences. Each country decides its public goods provision financed by taxes and public debt through probabilistic voting, reflecting the conflicting preferences of two successive generations. The prediction of this model is consistent with the empirical evidence from OECD countries for the past three decades.

DATA SOURCES, EMPIRICAL STRATEGY, AND RESULTS

The empirical strategy evaluates the hypothesis that a government that wants to be re-elected will try to avoid social conflict and class struggle related to increases in income inequality. Thus, it is expected that increasing social inequalities induce more political pressures the closer the next executive election is. The goal is to capture to what extent governments have incentives to use public debt instead of other fiscal policy alternatives to lessen increases in income inequality. To this end, we estimate the impact of income inequality on different fiscal policy options:

$$y_{i,t} = \beta_0 + \beta_1 y_{i,t-1} + \beta_2 INEQ_{i,t} + \beta_3 shr\_term_{i,t} + \beta_4 INEQ_{i,t} * shr\_term_{i,t} +$$
$$X_{i,t}\gamma + \mu_i + \tau_t + \varepsilon_{i,t} \tag{11.1}$$

where $y_{i,t}$ is a certain fiscal policy variable (public debt, government final consumption expenditure, progressive taxation, or fiscal primary balance) in country i in period t; $INEQ$ is the income inequality measured by the Gini coefficient (pre-tax, pre-transfer); shr_term is the share of the executive term completed; $X_{i,t}$ is a vector of control variables; μ_i is a country-specific fixed effect that captures all country-specific time-invariant determinants; τ_t is a time fixed effect that captures the influences of global shocks like those in international liquidity; and $\varepsilon_{i,t}$ is the error term.

The main variables of interest are $INEQ$ and its interaction with shr_term. For example, take the case where $y_{i,t}$ refers to the public debt. The coefficient β_4 is expected to be positive, suggesting that increasing income inequality induces governments to issue more public debt, and this effect is higher the closer the next executive election is.

The variable shr_term is constructed by using the information on the years left in the current term in the Database of Political Institutions (Cruz et al., 2021). Using that variable, we estimate the length of each executive term and then the proportion of the executive term completed as follows: $shr\_term = 1 - \frac{years\ left\ in\ current\ term}{term\ length}$. We drop the country-year observations that represent systems with unelected executives and those without a finite term in office. The dataset comprises annual data for 49 economies across the 1990–2015 period.[3]

We include a large set of control variables to isolate the effect of income inequality on our constrained fiscal policy mix. This set of control variables includes not only standard determinants taken from the literature, but also new potential determinants, which are listed along with the source of the information in Table 11A.1 in Appendix 11A.

RESULTS

The complete results of estimating Equation 11.1 using fixed effects and least squares dummy variables (LSDV-Kiviet) are presented in Table 11B.1 in Appendix 11B. We find that the interaction coefficient is only statistically significant in the case where the dependent variable is the public debt, although the linear term of the Gini coefficient is not statistically significant. The conjunction of these two terms gives the marginal effect that is plotted in Panel A of Figure 11.1.[4] The marginal effect of inequality on the public debt increases with the share of the executive term completed, and it becomes statistically significant after completing 85 percent of the corresponding term.

The interaction term is not statistically significant in the other three cases (government consumption, progressive taxation, and the primary balance), which suggests that the relationships between income inequality and those variables are not mediated by the political cycle. However, there is a statistically significant and negative (positive) linear effect of income inequality on government consumption (primary balance).

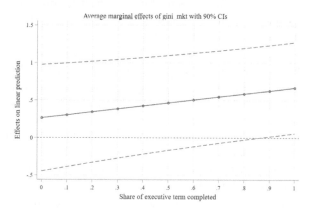

Note: The figure plots the marginal effect of the Gini coefficient on the public debt in terms of the share of the executive term completed. Dotted lines are 90 percent confidence intervals.
Source: Authors' elaboration.

Figure 11.1   Marginal effects of inequality on the public debt

ROBUSTNESS CHECKS

In recent years, the upper percentiles of the income distribution have generally been used as an alternative measure of income inequality. Various scholars have remarked that the high concentration of national income in the upper extreme of the distribution defines a new phase of modern capitalism (Piketty and Saez, 2006; Alvaredo et al., 2013; Piketty, 2014). Therefore, as a robustness check, we present our estimates substituting the Gini coefficient with the top 1 percent. As we illustrate in Figure 11.2, the marginal effect of the top 1 percent on the public debt increases with the share of the executive term completed, and it becomes statistically significant after completing around 15 percent of the corresponding term.

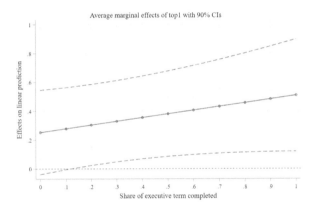

Note: The figure plots the marginal effect of the top 1 percent on the public debt in terms of the share of the executive term completed. Dotted lines are 90 percent confidence intervals.
Source: Authors' elaboration.

Figure 11.2   Marginal effects of top incomes on the public debt

Government policies aimed at addressing social problems tend to be guided by a more direct variable within voters' perceptions and possible experiences, such as the unemployment rate, which is a more direct indicator of social unrest and political instability. In that regard, as another robustness test, we performed our baseline regression, substituting the Gini coefficient for the unemployment rate. The marginal effect of the unemployment rate on the public debt also increases with the share of the executive term completed, and it becomes statistically significant after completing around 20 percent of the corresponding term (Figure 11.3).

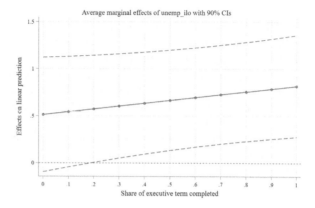

Note: The figure plots the marginal effect of the unemployment rate on the public debt in terms of the share of the executive term completed. Dotted lines are 90 percent confidence intervals.
Source: Authors' elaboration.

Figure 11.3   Marginal effects of unemployment on the public debt

HETEROGENEOUS EFFECTS

Openness of the Financial Account

To explore if our results vary for different levels of openness of financial accounts, proxied by NFAs, we consider an alternative specification with a three-way interaction:

$$y_{i,t} = \beta_0 + \beta_1 y_{i,t-1} + \beta_2 INEQ_{i,t} + \beta_3 shr\_term_{i,t} + \beta_4 INEQ_{i,t} * shr\_term_{i,t} + \\ \beta_5 INEQ_{i,t} * NFA_{i,t} + \beta_6 shr_{term_{i,t}} * NFA_{i,t} + \beta_7 INEQ_{i,t} * shr\_term_{i,t} * NFA_{i,t} + \\ X_{i,t}\gamma + \mu_i + \tau_t + \varepsilon_{i,t} \tag{11.2}$$

The political-cycle-mediated effect that we have seen in the baseline estimates (Figure 11.1) takes place where the external position of the whole country is increasingly negative (Figure 11.4). However, at higher levels of NFAs, the marginal effect of income inequality on the public debt, although statistically significant, does not depend on the political cycle.

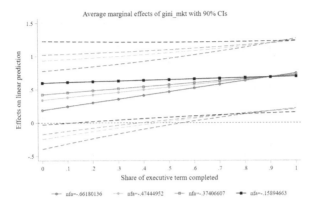

Note: The figure plots the marginal effect of the Gini coefficient on the public debt in terms of the share of the executive term completed for different values of the NFAs. Dotted lines are 90 percent confidence intervals.
Source: Authors' elaboration.

Figure 11.4   *Marginal effects of inequality on the public debt for different degrees of financial account openness*

LACs vs. Non-LACs

To explore if our results differ for LACs, we consider an alternative specification with a three-way interaction:

$$y_{i,t} = \beta_0 + \beta_1 y_{i,t-1} + \beta_2 INEQ_{i,t} + \beta_3 shr\_term_{i,t} + \beta_4 INEQ_{i,t} * shr\_term_{i,t} +$$
$$\beta_5 INEQ_{i,t} * LAC + \beta_6 shrterm_{i,t} * LAC + \beta_7 INEQ_{i,t} * shr\_term_{i,t} * LAC +$$
$$X_{i,t}\gamma + \mu_i + \tau_t + \varepsilon_{i,t} \tag{11.3}$$

As shown in Panel A of Figure 11.5, the effect on the public debt that we have seen in the baseline estimates (Figure 11.1) is evidenced for LACs, whereas it is not statistically significant for non-LACs. In Panel B of Figure 11.5, we also analyze if this effect is more pronounced in the case of the PED. We find a positive effect of inequality on the PED, but it is not mediated by the political cycle.

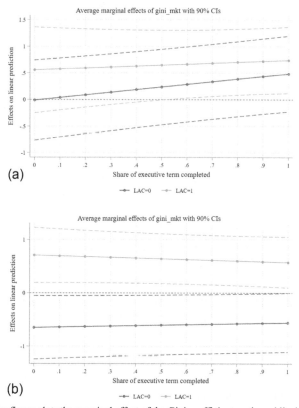

Notes: The figure plots the marginal effect of the Gini coefficient on the public debt (Panel A; central government debt, percent GDP) and on the PED (Panel B; percent GDP) in terms of the share of the executive term completed for different subsamples of countries. LAC = 1 refers to LACs, while LAC = 0 represents non-LACs.
Source: Authors' elaboration.

Figure 11.5   *(a) Dependent variable: central government debt (percent of GDP); (b) Dependent variable: public external debt (percent of GDP)*

CONCLUSIONS

We assess the different fiscal policy responses of EMDE governments to unexpected shocks that increase income inequality. Fiscal policy reactions are limited to choosing among a set of options. To lessen income inequality, EMDEs must decide among a constrained fiscal policy mix. We particularly focus on the relationship between income inequality and public expenditure, progressive taxation, and public debt. We highlight the strategic use of public debt to finance greater public expenditure targeted to lessen the negative effects of hikes in income inequality. We contribute to the literature by empirically showing that, in EMDEs, governments prefer this option when considering that preserving social and political stability enhances their chances of permanency in office.

We find that, for EMDEs, the interaction between the political cycle—proxied by the remaining time to complete the mandate—and income inequality is significant and positively related only to public debt. The marginal effect of inequality on the public debt increases with the share of the executive term completed, and it becomes statistically significant after completing 85 percent of the corresponding term. Our empirical approach takes some arguments from political economy contributions to prove that policymakers frequently opt for using public debt to face unexpected shocks that increase income inequality and to maximize their chances of being re-elected. The interaction term is not statistically significant in the other three fiscal policy alternatives (government consumption, progressive taxation, and the primary balance), which suggests that the relationships between income inequality and these variables are not mediated by the political cycle. However, there is a statistically significant and negative (positive) linear effect of income inequality on government consumption (primary balance).

According to our robustness checks, the marginal effect of the top 1 percent on the public debt increases with the share of the executive term completed, and it becomes statistically significant after completing around 15 percent of the corresponding term. The marginal effect of the unemployment rate on the public debt is also rising in the share of the executive term completed, and it becomes statistically significant after completing around 20 percent of the corresponding term.

Regarding the existence of heterogeneous effects, the political-cycle-mediated effect that we have seen in the baseline estimates takes place where the external position of the whole country is increasingly negative. However, at higher levels of NFAs, the marginal effect of income inequality on the public debt, although statistically significant, does not depend on the political cycle. The effect on the public debt that we have seen in the baseline estimates is evidenced for LACs, whereas it is not statistically significant for non-LACs. We also tested if this effect is more pronounced in the case of the PED. We identify a positive effect of inequality on the PED, but it is not mediated by the political cycle.

NOTES

1.   Theoretically, different political factors imply that a government behaves similarly to an agent with present-biased and dynamically inconsistent preferences

(Yared, 2018). An analytically tractable representation of such preferences is the quasi-hyperbolic case analyzed in Laibson (1997). The study of these political factors is beyond the scope of this chapter.

2. In small open financial economies, increasing progressive taxation has limitations due to international arbitrage reasons. Relating to the increasing capital and asset mobility such as intellectual property, as well as the new business models of the 21st century, Base Erosion and Tax Shifting (BEPS) has become a serious problem. In fact, the OECD Action BEPS refers to base erosion taxation and the transfer of profits caused by the existence of gaps or unwanted mechanisms between the different national tax systems through which multinational companies can make benefits disappear for tax purposes or transfer benefits to locations where there is little or no real activity. However, BEPS is weakly employed, resulting in little or null income for companies.

3. The countries included are: East Asia and Pacific (3): Indonesia, Malaysia, Mongolia; Europe and Central Asia (8): Armenia, Bulgaria, Croatia, Georgia, Hungary, Poland, Romania, Russia; Latin America and Caribbean (12): Argentina, Brazil, Chile, Colombia, Costa Rica, Ecuador, Jamaica, Mexico, Panama, Paraguay, Peru, Uruguay; Middle East and North Africa (1): Iran; South Asia (3): India, Pakistan, Sri Lanka; Sub-Saharan Africa (22): Benin, Botswana, Burkina Faso, Burundi, Cabo Verde, Cameroon, Chad, Côte d'Ivoire, Gabon, Guinea-Bissau, Kenya, Liberia, Mali, Mauritius, Namibia, Niger, Nigeria, Rwanda, Senegal, Tanzania, Togo, Uganda.

4. Intuitively, if the confidence interval (dotted lines) includes the zero (vertical axis), the marginal effect is not statistically significant. On the other hand, the slope of the solid curve indicates the magnitude of the interaction coefficient.

REFERENCES

Aghion, P. and Bolton, P. (1989). "Government Domestic Debt and The Risk of Default: A Political-Economic Model of The Strategic Role of Debt," Working Paper 541, Department of Economics, MIT.

Aksman, E. (2017). "Do Poverty and Income Inequality Affect Public Debt?" *Gospodarka Narodowa. The Polish Journal of Economics* 6: 79–93.

Alesina, A. and Passalacqua, A. (2016). "The Political Economy of Government Debt," in Taylor, J.B. and Uhlig, H. (eds): *Handbook of Macroeconomics* (Vol. 2), 2599–2651, Elsevier.

Alvaredo, F., Atkinson, A., Piketty, T. and Saez, E. (2013). "The Top 1 Percent in International and Historical Perspective," *Journal of Economic Perspectives* 27(3): 3–20.

Anderson E., D'Orey, M., Duvendack, M. and Esposito, L. (2017). "Does Government Spending Affect Income Inequality? A Meta-Regression Analysis," *Journal of Economic Surveys* 31(4): 961–87.

Arawatari, R. and Onoz, T. (2015). "Inequality and Public Debt: A Positive Analysis," Discussion Paper 15-01-Rev., Graduate School of Economics and Osaka School of International Public Policy, Osaka University.

Azzimonti, M., de Francisco, E. and Quadrini, V. (2014). "Financial Globalization, Inequality, and the Rising Public Debt," *American Economic Review* 104(8): 2267–2302.

Bank for International Settlements (2021, June). *Annual Economic Report.*

Bénétrix, A., Gautam, D., Juvenal, L. and Schmitz, M. (2020). "Cross-Border Currency Exposures. New Evidence Based on an Enhanced and Updated Dataset," Trinity Economics Papers 01/20, Department of Economics, Trinity College Dublin.

Brender, A. and Drazen, A. (2008). "How Do Budget Deficits and Economic Growth Affect Re-election Prospects? Evidence from a Large Panel of Countries," *American Economic Review* 98(5): 2203–20.

Carrera, J. and de la Vega, P. (2021). "The Impact of Income Inequality on Public Debt," *Journal of Economic Asymmetries* 24(November): e00216.

Cruz, C., Keefer, P. and Scartascini, C. (2021). "Database of Political Institutions 2020." Inter-American Development Bank Research Department.

Davtyan, K. (2014). "Interrelation among Economic Growth, Income Inequality, and Fiscal Performance: Evidence from Anglo-Saxon Countries," Working Paper 2014/05, Research Institute of Applied Economics, Barcelona.

Doumbia, D. and Kinda, T. (2019). "Reallocating Public Spending to Reduce Income Inequality: Can It Work?" IMF Working Paper 19/188.

Duncan, D. and Peter, K. (2012). "Unequal Inequalities: Do Progressive Taxes Reduce Income Inequality?" IZA Discussion Paper Series No. 6910.

Hager, S. (2016). *Public Debt, Inequality and Power. The Making of a Modern Debt State*. University of California Press.

Hollar, I. and Cubero, R. (2010). "Equity and Fiscal Policy: The Income Distribution Effects of Taxation and Social Spending in Central America," IMF Working Paper 10/112.

International Monetary Fund (2021, May). *Outlook for Latin America and the Caribbean*.

Jabłoński, Ł. (2013). "Nierówności Dochodowe A Zadłużenie Publiczne Krajów," OECD, Management and Business Administration, *Central Europe* 21(2): 64–81.

Laibson, D. (1997). "Golden Eggs and Hyperbolic Discounting," *Quarterly Journal of Economics* 112(2): 443–78.

Lane, P., and Milesi-Ferretti, G. (2007). "The external wealth of nations mark II: Revised and extended estimates of foreign assets and liabilities, 1970–2004," *Journal of International Economics* 73(2): 223–50.

Larch, M. (2012). "Fiscal Performance and Income Inequality: Are Unequal Societies More Deficit-Prone? Some Cross-Country Evidence," Economic Papers 414, European Commission.

Martorano, B. (2016). "Taxation and Inequality in Developing Countries: Lessons from the Recent Experience of Latin America," Working Paper No 98, WIDER Working Paper Series from World Institute for Development Economics Research.

Meltzer, A. and Richard, S. (1981). "A Rational Theory of the Size of Government," *Journal of Political Economy* 89(5): 914–27.

Muinello-Gallo, L. and Roca-Sagalés, O. (2011). "Economic Growth and Inequality: The Role of Fiscal Policies," *Australian Economic Papers* 50(2–3): 74–97.

Muinello-Gallo, L. and Roca-Sagalés, O. (2013). "Joint Determinants of Fiscal Policy, Income Inequality and Economic Growth," *Economic Modelling* 30(2013): 814–24.

Nordhaus, W. (1975). "The Political Business Cycle," *Review of Economic Studies* 42(2): 169–90.

Nordhaus, W. (1989). "Alternative Approaches to the Political Business Cycle," *Brookings Papers on Economic Activity* 2(1989): 1–68.

Organisation for Economic Co-operation and Development (2021, May). *OECD Economic Outlook*.

Persson, T. and Svensson, L. (1989). "Why a Stubborn Conservative Would Run a Deficit: Policy with Time-Inconsistent Preferences," *The Quarterly Journal of Economics* 104(2): 325–46.

Persson, T. and Tabellini, G. (2000). *Political Economics: Explaining Economic Policy*. MIT Press.

Piketty, T. (2014). *Capital in the Twenty-First Century*. Harvard University Press.

Piketty, T. and Saez, E. (2006). "The Evolution of Top Incomes: A Historical and International Perspective," *American Economic Review* 96(2): 200–205.

Rogoff, K. (1990). "Equilibrium Political Budget Cycles," *American Economic Review* 80(1): 21–36.

Rogoff, K. and Sibert, A. (1988). "Elections and Macroeconomic Policy Cycle," *Review of Economic Studies* 55(1): 1–16.

Röhrs, S. and Winter, C. (2014). "Reducing Government Debt in the Presence of Inequality," Unpublished Manuscript.

Shi, M. and Svensson, J. (2006). "Political Budget Cycles: Do They Differ Across Countries and Why?" *Journal of Public Economics* 90(8–9): 1367–89.

Song, Z., Storesletten, K. and Zilibotti, F. (2012). "Rotten Parents and Disciplined Children: A Politico-Economic Theory of Public Expenditure and Debt," *Econometrica* 80(6): 2785–2803.

Tabellini, G. and Alesina, A. (1990). "Voting on the Budget Deficit," *American Economic Review* 80(1): 37–49.

World Bank (2021, June). *Global Economic Prospects*.

Yared, P. (2018). "Rising Government Debt: Causes and Solutions for a Decades-Old Trend," NBER Working Paper 24979.

APPENDIX 11A: VARIABLES AND SOURCES

Table 11A.1   Variables and sources

Name	Description	Source
Public Debt	Total stock of debt liabilities issued by the central government as a share of GDP	Global Debt Database (IMF)
Primary fiscal balance (% GDP)	General government primary net lending/borrowing	IMF WEO
Real GDP growth (annual %)	Annual percentage growth rate of GDP at market prices based on constant local currency	World Bank WDI
Log of GDP per capita	GDP per capita based on purchasing power parity (PPP; constant 2017 international dollars)	World Bank WDI
Log of terms of trade	Net barter terms of trade index	World Bank WDI
Inflation	Inflation, consumer prices (annual percentage). As is usually done in the literature, we use the transformation: $\ln(1 + \text{inflation}/100)$	World Bank WDI
Credit to the private sector (% GDP)	As a proxy for the size of the domestic financial market	World Bank
Fiscal rules	We include categorical variables that indicate the presence of four types of fiscal rules: balanced budget rules, debt rules, expenditure rules, and revenue rules, which apply to the central or general government or the public sector	IMF Fiscal Rules Dataset, 2016
Institutions (constraints on the executive)	We use a measurement of the institutionalized constraints on the decision-making powers of chief executives, whether individuals or collectivities. This variable contains a seven-category scale ranging from the most authoritarian regimes up to those that have the most exhaustive mechanism of control on the executive powers. We grouped these into four categories to facilitate the analysis	Polity IV dataset
Old dependency ratio	Age dependency ratio, old (percentage of working-age population)	World Bank WDI
De facto capital account openness	International Financial Integration (IFI; % GDP) is defined as: $IFI_{it} = \frac{FA_{it} + FL_{it}}{GDP_{it}}$, where FA (FL) denotes the stock of external assets (liabilities)	Lane and Milesi-Ferretti (2007), Bénétrix et al. (2020)

Name	Description	Source
Unemployment rate	Unemployment, total (percentage of total labor force; modeled ILO estimate)	ILO
Top incomes	Share of the top 1 percent in the pre-tax national income	WID Database

APPENDIX 11B: RESULTS

Table 11B.1   Estimation results

	(1) Public debt (% of GDP)		(2) Government final consumption expenditure (% of GDP)		(3) Taxes on income profits and capital gains (% of GDP)		(4) Primary balance (% of GDP)	
	FE	LSDV-Kiviet	FE	LSDV-Kiviet	FE	LSDV-Kiviet	FE	LSDV-Kiviet
Lagged dependent variable (−1)	0.667***	0.720***	0.673***	0.745***	0.490***	0.550***	0.199***	0.270***
	(0.062)	(0.024)	(0.034)	(0.033)	(0.086)	(0.066)	(0.074)	(0.089)
Gini coefficient	0.264	0.296	−0.101***	−0.089*	−0.056	−0.041	0.221*	0.212***
	(0.432)	(0.470)	(0.036)	(0.052)	(0.048)	(0.045)	(0.112)	(0.046)
Share of executive term completed	−0.199*	−0.211**	−0.002	−0.002	−0.013	−0.014	0.021	0.020*
	(0.118)	(0.095)	(0.012)	(0.003)	(0.015)	(0.022)	(0.020)	(0.011)
Gini * Share of executive term completed	0.402*	0.423**	0.004	0.004	0.030	0.031	−0.055	−0.053
	(0.235)	(0.182)	(0.025)	(0.005)	(0.031)	(0.049)	(0.041)	(0.033)
Primary fiscal balance	−0.485***	−0.549						
	(0.141)	(0.394)						
GDP growth (annual %)	−0.559***	−0.622***	−0.054***	−0.054***	−0.005	−0.005	0.104**	0.106***

	(1)		(2)		(3)		(4)	
	Public debt (% of GDP)		Government final consumption expenditure (% of GDP)		Taxes on income profits and capital gains (% of GDP)		Primary balance (% of GDP)	
	FE	LSDV-Kiviet	FE	LSDV-Kiviet	FE	LSDV-Kiviet	FE	LSDV-Kiviet
	(0.184)	(0.218)	(0.013)	(0.002)	(0.011)	(0.003)	(0.047)	(0.014)
GDP per capita	−0.023 (0.094)	0.044 (0.085)	0.003 (0.004)	0.006*** (0.001)	0.008 (0.006)	0.006*** (0.001)	0.019 (0.016)	0.015*** (0.003)
Terms of trade	0.010 (0.031)	0.025 (0.047)	−0.001 (0.003)	−0.002*** (0.001)	0.002 (0.004)	0.001** (0.001)	0.012 (0.007)	0.012*** (0.001)
Inflation	0.345* (0.188)	0.332 (0.203)	−0.009*** (0.002)	−0.008 (0.005)	−0.009*** (0.003)	−0.008 (0.005)	0.015 (0.025)	0.013 (0.031)
Domestic credit to private sector (% of GDP)	−0.024 (0.100)	−0.036 (0.068)	0.008 (0.007)	0.003 (0.003)	−0.000 (0.008)	−0.001 (0.000)	−0.019 (0.017)	−0.017 (0.028)
Expenditure rule in place (1 if yes)	0.045** (0.022)	0.043*** (0.012)	−0.007*** (0.002)	−0.007*** (0.001)	−0.002 (0.002)	−0.002 (0.002)	0.013*** (0.004)	0.013*** (0.001)
Revenue rule in place (1 if yes)	−0.030 (0.033)	−0.029*** (0.011)	−0.005 (0.004)	−0.005 (0.004)			−0.006 (0.009)	−0.007 (0.006)
Budget balance rule in place (1 if yes)	0.014 (0.017)	0.013 (0.011)	−0.001 (0.001)	−0.001 (0.002)	0.001 (0.002)	0.002 (0.004)	0.004 (0.003)	0.004*** (0.001)

	(1) Public debt (% of GDP)		(2) Government final consumption expenditure (% of GDP)		(3) Taxes on income profits and capital gains (% of GDP)		(4) Primary balance (% of GDP)	
	FE	LSDV-Kiviet	FE	LSDV-Kiviet	FE	LSDV-Kiviet	FE	LSDV-Kiviet
Debt rule in place (1 if yes)	−0.023	−0.016	−0.003	−0.002**	−0.004	−0.004	0.006	0.006
	(0.018)	(0.016)	(0.002)	(0.001)	(0.003)	(0.003)	(0.004)	(0.004)
Constraint on the executive 2	−0.014	−0.008	0.004	0.004***	−0.001	−0.001	−0.018*	−0.017***
	(0.014)	(0.028)	(0.005)	(0.000)	(0.002)	(0.002)	(0.009)	(0.005)
Constraint on the executive 3	−0.017	−0.004	0.010*	0.010	0.004	0.004***	−0.008	−0.008***
	(0.028)	(0.033)	(0.006)	(0.007)	(0.003)	(0.000)	(0.010)	(0.002)
Constraint on the executive 4	−0.019	−0.014	0.006	0.005***	0.003	0.004	−0.023**	−0.022***
	(0.030)	(0.084)	(0.005)	(0.000)	(0.003)	(0.008)	(0.011)	(0.004)
Age dependency ratio (percentage of working-age population)	−0.357**	−0.404*	0.033	0.023*	0.005	0.002	0.003	0.001
	(0.172)	(0.230)	(0.026)	(0.013)	(0.014)	(0.006)	(0.044)	(0.085)

	(1) Public debt (% of GDP)		(2) Government final consumption expenditure (% of GDP)		(3) Taxes on income profits and capital gains (% of GDP)		(4) Primary balance (% of GDP)	
	FE	LSDV-Kiviet	FE	LSDV-Kiviet	FE	LSDV-Kiviet	FE	LSDV-Kiviet
Net Foreign Assets (NFAs)	-0.126^{**}	-0.103^{***}	-0.000	-0.000	0.000^{**}	0.000	0.000	0.000
	(0.058)	(0.020)	(0.000)	(0.001)	(0.000)	(0.001)	(0.001)	(0.001)
Observations	635	635	745	745	458	458	674	674
Number of countries	45	45	49	49	39	39	49	49

Notes: Robust standard errors in parentheses; *** $p < .01$; ** $p < .05$; * $p < .10$; Period: 1991–2015; Estimates are obtained through fixed effects and least squares dummy variable (LSDV)-Kiviet estimations. All models include time-fixed effects.
Source: Authors' elaboration.

12. Fiscal and monetary policy challenges after COVID-19: The Argentinean case

Damián Pierri

INTRODUCTION

This chapter studies the connection of monetary policy and capital markets in Argentina since 2019. After the sudden stop observed in 2018, there had been several fundamental changes in the design of economic policy, especially following the 2019 national election, which implied a turnover in the ruling party. These changes have major implications in the relative behavior of Argentina with respect to other middle-income countries.

The first important measure of President Fernández's administration was a sobering debt swap, which implied a reduction in the burden associated with dollar-denominated debt but was followed by a sharp drop in the price of bonds. Even in a context of zero interest rates around the world, this juncture precludes debt issuances. In this context, COVID-19 forced the government to restrict the mobility of citizens, which implied the need for an unprecedent monetary and fiscal stimulus (Bortz et al., 2020). Thus, the Argentinean economy now has misalignments in relative prices and liquidity levels with a banking sector that significantly increased its exposure to the issuance of the public sector debt. In addition, Argentina established capital and exchange rate controls, and there is no formal monetary program.

Due to the financing needs implied by the COVID-19 stimulus, there was an impressive jump in the transferences from the central bank to the Treasury, with a minor impact on the money base affecting the balance sheets of banks. Coupled with the implications of the debt swap, the government now faces important restrictions when it comes to financing the deficit. Although there was an improvement in local currency debt issuances, mainly bought by residents, the composition of deficit financing is still tilted toward money printing.

Due to capital and exchange rate controls, the foreign exchange (FX) premium jumped. The lack of access by the public sector to non-monetary financing sources and the mentioned premium generated a misalignment in inflation expectations, which severely affects the stance of monetary policy to fight inflation. Of course, this is a consequence of the sudden stop suffered in 2018 and it is by no means clear that keeping the balance of payments completely deregulated would have been a better option (Bortz et al., 2021; Libman and Palazzo, 2020). Moreover, the previous administration received an unprecedented loan from the International Monetary Fund (IMF) in the form of a Stand-By program. Now, the current administration must renegotiate the loan under a new type of program, which implies long-term commitments.

This macroeconomic outlook implies that Argentina constitutes a unique case among modern middle-income countries as it combines a persistent moderate inflation regime, capital and exchange rate controls, high deficits, and volatility of relative prices. These facts are rarely observed in comparable countries, thus motivating Argentina as a case study, especially in a zero-interest-rate world. The objective of this chapter is to better understand the current Argentinean situation. Having a clear analysis will permit us to anticipate the future macroeconomic outlook of the country, especially considering the limitations to restoring macroeconomic stability implied by COVID-19.

STRUCTURAL MACROECONOMIC SITUATION

Argentina suffered a major macroeconomic crisis between 2001 and 2003. Authorities decided to default sovereign debt, there was a banking crisis, and the social situation was critical. Between 2003 and 2007, however, the country grew rapidly, the social situation improved, and inflation was contained.
Between 2008 and 2011 the social situation also improved but by means of a series of redistributive policies that, as is well known, affected the macro stability of the country. Among other factors, it is important to highlight a massive moratorium on the pension system, the presence of a collective wage bargaining process that was established by law, and an unprecedented hike in wages expressed in current dollars. The figures in this chapter illustrate the situation.

If we define macro sustainability as an intertemporally balanced external sector, one of its main determinants is the level of competitiveness. Figure 12.1 illustrates the gap between wages expressed in constant local currency units and in (official) dollars. It is interesting to note at least four periods after 2003: (a) up to 2010, there was a moderate reduction in the gap, which of course mimicked a slow appreciation of the real exchange rate; (b) between 2011 and 2012 the gap disappeared and, as we will see below, this situation severely affected macro stability and Argentina's performance relative to comparable countries in the region; (c) between 2013 and 2018 the gap was stable around

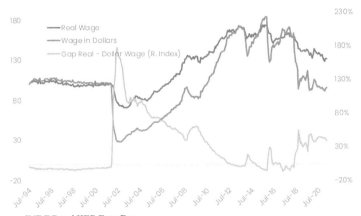

Source: INDEC and IIEP Data Base.

Figure 12.1   *Real wage vs. wage in dollars*

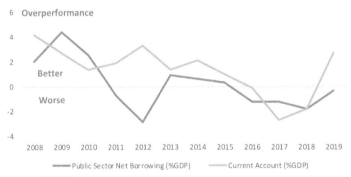

Source: World Bank.

Figure 12.2   *Argentina: difference in fundamentals, WRT Latam*

zero and the macro situation was characterized by secular stagnation with rising inflation; and (d) when COVID-19 struck, the wage bargaining process was suspended, de facto, and the gap was (and is currently) sustained at levels observed at the end of phase b and the beginning of phase c.

To illustrate the impact of this gap on the macroeconomic performance, we show the relative fundamentals of Argentina compared to Brazil, Chile, and Colombia.

Figure 12.2 depicts the difference between the net borrowing position of the public sector in Argentina scaled by gross domestic product (GDP) and the average of the same variable observed in Brazil, Chile, and Colombia. It also illustrates the gap between the current over GDP in Argentina and these countries: when the value is above zero, Argentina has better fundamentals than the other countries in the region. Note that between 2008 and 2010, in phase a of the gap between the real and dollar-denominated wage, Argentina overperformed the region in terms of fundamentals. Figure 12.3 illustrates the effect of the structure of relative prices and fundamentals on the macroeconomic performance of the country.

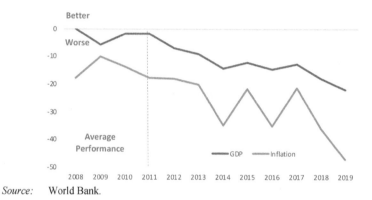

Source: World Bank.

Figure 12.3   Argentina: difference in performance WRT Latam

It is clear from Figure 12.3 that, when Argentina overperformed the region, it had a relatively stable comparative performance measured by the gap between the GDP per capita at constant local currency prices and the inflation rate. Having an average fundamental structure is not enough to sustain macro stability and keep the growth rate comparable to that of other middle-income countries.

Why? Argentina is the only country in Latin America with a recent default in its sovereign debt. Thus, the ability to finance the external imbalance is smaller when compared with other countries in the region. Moreover, after the banking crisis and due to the nationalization of the private pension system, the sovereign has only two options to finance its deficit: the rest of the world and the central bank. Moreover, the public sector typically crowds out external borrowing by local firms. Thus, it is not surprising to see that the fiscal deficit and the current account balance move in line with each other.

Argentina was recovering from a sudden stop suffered in 2018 when COVID-19 hit the economy. This generated the need for redistributive policies. However, there is no room for them due to the average position of fundamentals. If Argentina would pursue this type of policies, the regulations would reduce the country's fiscal and external positions below the region's average, something that the country cannot afford. Figures 12.4a and 12.4b depict the current situation.

COVID-19 pushed the poverty line to a critical level, with no room for redistributive policies. After the default in 2001 and an unfriendly debt swap, the country cannot afford twin deficits. The level of inflation and the nominal instability associated with tight capital and exchange rate controls would suggest taking the fundamentals to the overperforming region, which would severely affect the fragile social situation.

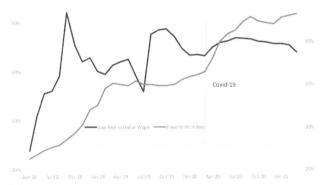

Source: INDEC.

Figure 12.4A   Macro vs. social stability

Thus, Argentina needs to return to a stable macro situation but is trapped with implementation problems because of COVID-19 and three major exchange rate depreciations (two in 2018 and one in 2019). This fact explains the delay in closing a deal with the IMF, something that will flatten the debt services profile in the coming years.

Moreover, COVID-19 generated a major reduction in the scale of the economy. Figure 12.4b shows that GDP per capita is more than 15 percent below the level observed in 2013. When restricted to industrial production, the situation is even worse.

This situation affects: (a) mark-ups, real wages, and employment; (b) exports; and (c) inflation. The first point can be explained by noting that average costs in this economy are higher than in previous years, especially

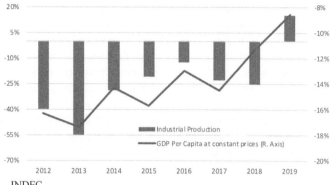

Figure 12.4B   Scale problems: variation in 2021 WRT previous years

before 2017. This entails higher mark-ups and lower investment. Due to the complementarity between capital and labor, employment creation is insufficient. Lower productivity links to lower real wages.

The second point relates to the first: scale problems affect the competitiveness of prices in a non-protected environment. The lack of investment and its effects on productivity make things even worse.

Finally, scale problems generate a higher price and inflation levels due to higher mark-ups and nominal exchange rates. As average costs increase, firms in the tradable sector require higher exchange rates to compensate the reduction in productivity inherited from a lower scale.

The social situation does not allow authorities to pursue a correction in the fundamentals. Macro instability and scale problems do not generate the proper incentives for investment, exports, and highly skilled employment creation. Furthermore, the insufficient access to voluntary financing in hard currency creates difficulties that begin a disinflationary process, which are typically characterized by either current account deficits or real appreciation of the exchange rate, and generally both. Finally, the mentioned redistributive policies put a high lower bound on public expenditure and, thus, on taxes. Collective wage bargaining and unions imply a high level of labor costs beyond the real wage.

In summary, the country has a reduced local market and is not suitable to become an export platform. Macroeconomic instability and COVID-19 act as barriers against: (a) investment, exports, and quality employment creation; and (b) the structural and macroeconomic reforms necessary to curb inflation. Argentina is thus immersed in a stagnation loop and it is not clear how to break it.

In the next section, I will describe the juncture in detail to highlight the challenges ahead for the country. Finally, I will conclude with some ideas about the next steps to follow to break the mentioned loop.

MONETARY POLICY, FINANCIAL MARKETS, CAPITAL CONTROLS, AND NOMINAL INSTABILITY

In this section I will cover a series of topics that are typical of the Argentinean economy and the implications for the macroeconomic performance of the country.

Cyclical Instability

The lack of external financing affects the ability of the country to reduce nominal and real volatility. This fact interacts with a peculiar pattern of net exports and public expenditure: (a) due to the dependence of the current account on soybean exports (every year between September and March there is a shortage of dollars in the FX market); and (b) in the second half of the year, the fiscal deficit is higher than during the first half of the year.

This situation creates, at the same time, abundant liquidity due to the need to finance the Treasury by means of transfers from the central bank, and dollar scarcity, something that typically implies a depreciation of the nominal and real exchange rates.

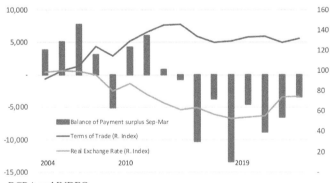

Source: BCRA and INDEC.

Figure 12.5   *Balance of payments: seasonal behavior*

Figure 12.5 illustrates the implications of the overperformance in fundamentals observed in Figure 12.2: except between 2003 and 2010, when competitiveness was extremely high and stable and there were twin surpluses—an exception in the region—there has been a seasonal pattern in the net dollar supply coming from the trade balance. This happens even if the real exchange rate and the terms of trade are stable but not (exceptionally) high. On top of that, it comes along with a seasonal pattern in fiscal accounts.

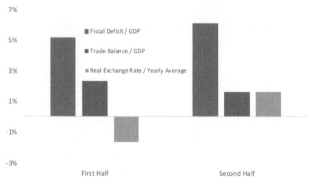

Source: Ministry of Economy, BCRA and INDEC.

Figure 12.6   Seasonal fundamentals

Figure 12.6 depicts the cyclical pattern of fundamentals and the real exchange rate. In the absence of external financing, it is not possible to smooth the seasonal shortage of dollars. Without local and external capital markets' founding, the country must rely on the central bank. Both factors imply an anticipated depreciation of the exchange rate. More to the point, elections take place in the second half of the year every two years. Thus, political and macro instability interact with each other, affecting real allocations, especially concerning exports, investment, and formal employment; all these variables involve long-term decisions that are postponed due the presence of periodic risks.

Unanchored Inflation

After the national election in August 2019, inflation expectations jumped well above current inflation. As time passed, expectations became less dispersed, which suggests an agreement between market participants who are periodically surveyed by the central bank.

There are several reasons behind this disagreement. Note that between 2017 and 2019, the situation was reversed: the market underestimated inflation systematically (Figure 12.7). During that period, Argentina had an inflation target,

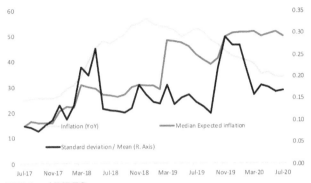

Source: BCRA and INDEC.

Figure 12.7   *Inflation expectations*

and authorities, especially in the central bank, were clear about the objective of monetary policy: contain inflation (Sturzenegger, 2019). Since 2020, the central bank has not clearly signaled its stance with respect to inflation. Several times after inflation peaked, there was neither a statement nor a change in interest rates/monetary aggregates. Besides, after capital and exchange rate controls were established, and considering their transitory nature, market participants have always expected an additional depreciation of the exchange rate. Moreover, after COVID-19 hit the economy, as Argentina has neither a wealth fund (as Chile) nor market financing (like Brazil), the associated fiscal stimulus was paid with central bank transfers, which implied an important hike in the interest-paying liabilities of the central bank. Market participants may interpret this fact as signaling future money printing and, thus, inflation.

Finally, the government does not have a clear strategy to fight inflation. On the one hand, there was a delay in closing a deal with the IMF, which could imply a tighter commitment with respect to nominal stability. Moreover, the fiscal stance is confusing. After the first wave of COVID-19, there was a windfall of fiscal revenues, more than 1 percent of GDP, associated with extraordinary international prices and taxes. The Treasury did not change its target for the primary deficit; instead, they decided to spend it all before the midterm elections. Furthermore, we observed an appreciation of the real exchange rate and a reduction in real regulated prices. Considering a future agreement with the IMF, all these features suggest future inflation, as relative prices must be restored to their previous levels to ensure macro stability. On the other hand, after consolidating the transactions between the Treasury and the central bank" Including FX operations, fiscal policy generated a contraction of the money base. This is mainly because the Treasury is obtaining more funds than needed to cover local currency debt services.

Tight Capital and Exchange Rate Controls

In a first stage, capital and exchange rate controls intended to contain the volatility of the capital account of the balance of payments. In this sense, the government set an upper bound for dollar purchases for households. Importantly, firms were allowed to request, almost freely, imports at the official exchange rate.

After COVID-19 forced the government to run an important fiscal deficit, the blue-chip swap (i.e., a legal way to purchase dollars freely using the bond market) and its gap with respect to the official dollar surged; this forced authorities to tighten capital and exchange rate controls. This is depicted in Figure 12.8.

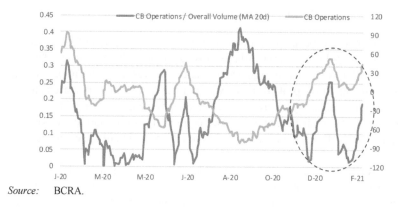

Source: BCRA.

Figure 12.8   Tight capital controls

Figure 12.8 shows the ratio between the overall volume in the FX market and interventions of the central bank: the higher the ratio, the tighter the degree of capital and exchange rate controls. These restrictions were implemented through a series of central bank regulations that especially affected firms.

This situation puts a lower bound on the FX premium and, as discussed before, does not allow authorities to anchor inflation, considering that market participants interpret capital and exchange rate controls as transitory measures that are typically followed by a sudden depreciation of the (official) exchange rate. Moreover, as imports are being restricted, GDP cannot grow sustainably.

Thus, the stance of the monetary/exchange rate policy perpetuates the current stagflation in Argentina. Of course, abandoning capital and exchange rate controls is not an option due to the scarcity of foreign reserves and the impossibility of accessing voluntary and massive foreign capital markets. It is still an open question how to stabilize an economy with capital and exchange rate controls and relatively loose monetary and fiscal policy without external support, either in the form of debt issuances or foreign direct investment.

Money Overhang

After COVID-19 hit the economy, Argentina was in a relatively weak situation. Before leaving, in 1Q19, the previous administration defaulted on the local currency-denominated debt and there was an important depreciation of the nominal exchange rate. Moreover, the incoming authorities had decided to renegotiate the dollar-denominated debt services with both types of lenders: private and international organizations. The country suspended the ongoing Stand-By program with the IMF and committed to a tough renegotiation with private creditors.

To finance an unprecedented fiscal stimulus, authorities had to rely on transfers from the central bank. Monetary aggregates did not increase accordingly, due to an ongoing sterilization process that had two phases. First, when mobility restrictions were at peak, money demand was abnormally high, a fact that helped to contain inflation. This was followed by a reduction in interest rates. Second, when restrictions started to be lifted, money demand lowered in line with addicted-to-dollars behavior (Reinhart et al., 2003), which generated tensions in the FX market. The first reaction was to tighten capital and exchange rate controls further, something that was not effective.

Since then, the central bank started to reduce slowly monetary aggregates until reaching an implicit target. They also adjusted the interest rate level, especially for overnight loans to firms. However, there is still excess liquidity, especially in term deposits. Figure 12.9 illustrates the ratio of term deposits

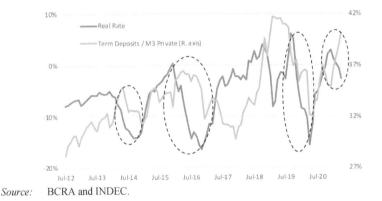

Source: BCRA and INDEC.

Figure 12.9   Money overhang

with respect to M3, which include money and coins, sight, and term deposits. Moreover, the real rate is lowering. Typically, those situations were followed by a marked reduction in term deposits to restore the equilibrium in money market operations.

Argentina is still facing some distortions associated with the monetary and fiscal policy implications of COVID-19. To restore macro stability, some corrections are needed, especially in term deposits.

FX Premium

Argentina restored capital and exchange rate controls in 4Q19. Given the current inflationary juncture, the non-anchored expectations, and the decreasing real rates in local currency-denominated assets, households and firms prefer to save in hard currency. However, they cannot purchase dollars from the official window freely; there is a monthly upper bound, which was set well below the median wage.

This fact generates a demand for the "blue-chip-swap" dollar. Households and firms, with restrictions, can purchase dollars by buying bonds with local currency and selling it against dollars. Thus, a premium emerges between the blue-chip and the official dollar.

However, contrary to past experiences, the level of this premium is abnormally high. Figure 12.10 shows the empirical distribution of the FX premium between 2011 and 2020. There was a period with no capital and exchange rate controls between 2016 and 2019. Thus, as the premium was zero, those observations were removed. The premium has been oscillating between 60 percent and 80 percent. Not only that, but authorities also charge taxes to expenditures in dollars paid with credit cards. This fact generates a lower bound for the premium around 65 percent.

From this picture, it is clear that the current capital and exchange rate control regime is working with a substantially higher level of FX premium. In the column labeled "84%," you can see the current figure as against the entire distribution. Considering that the past capital controls regime lasted four years but with a substantial lower level of premium, it is still an open question how to curb instability in the current situation. Besides the effect on inflation expectations, the premium regenerates important misallocations, especially in the demand of tradable goods.

To reduce the FX premium, authorities must accumulate FX reserves. The current peak in international (soybean) prices generated a significant hike in FX reserves. However, considering the previous scarcity of dollars in the central bank and the upcoming elections, authorities tightened capital and exchange rate controls even further. The future behavior of the FX premium, without COVID-19, is an open question. It is not possible to imagine a reduc-

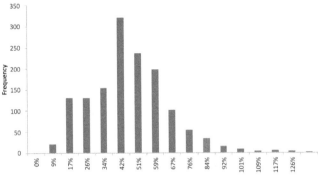

Source: BCRA and IAMC.

Figure 12.10   FX premium: empirical distribution (2011–2020)

tion in nominal and real instability unless the FX premium is reduced to normal figures, around 34–51 percent.

CONCLUSIONS

I have described the structural challenges ahead for Argentina. I also focused on the juncture. The analysis is clear: to reduce macro instability and to curb inflation, the country needs to implement a series of reforms aimed at pushing the fundamentals (current account and borrowing requirements) well above the average of comparable countries in the region. However, the social situation and the aftermath of COVID-19 act as barriers to such a program.

The country is and will be, at least in the near future, trapped in a stagflationary loop. Moreover, this fact worsens the scale problems that are now affecting the country, making the need for corrections stronger as time passes. It is necessary to refine this analysis and use it to develop corresponding restrictions. Thus, we can think in a two-step procedure for the next two years.

In the first step, authorities must deal with money overhang, close a deal with the IMF, and send a clear fiscal and monetary signal to contain the inflationary impact of the relative price adjustments associated with the agreement. After that, the government must redefine its priorities. From a dichotomous perspective, it must choose between redistributive policies and measures oriented to reduce macroeconomic volatility and to curb inflation. However, authorities will prefer a middle-ground stance as, after COVID-19, the Argentinean economy cannot tolerate additional shocks, especially those affecting relative prices.

Considering the constrained scope for redistributive policies at the current juncture, especially challenges in the nominal side of the economy, the best option is to pursue a modest stabilization plan aimed at reducing the FX premium to the 35–50 percent range and inflation to 25–30 percent, which is an average, moderate inflation regime with capital and exchange rate controls.

REFERENCES

Bortz, P., Michelena, G., and Toledo, F. (2020). "A Gathering of Storms: The Impact of COVID-19 Pandemic on the Balance of Payments of Emerging Markets and Developing Economies (EMDEs)", *International Journal of Political Economy* 49(4): 318–35.
Bortz, G., Toftum, N., and Zeolla, N. (2021). "Old Cycles and New Vulnerabilities: Financial Deregulation and the Argentine Crisis", *Development and Change* 52(3): 598–626.
Libman, E., and Palazzo, G. (2020). "Inflation Targeting, Disinflation, and Debt Traps in Argentina", *European Journal of Economics and Economic Policies* 17(1): 78–105.
Reinhart, C., Rogoff, K., and Savastano, M. (2003). "Addicted to Dollars", NBER Working Paper 10015.
Sturzenegger, F. (2019). "Macri's Macro: The Meandering Road to Stability and Growth", Brookings Papers on Economic Activity Conference Drafts, September 5–6.

13. International reserves, repurchase agreements, and the Brazilian monetary policy

Sylvio Antonio Kappes

INTRODUCTION

The commodity boom of the first decade of the 21st century allowed many developing countries to accumulate international reserves.[1] In Brazil, this process was very intense. The accumulation of foreign exchange reserves had a side effect, namely, an increase in the liquidity of the domestic monetary system, which forced the Central Bank of Brazil (BCB) to use its monetary policy instruments to drain such liquidity. Due to the problem, repurchase agreements (repos) were the main instrument used, and they had several negative implications for public debt. Finally, in the face of exchange rate volatility, the prevailing legislation obliged the accounting revaluation of international reserves that, in turn, inflated the BCB's balance sheet: accounting gains resulted in contributions to the Treasury Account, while losses caused an increase in the public securities portfolio of the BCB.

Taking the BCB's balance sheet as a benchmark, the four items described above (international reserves, repo operations, Treasury Account, and public securities portfolio) make up almost the entire asset side and two-thirds of the liability side. In light of that, the purpose of this chapter is to briefly discuss the recent evolution of these four items, and to explain the connections between them. The following section briefly summarizes the main elements of the Brazilian monetary policy. The third section explores the evolution of these items and their links. Finally, we present our final remarks.

MONETARY POLICY OPERATION IN BRAZIL – AN OVERVIEW

The BCB has adopted an inflation-targeting regime that was implemented in 1999. The National Monetary Council (CMN) defines the inflation target. This

Council is currently composed of three members: the Minister of Economy
(the Council's chairman), the Special Secretary of Treasury and Budget of the
Ministry of Economy, and the Governor of the BCB. The inflation target is
set for the next three years. As an example, the inflation target for 2022 was
defined in 2019, whereas in 2022 the CMN defined the target until 2025.[2]

Along with the target, the CMN also defines its upper and lower limits.
Figure 13.1 presents both the center target and the range around it. From 2006
to 2016, the inflation target was 4.5 percent, with a 2 percent tolerance band.
Since 2017, the range has been narrower, at 1.5 percent, and the center target
is being gradually reduced, aiming for a center target of 3 percent for 2024. If
current inflation goes below or above the tolerance range in a given year, the
Central Bank governor must write an open letter to the Minister of Economy
explaining the reasons for not achieving the target, and the actions that will be
taken to bring inflation back to the range. Finally, the official targeted price
index is presented by the Broad National Consumer Price Index (IPCA), which
measures, in 16 metropolitan regions, the consumer inflation for households
with incomes between 1 and 40 times the minimum wage.[3]

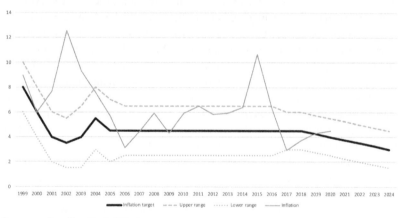

Source: Brazilian Central Bank.

Figure 13.1   Brazilian inflation target regime

To reach the inflation target, the Monetary Policy Committee (Copom), which
is formed by the BCB's Board of Directors and its governor, defines the target
for the policy interest rate – it is called Selic in Brazil; this is the interest rate
paid on overnight repo operations, which are collateralized by federal government bonds. The Committee meets eight times a year (every 45 days), and each
meeting lasts two days. The first day is reserved for the BCB's staff technical

reports on recent developments and forecasts for both the Brazilian and global economies. On the second day, in a closed-door meeting, the Committee decides the Selic target rate.

The instrument to ensure that the effective Selic rate stays at the target is the use of open market operations. The BCB performs these operations exclusively with federal public debt, composed by Treasury bonds.[4] The vast majority of the open market operations are repurchase agreements, a topic that the next section covers.

Compulsory reserves requirements are charged on demand, savings deposits, and certificates of deposit. In the first, no remuneration is paid. For savings deposits, the remuneration is set at the same rate that the banks pay their customers. Finally, the reserves requirements for certificates of deposit are remunerated at the Selic rate. The required reserve is calculated over the financial institution's average reception of each kind of deposit, over two weeks. The compulsory deposits, in turn, are held at the BCB for a period of two weeks, in the so-called maintenance period. Figure 13.2 presents the required reserve ratios. The ratios have been relatively constant from 2003 to 2015, so required reserves have not been a major force driving the BCB's balance sheet.

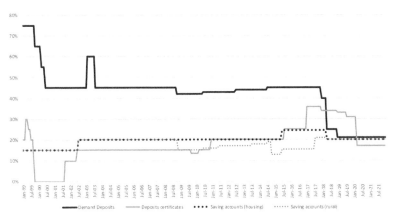

Source: Brazilian Central Bank.

Figure 13.2   Required reserve ratios

As for the standing facilities, the rediscount rate is set as the base rate, plus 35 basis points.[5] There is also the recently implemented voluntary reserves, authorized by the Brazilian congress in July 2021.[6] At the time of writing, this instrument is still being implemented.

Table 13.1   Brazilian Central Bank's balance sheet

Percentage of total assets and liabilities					
Assets	2005	2020	Liabilities	2005	2020
International reserves	29.0%	49.3%	Repos	13.0%	31.0%
Treasury bills	58.2%	48.3%	Treasury Account	43.6%	36.5%
Others	12.8%	2.4%	Others	43.4%	32.5%
Percentage of GDP					
Assets	2005	2020	Liabilities	2005	2020
International reserves	7.2%	26.4%	Repos	3.2%	16.6%
Treasury bills	14.4%	25.8%	Treasury Account	10.8%	19.5%
Others	3.2%	1.3%	Others	10.7%	17.4%

Source: Brazilian Central Bank.

Having discussed the main monetary policy instruments, let us now turn to the BCB's balance sheet. Table 13.1 presents the data as a percentage of total assets and liabilities (upper panel) and as a percentage of gross domestic product (GDP; lower panel) for 2005 and 2020. Data for 2005 are presented to show the changes in the BCB's balance sheet composition, including the period when the accumulation of international reserves happened.

The asset side has been comprised basically of two items: international reserves and Treasury bills. In 2005, other items summed to 12.8 percent, while in 2020 it was only 2.4 percent, evidencing the accumulation of international reserves. As the next section elucidates, repos sterilized the liquidity created by mounting foreign reserves, which explains the increased number of Treasury bills in the Central Bank's portfolio. Notice the close numbers, relative to the GDP, of these two items in 2020. As for the liabilities, two items are also the focus (although not to the same degree as the asset side): two-thirds of them are repos and the Treasury Account. The major development is the greater importance of repos: they rose from 13 percent of total liabilities to 31 percent, and from 3.2 percent of GDP to 16.6 percent.

These four items – international reserves, treasury bills, repos, and the Treasury Account – evolved due to the same policy decisions and institutional features. Their evolution began with the decision to accumulate international reserves. A second decision, the sterilization of the liquidity created by this reserve accumulation, explains both the increase in repos and in Treasury bills. Finally, the legal framework connects the first decision to the increase in the Treasury Account. The next section analyzes all these developments.

THE CONNECTION BETWEEN INTERNATIONAL RESERVES, REPURCHASE AGREEMENTS, AND THE TREASURY ACCOUNT

In the past two decades, Brazil has accumulated an outstanding amount of international reserves. Figure 13.3 shows their value, both in millions of US dollars (left axis) and as a percentage of GDP (right axis). From 2006 to 2012, the process of reserves accumulation was intense, and their total amount jumped from US$56.9 billion to US$373 billion, which was equivalent to 6 percent of GDP in 2006 and 15 percent in 2012.

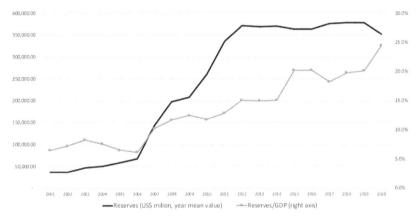

Source: Brazilian Central Bank.

Figure 13.3   Brazilian international reserves, in millions of US dollars and as a percentage of GDP

Holding such a large amount of reserves has both advantages and problems. Some of the advantages are (i) guaranteeing imports even in the presence of balance-of-payments constraints; (ii) maintaining the ability to repay external debt, even if capital flows suddenly stop coming; and (iii) constituting an insurance against capital flights, speculation, and exchange rate volatility. In sum, reserves are a buffer against external constraints.

However, reserves also have costs. They are basically related to a greater government debt resulting from the sterilization of liquidity coming as a counterpart of acquiring reserves. When the BCB bought the dollars to create its international reserves, it augmented the supply of money, forcing the Selic rate down. Due to its commitment to the stability of the interest rate between the Copom meetings, the BCB must drain this extra money in circulation to keep the interest rate stable at its target. It does so via open market operations performed by repo. Therefore, repurchase agreements enabled the Central Bank to withdraw the excess of reserves from the money market and stabilize the Selic rate.

The use of repos to sterilize the liquidity created by the accumulation of international reserves generated three interrelated problems. The first is the interest rate differential between international reserves' yield and repos' cost. Since the Brazilian Selic rate, which is the cost of repos, has always been higher than the Federal Funds Rate, which is the main rate remunerating the Brazilian international reserves, the carrying cost of the foreign reserves is high. However, being part of the interest paid by the central government, this cost is not accounted for in the Treasury budget because it is generated and paid by the Central Bank, who pays it by issuance of money.

The second problem is the increase in government indebtedness. In Brazil, there are two alternative methodologies for the assessment of public debt: (i) the BCB method, which considers the repos as part of government debt; and (ii) the International Monetary Fund (IMF) method, a broader measure that treats as public debt all government bonds the BCB possesses.[7] The use of Treasury bonds for repos can increase indebtedness in both measures. The effect in the first methodology is more straightforward: the more repos needed to control liquidity, the higher the government debt. In the second method, the effect is indirect: government debt will increase as long as the BCB needs more Treasury bonds to keep doing repos. According to Tesouro Nacional (2019, 17), from 2001 to 2018, the Treasury had to issue bonds to the BCB four times in order to maintain its portfolio of bonds.[8] It is not possible to identify if this issuance was directly related to the repos used to sterilize the reserves acquisition, but the simultaneity of events – reserves and repos were increasing while the Treasury was transferring more bonds to the BCB – makes us believe that this was the case.

Finally, the third problem is that repos are performed on a short-term basis. Since they are part of government debt, it follows that they influence public debt's maturity. For instance, Figure 13.4 shows that repos' mean term (presented in the left axis) has persistently been reduced. From operations maturing in more than one month, their recent average term is by five days. The figure also shows that repos represent a significant portion of government debt (right axis).

In short, there are benefits as well as shortcomings in accumulating international reserves, and it is not straightforward to assess whether the process is positive or negative overall. There are a number of metrics used to evaluate the optimum size of a country's international reserves that give precise numbers for this type of evaluation.[9] According to the majority of them, Brazil is well

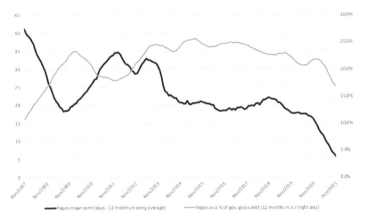

Source: Brazilian Central Bank.

Figure 13.4   *Repos' mean term and as a percentage of government gross debt*

above any meaningful criteria. Pellegrini (2017a) estimates four of these metrics. The first is the months of imports rule, which jumped from less than 8 months in 2005 to more than 20 months in 2016. The second metric is reserves in relation to the short-term external debt, according to which the Brazilian international reserves were 3.4 times larger than all the country's short-term external debt in 2016. The third measure is reserves in relation to the monetary aggregate (M3), indicating the potential size of liquid assets that could quickly fly out of the country in face of any negative shock. In this case, Brazilian reserves jumped from 10 percent of M3 in 2005 to 20 percent of M3 in 2016. Finally, the author also computes the IMF's Assessing Reserve Adequacy, which is a composite index that includes exports, broad money (like M3), and measures of external debt. Again, the numbers present a strong increase: reserves jumped from 60 percent of the adequate level in 2005 to 160 percent in 2016. In an earlier study, Vonbun (2013) found that the international reserves have been at an excessive level at least since the second quarter of 2010. According to the majority of his measures, the Brazilian economy could enjoy all the benefits of large international reserves even if it had half of its observed level. This raises the question of whether or not the BCB has gone too far on this matter.

Other comparative works were devoted to analyzing the increased usage of repos as the main monetary policy instrument. Blikstad (2020) compares the monetary policy implementations of Brazil, Mexico, Russia, and Turkey, four developing countries that accumulated international reserves during the same period. As is clear from his study, the Brazilian monetary policy presents many unique features. First, it is the only one to have exclusively used repos in its open market operations, while the other countries have used, to varying degrees, outright operations. Second, when measured as a percentage of GDP, Brazilian repos are by far the largest of the group. Finally, it is important to point out that the BCB has basically resorted to repos and reserve requirements as its policy instruments, while the other countries have used a wider array of instruments, such as reserves' remuneration, Central Bank bills, and so on. Pellegrini (2017b), in turn, compares the Brazilian experience with 14 other countries that also accumulated international reserves, and finds that it is by far the country that used the most repos.

Finally, the last aspect related to the process of international reserves accumulation is the evolution of the Treasury Account at the Central Bank. As the exchange rate varies, the value of international reserves is revalued: if there is a depreciation, the value of the reserves measured in Brazilian reais increases and generates an accounting gain for the BCB; on the other hand, if an appreciation occurs, the value of the reserves in Brazilian reais decreases, creating an accounting loss. Over the period analyzed in this chapter, these accounting results were the main component of the BCB's financial result, as presented in the Tesouro Nacional (2019, 9).

Until 2008, there was no distinction between the result arising from revaluations of international reserves and the result arising from other BCB operations. The law 11 803 of 2008 establishes the separation between these two components. There was, however, no other practical consequence: both components were added together to compose the BCB result. The legislation in force when dealing with this result created a growth bias for the BCB's balance sheet: during the semesters in which the BCB obtained a positive result, the gain should be transferred to the Treasury Account; during the semesters in which a loss occurred, the Treasury should add government bonds to the BCB's portfolio in an amount equal to the loss. In this way, the BCB's balance either grew or remained constant. This is because, in semesters with positive results, both assets (due to international reserves) and liabilities (via the Treasury Account) grew. In the semesters with negative results, the balance did not change, as the reduction in assets caused by the devaluation of reserves was offset by an increase of the same amount in the BCB's securities portfolio.

This bias was only corrected with Law 13 820 of 2019. With this law, the difference in the results between, on the one hand, the revaluations of international reserves and, on the other hand, other operations of the Central Bank started to have practical consequences, since each component became treated differently. According to the new law, the results of the international reserves' revaluations are now allocated to or discounted from a reserve account at the BCB. In periods when a positive result occurs, this is added to the reserve account; in the face of negative results, the amount is debited from this account. The results of the other BCB operations follow the previous methodology: positive results are transferred to the Treasury Account, while negative results are covered by the Treasury via the injection of public bonds in the BCB's portfolio.

CONCLUDING REMARKS

Now we can list the reasons that explain the relevance of each of the items presented in Table 13.1. The first – and main – reason is the economic policy decision to accumulate international reserves. The second relevant reason is also a political decision by the BCB: the liquidity generated by the reserve accumulation process was drained with repo operations. The use of these, in turn, requires that the BCB holds a portfolio of public securities at least equal to the amount of repos. Finally, the last reason is a regulatory aspect: the fluctuation in the value of international reserves, combined with the legislation in force throughout the period, meant that both the Treasury Account (in the semesters with positive results) and the portfolio of securities (in the semesters with negative results) grew sharply.

This set of decisions presents a series of costs and challenges for both the Central Bank and national debt management. First, the interest rate differential between the remuneration of international reserves and the Selic rate means that the process of accumulating reserves has a fiscal cost for the government. Second, the need to sterilize the extra liquidity with government bonds has implications for public debt. Finally, the accumulation of positive results inflated the balance of the Treasury Account at the Central Bank.

At least two major implications that go beyond mere technical issues related to public debt metrics and the relationship between the Central Bank and the Treasury arise from these problems. The first implication is distributive: if repos are a major public debt management component for the Treasury, for the financial sector they are a very short-term asset with high returns and plenty of liquidity. It is difficult not to point to this sector as the main beneficiary of the entire process described in this chapter. The second implication is ideological: by raising public indebtedness, this process feeds the discourse of fiscal austerity defenders who call for fiscal surpluses to reduce public debt, while advocating the use of the positive balance in the Treasury Account exclusively for the repayment of the debt.

It is interesting to point out an apparent contradiction that emerges from this last point. The relationship between the Central Bank and the financial system is organized in such a way that any attempt to reduce public debt is useless. Suppose, for example, that part of the balance in the Treasury Account is actually used to reduce the public debt. One plausible consequence of this is that banks are left with more reserves. This pressures the Selic rate down, forcing the Central Bank to drain the extra liquidity. As the monetary policy option is always the use of repos, and as these compose the public debt, the drying up of liquidity ends up raising the public debt, making the first move useless. Nevertheless, the public debt, despite not having its level changed, has had its maturity period reduced. The National Treasury admits this in an official publication (Tesouro Nacional, 2019, 21).

Anyone advocating these policies might say that these were the best options available. However, one cannot say that it was the only possible alternative. Some questions exemplify this point: Why was the process of accumulation of international reserves so intense? Why was the liquidity generated in this process not drained with another instrument, such as an increase in the reserve requirement rate or the implementation of remunerated reserves? Why cannot the positive balances in the Treasury Account be used for other purposes, and why does it become useless even for the reduction of public debt? Answering these questions will certainly contribute to a better understanding of Brazilian monetary policy and will help to overcome its limitations.

NOTES

1.   The chapter benefited from insightful comments and suggestions by Fábio Terra. All the remaining errors are mine.
2.   From 1999 to 2016, the target was chosen two years in advance. The three-year horizon was introduced in 2017.
3.   The Brazilian regime considers the headline index as its reference. Some countries, like the US, use instead a measure of core inflation.
4.   The law of fiscal responsibility (Lei Complementar no 101, May 4, 2000) prohibits the BCB from issuing its own securities.
5.   "Resolução BCB 175, de 15 de dezembro de 2021" regulates this matter.
6.   "Lei no 14.185, de 14 de julho de 2021" sets this regulation.
7.   For further discussion of this topic, see Tesouro Nacional (2019, 19).
8.   This has happened in 2008, 2009, 2015, and 2016, with issuances ranging from around R$10 billion to nearly R$70 billion.
9.   A classical work on this subject is Jeanne and Ranciére (2006).

REFERENCES

Blikstad, N. M. D. (2020), O balanço patrimonial do Banco Central e a implementação da política monetária em economias emergentes. Ph.D. thesis, Universidade Estadual de Campinas (Unicamp).
Jeanne, O., & Ranciére, R. (2006), The optimal level of international reserves for emerging market economies: formulas and applications. IMF Working Paper no 229.
Pellegrini, J. A. (2017a), Reservas Internacionais do Brasil: Evolução, Nível Adequado e Custo de Carregamento. Instituição Fiscal Independente, special study n. 1.

Pellegrini, J. A. (2017b), As Operações Compromissadas do Banco Central. Instituição Fiscal Independente, special study n. 3.

Tesouro Nacional (2019), Relacionamento entre o Tesouro Nacional e o Banco Central. Relatório especial da Secretaria do Tesouro Nacional.

Vonbun, C. (2013), Reservas Internacionais Revisitadas: Novas Estimativas de Patamares Ótimos. Instituto de Pesquisa Econômica Aplicada: texto para discussão n. 1885.

14. External debt and economic growth in Latin America and the Caribbean

Alfredo Schclarek Curutchet

INTRODUCTION

The preoccupation with the negative impact of public debt on economic growth is a recurrent theme in macroeconomic discussions.[1] This is especially true around crisis times when the responsibility of the crises is often attributed to high public debt levels or when the crisis resolution strategies involve large increases in public debt to bail out the private sector. Similarly, the relevance of distinguishing between external debt and domestic debt has also been the subject of a long debate.[2] An argument that has been put forward is that external debt is much more difficult to service than domestic debt because it requires not only a fiscal surplus to service government debt, or positive returns for companies to service private debt, but also sufficient access to foreign currency. In this sense, excessive foreign indebtedness is associated with currency crises and low growth.

Concurrently, the economic literature on the nature of the relationship between debt and growth, though large, remains partly equivocal. Theoretical works such as Cohen (1991) suggest that low debt levels are positively associated with growth, even if countries are not able to borrow freely due to the risk of debt repudiation; an underlying assumption in these cases is that borrowed funds are associated with productive investment. In contrast, other theoretical contributions, including Tornell and Velasco (1992) and Sachs (1989), show that large public debt levels may have a significant negative impact on economic activity if the cost of high taxes associated with debt servicing is not internalized or there is some probability that future debt obligations exceed an economy's repayment ability. In this case, expected debt servicing costs imply higher taxes or real interest rates, ultimately crowding out private investment. Note that these papers suggest that non-linearities may be present in the relationship between debt and growth: a positive or negligible relationship between debt and growth at low levels of debt, and a negative causation at high levels of debt.

In addition, there is a growing theoretical literature that highlights the relevance of the external component of debt (Aghion et al., 2004; Jeanne, 2000; Korinek, 2011; Moreno-Brid, 2003; Rocha and Oreiro, 2013; Schclarek and Xu, 2022). In general terms, this literature argues that external debt may be detrimental to growth due to debt defaults and currency crises, caused by the interplay between the exchange rate and the currency mismatch of the balance sheets of debtors; while debt has to be paid in USD, the revenues of the government or private agents are collected in domestic currency. This literature stresses the importance of issuing debt in domestic currency and fostering export-led growth. In terms of the empirical literature studying the relationship between debt and growth, only a limited number of studies have found evidence of a non-linear relationship between debt and growth, including Checherita-Westphal and Rother (2012), Cohen (1997), Elbadawi et al. (1997), Patillo et al. (2002), Smyth and Hsing (1995), and Woo and Kumar (2010). The non-linear relationship implies that there is no significant relationship at low levels of debt and a negative relationship after a certain debt-to-GDP (gross domestic product) threshold has been passed. In addition, Calderon and Fuentes (2013) find a negative relationship between public debt and economic growth, and evidence of non-linearity in this relationship by the level of development and public debt. An interesting feature of this study is that it uses the historical public debt database published by the International Monetary Fund (IMF, 2010), which allows us to study both external and domestic public debt for a large sample of developing and industrial countries, and not only public external debt, as most of the studies do.

In contrast to the empirical literature that finds non-linear evidence, Schclarek (2004) identifies a negative linear relationship between external debt and growth for developing countries (no evidence of non-linear effects), and that this negative relationship is driven by the incidence of public external debt, and not by private external debt. For industrial countries, he finds no significant relationship between gross government debt and economic growth. These results are confirmed by Afonso and Jalles (2013), who find a negative relationship and no non-linear evidence using a sample including both developed and developing countries. In addition, Qureshi and Liaqat (2020), Levy-Yeyati (2014), and Rocha and Oreiro (2013) confirm the negative relationship between external debt and growth for developing countries. De Vita et al. (2018) find that the causal relationship between debt and growth for 13 developed countries is very weak. Finally, Heimberger (2022) performs a meta-regression analysis for 47 papers and cannot reject a zero-average-growth effect. Thus, he concludes that the econometric literature has so far not provided robust evidence for consistently negative growth effects of higher public debt levels.

This chapter sheds light on these issues by redressing the relationship between external debt and growth in a Latin American and Caribbean context. The chapter provides a comprehensive treatment of this issue by using alternative explanatory variable sets, which include debt ratios not commonly used (such as debt to years of government revenues) as well as a distinction between public and private external debt. To uncover these relationships, we use the generalized method of moments (GMM) dynamic panel econometric technique proposed by Arellano and Bover (1995) and Blundell and Bond (1998). Previous applied growth studies that use this econometric methodology include Beck et al. (2000), Levine et al. (2000), and Patillo et al. (2002). The data set consists of a panel of 20 Latin American and Caribbean countries with data averaged over each of the seven five-year periods between 1970 and 2002.[3] There are several data sources, but our main source is the World Development Indicators 2004 of the World Bank.

Our results suggest that higher total external debt levels are associated with lower growth rates, and that this negative relationship is driven by the incidence of public external debt levels, and not by private external debt levels. We do not find evidence of non-linear effects for these relationships.

The rest of the chapter is organized as follows. In the second section we present some descriptive statistics for the debt and growth data that we use. The empirical methodology and the data are discussed in the third and fourth sections, respectively. Next, the chapter presents the estimation results for the different debt indicators. Further, we also explain the results of considering non-linear effects on GDP growth. In the sixth section, we discuss and present the results from some consistency tests that were conducted to confirm the results from the benchmark case. The final section concludes.

DESCRIPTIVE STATISTICS

In this section we present some descriptive statistics of the values of some of the debt and growth variables in selected countries in Latin America. In Figure 14.1 we illustrate the average total external debt as a ratio to GDP for the period 1970–2002. The total external debt is divided between public external debt and private external debt. The first conclusion from this figure is that the largest part of total external debt is composed of public external debt in contrast to private external debt. Note that the relatively low level of private external debt might be partially influenced by the large bailout of the private sector by the governments in the debt crisis of the 1980s. Further, the average total debt-to-GDP ratio for these Latin American countries has remained between 30 percent and 66 percent, which from an international perspective cannot be considered excessively disproportionate.

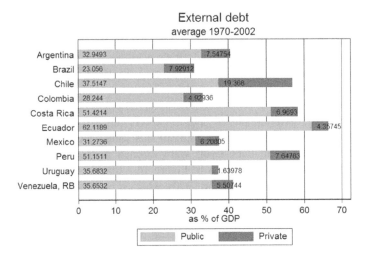

Source: World Bank.

Figure 14.1   *External debt-to-GDP ratio*

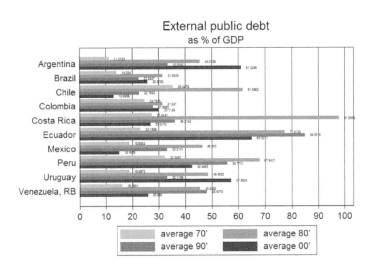

Source: World Bank.

Figure 14.2   *Public external debt-to-GDP ratio 1970–2002*

Monetary policy challenges in Latin America

In Figure 14.2 we present the external public debt-to-GDP ratio for the same selected countries, but now taking the average for each of the four decades between 1970 and 2002. Besides the fact that the values of the external public debt variable show a larger dispersion than in Figure 14.1, it is interesting to note that, in general, the 1980s and 1990s were the decades with the largest average debt levels. Further, when comparing the 1970s with the 2000s, we see that, in general, the debt levels have increased in these Latin American countries.

The average external public debt-to-exports ratios for each of the four decades are presented in Figure 14.3. In this figure we again see that, in general, the maximum debt levels were reached in the 1980s and 1990s. Nonetheless, it is less clear than in Figure 14.2 that the ratio has increased when comparing the 1970s and the 1990s, which is probably a consequence of increasing exports in the last two decades.

Figure 14.4 presents the per capita GDP growth rate for each of the four decades between 1970 and 2002. In general, we can conclude that the 1970s was a decade of high growth, and the 1980s was one of low growth. For the other two decades, the evidence is mixed and no general pattern can be observed.

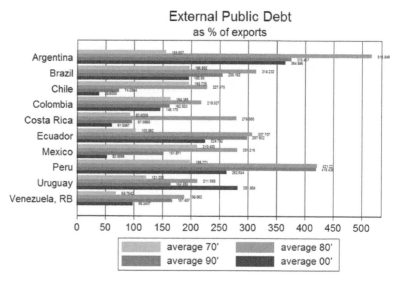

Source: World Bank.

Figure 14.3   Public external debt-to-exports ratio 1970–2002

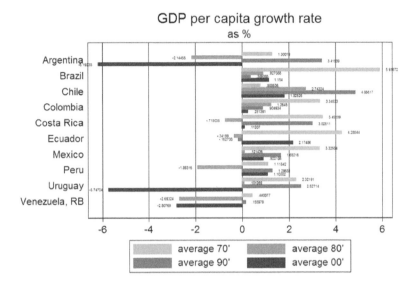

Source: World Bank and other (see text).

Figure 14.4   GDP per capita growth rate

ECONOMETRIC METHODOLOGY

The basic regression equation that we use to uncover the relationship between
external debt and economic growth is of the type:

$$Y_{i,t} = aX_{i,t} + yD_{i,t} + \eta_i + \lambda_t + \varepsilon_{i,t} \tag{14.1}$$

where $Y_{i,t}$ is the dependent variable, $X_{i,t}$ represents the set of explanatory variables, $D_{i,t}$ is the debt variable, η_i is an unobserved country-specific effect, λ_t is
an unobserved time-specific effect, $\varepsilon_{i,t}$ is the error term, and the subscripts i and
t represent country and time period, respectively.

When estimating Equation 14.1, we use the real growth rate of GDP per
capita as the dependent variable. Regarding $X_{i,t}$, we will use five alternative
explanatory variable sets. The first set, which is the base set, includes initial
income per capita[4] and educational attainment. The second set adds to the base
set government size, openness to trade, and inflation. The third set is like the
second set, but also includes the level of financial intermediary development.
The fourth set is equal to the first set plus population growth and the level of
investment. The fifth set adds to the fourth set openness to trade, terms of trade

growth, and fiscal balance. Note that the second and third set are very similar to each other and to the fourth and fifth sets. The sources and definitions of these variables are defined more thoroughly in the next section.

Evidently, Equation 14.1 is linear in nature. However, we are also interested in investigating if there is any non-linear relationship between external debt and economic growth.[5] Therefore, to allow for non-linear effects of external debt, we include a linear spline function in Equation 14.1. In this case, Equation 14.1 becomes:

$$Y_{i,t} = aX_{i,t} + yD_{i,t} + \delta_{di,t}\left(D_{i,t} - D^*\right) + \eta_i + \lambda_t + \varepsilon_{i,t} \tag{14.2}$$

where $d_{i,t}$ is a dummy variable that equals one if the value of the debt variable is above a certain threshold value D^*, and zero otherwise. If δ is significantly different from zero, we can conclude that there is a non-linear relationship. In this case, the impact of debt will be different above and below the threshold D^* (i.e., there will be a structural break). The specific threshold values for D^* will depend on the specific debt indicator that is used. The benchmark case values are introduced in the subsection "Non-Linear Effects on GDP Growth." Further, for each debt indicator, a series of threshold values are used to corroborate the results of the benchmark case (see the section "Consistency Tests" for more details).

Methodologically, the chapter uses the dynamic system GMM panel estimator developed by Arellano and Bover (1995) and Blundell and Bond (1998).[6] Further, we use the robust one-step estimates of the standard errors, which are consistent in the presence of any pattern of heteroskedasticity and autocorrelation within panels.[7] There are two conditions that are necessary for the GMM estimator to be consistent: that the error term, ε, does not exhibit serial correlation, and that the instruments used are valid. We use two tests proposed by Arellano and Bond (1991) to validate these assumptions. The first test examines the assumption that the error term is not serially correlated. As this test uses the differenced error term, by construction, AR(1) is expected to be present. Therefore, the Arellano–Bond test for autocorrelation determines whether the differenced error term has second-order, or higher, serial correlation. Under the null hypothesis of no second-order serial correlation, the test has a standard normal distribution. The second assumption is corroborated by a test of over-identifying restrictions, which tests the overall validity of the instruments. Specifically, we use the Hansen J statistic, which is the minimized value of the two-step GMM criterion function. Under the null hypothesis of the validity of the instruments, this test has a χ^2 distribution with $(J\ K)$ degrees of freedom, where J is the number of instruments and K the number of regressors. The reason for using this statistic, as opposed to the Sargan statistic, is that it is robust to heteroskedasticity and autocorrelation.

There are several reasons for using cross-sectional time-series data. First, adding the time-series dimension to the data augments the number of observations and the variability of the data. This is especially important for us given that we have a limited number of Latin American and Caribbean countries. Second, we are able to control for unobserved country-specific effects and thereby reduce biases in the estimated coefficient estimates. Third, the GMM estimator controls for the potential endogeneity of all explanatory variables.[8] This is because the estimator controls for endogeneity by using "internal instruments" (i.e., instruments based on lagged values of the explanatory variables). Note that it controls for "weak" endogeneity and not for full endogeneity (Bond, 2002).

DATA

The data set consists of a panel of 20 Latin American and Caribbean countries, with data averaged over each of the seven five-year periods between 1970 and 2002 (1970–74; 1975–80; etc.).[9] All the variables that we use are averaged data over non-overlapping five-year periods, as we want to capture the long-run relationship between growth and debt, and not be subject to short-run cyclical movements. Therefore, the total number of observations is 140. However, due to data availability, for some samples we had fewer than 140 observations, and in some cases we had unbalanced panels.

The dependent variable is the real per capita GDP growth rate (*growth*). For the debt variable, $D_{i,t}$, we use 15 debt indicators: total external debt-to-GDP ratio (*dbtgdp*), total external debt-to-exports ratio (*dbtexp*), total external debt-to-revenues ratio (*dbtrev*), public external debt-to-GDP ratio (*pubdgdp*), public external debt-to-exports ratio (*pubdexp*), public external debt-to-revenues ratio (*pubdrev*), private external debt-to-GDP ratio (*privdgdp*), private external debt-to-exports ratio (*privdexp*), private external debt-to-revenues ratio (*privdrev*), interest payment-to-GDP ratio (*intgdp*), interest payment-to-exports ratio (*intexp*), interest payment-to-revenues ratio (*intrev*), debt service-to-GDP ratio (*dbtsergdp*), debt service-to-exports ratio (*dbtserexp*), and debt service-to-revenues ratio (*dbtserrev*). Besides the debt variable, the regressors include several variables to control for other factors associated with economic development. Specifically, we have five explanatory variable sets. The first set consists of the initial income per capita to control for convergence (*linitial*) and average years of schooling as an indicator of the human capital stock in the economy (*lschool*). The second set includes the variables from the first set, as well as government size (*lgov*) and inflation (*lpi*), which are used as indicators of macroeconomic stability, and openness to trade (*ltrade*) to capture the degree of openness of an economy. The third set adds to the second set a variable for financial intermediary development (*lprivo*).

The fourth set includes, apart from initial income and schooling, population growth (*lpop*) and the investment-to-GDP ratio (*linv*). The fifth set includes the variables from the fourth set plus openness to trade (*ltrade*), terms of trade growth (*ltot*), and the fiscal balance-to-GDP ratio (*lfbal*).[10]

The source for the data is mainly the World Development Indicators 2004 of the World Bank. However, we also used data from the International Financial Statistics database of the IMF, the Penn World Tables 6.1, the Barro-Lee database on educational attainment, and the Financial Development and Structure database of the World Bank. Appendix 14A presents more detailed information about the sources and definitions of the variables.

ESTIMATION RESULTS

Linear Effects on GDP Growth

Table 14B.1 in Appendix 14B displays the estimation results for Equation 14.1 when the dependent variable is the GDP growth rate and the debt indicator is the total external debt-to-GDP ratio. The debt coefficient is negative and significant at the 1 percent level for all five independent variable sets. Specifically, the coefficient values range from −1.372 (column 2) to −1.671 (column 4). In the case of the total external debt-to-exports ratio (Table 14B.2), the debt coefficients are also negative and significant at the 1 percent level, with values ranging from −1.107 (column 4) to −1.493 (column 3). These results are confirmed when using the total external debt-to-revenues ratio.[11] Thus, for Latin American and Caribbean countries, there is a significant negative relationship between the level of total external debt and the growth rate of the economy.

The results for the public external debt-to-GDP ratio are presented in Table 14B.3. We find a negative relationship with economic growth, with all the coefficients for the independent variable sets being significant at the 1 percent level and ranging from −1.235 (column 5) to −1.550 (column 4). We find identical results in the case of the public external debt-to-exports ratio, with coefficients ranging from −1.190 to −1.469 (Table 14B.4). Further, these results are corroborated for the public external debt-to-revenues ratio.

When analyzing the results for the private external debt indicators, we find that the relationship with growth is not significant. In Table 14B.5, for example, we present the results when using the private external debt-to-GDP variable. Here, none of the debt coefficients are significant. These results are supported by findings for the private external debt-to-exports ratio (Table 14B.6) and the private external debt-to-revenues ratio. As total external debt is composed of public external debt and private external debt, this suggests that the negative relationship between total external debt and growth is driven by the negative relationship with public external debt, and not by the private component of it. In other words, it seems that high levels of public external debt (but not necessarily private external debt) are associated with low economic growth.

The results of the linear relationship between GDP growth and the interest payment-to-GDP ratio, interest payment-to-exports ratio, and interest payment-to-revenues ratio are not presented due to space considerations.[12] However, the findings for the interest payment indicators for all five independent variable sets suggest that there is no significant relationship between GDP growth and interest payments. We have also chosen not to present the findings for the debt indicators involving debt services, again to save space. The results for all three debt service ratios, and for all five independent variable sets, show that there is an insignificant association between them and the growth rate of the economy.

Non-Linear Effects on GDP Growth

In this subsection we present the estimation results for the non-linear relationship between the debt indicators and economic growth using Equation 14.2. We have estimated this equation for the total external debt indicators, the interest payment indicators, and the debt service indicators. For each of these debt indicators, specific threshold values, D^*, must be chosen to specify the non-linear relationship. As there is no theoretical or empirical indication on any specific threshold value, we chose to estimate Equation 14.2 from each debt indicator with a benchmark value selected ad hoc. However, we also performed a consistency test by estimating Equation 14.2 with eight alternative threshold values. The specific threshold values for each debt indicator are presented in the next section. Further, we note that the results from the benchmark case were confirmed when using theses alternative threshold values.

When using the total external debt-to-GDP ratio, the total external debt-to-exports ratio, and the total external debt-to-revenues ratio, we use threshold values of 60 percent, 250 percent, and 300 percent, respectively. In the next section we will confirm these results using other threshold values. In Table 14B.7 we see that the significance of the debt variable *dbtgdp* for all the samples is similar to the results in Table 14B.1. Further, the debt dummy variable, *dbtgdp3d1060*, is not significantly different from zero for all the independent variable sets, except for the first set. Therefore, there is no convincing evidence of non-linear effects of the total external debt-to-GDP ratio on economic growth. This result is confirmed in Table 14B.8, when using the total external debt-to-export ratio as the relevant debt variable. In this case, the debt dummy variable is *dbtexp3d2250*, which is also not significant for all sets. We performed the same non-linear estimation using the total external debt-to-revenues ratio with a threshold value of 300 percent. Again, we did not find any evidence of non-linear effects, as the variable *dbtrev3d3300* is insignificant for all five sets. Concluding, we can assert that none of the considered total external debt variables have non-linear effects on economic growth.

In the cases of the interest payment-to-GDP ratio, interest payment-to-exports ratio, and interest payment-to-revenues ratio, we used the following benchmark case threshold values to control for the existence of non-linear effects on growth: 2.5 percent, 12 percent, and 12 percent, respectively. For the interest payment-to-GDP ratio we found some mixed evidence of non-linear effects. The results are displayed in Table 14B.9, where we see that the dummy variable coefficient is positive and significant for the first three independent variable sets. These positive and significant coefficients suggest that, when the interest payment-to-GDP ratio is higher than 2.5 percent, there is a positive relationship between it and the growth rate of the economy. Similar results are also obtained for the interest payment-to-exports ratio, where the dummy variable coefficient is positive and significant for the first three independent variable sets. Conversely, in the case of the interest payment-to-revenues ratio, none of the dummy variable coefficients of the sets are significantly different from zero. Thus, we can conclude that, although there is some evidence of non-linear effects, the findings are not very robust. Further, the positive coefficient contradicts the common belief that the higher the level of interest payment, the worse its effects, if any, on growth. Therefore, caution should be taken in interpreting these results.

For the debt service indicators, we used as a benchmark case the following values: 6 percent for the debt service-to-GDP ratio, 25 percent for the debt service-to-exports ratio, and 30 percent for the debt service-to-revenues ratio. We do not find any evidence that the debt service indicators had non-linear effects on GDP growth.

CONSISTENCY TESTS

To corroborate the results of the previous section, we performed several consistency tests. First, all the estimated equations were estimated without outliers. We identified outliers using the method from Hadi (1994). Second, we also used three-year averages instead of five-year averages, which increased the time span to 11 periods and the sample size to 220 observations. Third, in the case of the non-linear effects, Equation 14.2 was estimated using alternative threshold values for the dummy variables. In Appendix 14B, we display the specific threshold values for each debt indicator. After performing all these consistency tests, the results obtained did not change from the benchmark case results presented in the previous section. Consequently, the benchmark case results could not be refuted and are robust to all the consistency tests.[13]

CONCLUSIONS

This chapter has investigated both the linear and non-linear relationships between external debt and economic growth for a sample of 20 Latin American and Caribbean economies.

The results show that higher total external debt levels are associated with lower growth rates, and there is no evidence of non-linear effects for these relationships. In addition, the negative relationship is driven by the incidence of public external debt levels, and not by private external debt levels. Note, however, that overall private external debt levels are relatively low, meaning that the insignificance of external private debt may be due to its low levels and perhaps not by it being intrinsically irrelevant for growth. In any case, more research should be conducted.

Although these results give only partial responses to why public external debt affects growth, one possible answer is that the government, by taking on too much external debt, may crowd out private investment and reduce economic activity. Alternatively, it may also be that private investment is discouraged by recurrent exchange rate instabilities and currency crises due to having insufficient hard currency to service external public debt. The reduction in private investment may be because (1) private companies are unwilling to invest due to exchange rate and currency crisis risks, or (2) because both domestic and foreign creditors are unwilling to lend and finance private companies due to these risks.

In terms of policy implications, the results of the chapter suggest that external debt should be avoided, particularly public external debt. Although more research needs to be done, it seems that taking on debt in external currency is much more problematic for growth than taking on debt in domestic currency. A big question that is still unanswered is whether public debt is intrinsically bad for growth, or if it is external debt that is problematic due to its consequences for the exchange rate and the balance of payments. A suitable avenue for further research on this issue is to compare the empirical results when using external public debt from the World Development Indicators and gross public debt from the historical public debt database published by the IMF (2010).

Another policy implication is that, to reduce public external debt, it is not sufficient to increase the fiscal surplus, but it is necessary to increase the current account surplus. This is a direct consequence of the public debt being external, which requires hard currency to repay the debt, not only being a surplus agent. Furthermore, although private external debt could be thought of as a non-issue for the government, this is not true. When private debt is external, the demand of hard currency by companies to repay external debt may have consequences for the exchange rate and the balance of payments.

NOTES

1. I am grateful for comments and suggestions from Steven Durlauf, Luis Rivera Batiz, and Fernando Toledo.
2. Note that "external" debt may be analyzed in terms of debt denominated in a foreign currency (currency denomination) or debt held by foreign investors (origin of creditors). In this chapter, when analyzing "external" debt, we are considering the currency denomination of debt definition.
3. Note that we have only used data until 2002 because that was the database we had access to. The econometric analysis with an updated database that includes more years is left for future research. However, if the results are robust, as it is claimed, the main results should not change if we add more years/observations.
4. The inclusion of initial income per capita when the dependent variable is the real growth rate of GDP per capita makes Equation 14.1 become dynamic in nature (e.g., Durlauf et al., 2004).
5. It has been claimed by Patillo et al. (2002) that such a non-linear relationship is present.
6. See Bond (2002) for an introduction to the use of GMM dynamic panel data estimators.
7. The two-step estimates of the standard errors are asymptotically more efficient than the one-step variant. However, in a finite sample, the two-step estimates of the standard errors tend to be severely downward biased (Arellano and Bond, 1991; Blundell and Bond, 1998). Windmeijer (2000) derives a finite-sample correction to the two-step covariance matrix, which can make the two-step variant more efficient than the one-step variant. We are, however, unable to implement the Windmeijer finite-sample correction because we have a limited number of cross-sections (countries).
8. Recall that, by including initial income per capita, growth regressions become dynamic in nature.
9. Note that, for the last period (2000–02), only three observations are available. The countries are Argentina, Bolivia, Brazil, Chile, Colombia, Costa Rica, Dominican Republic, Ecuador, El Salvador, Guatemala, Haiti, Honduras, Mexico, Nicaragua, Panama, Paraguay, Peru, Trinidad and Tobago, Uruguay, and Venezuela.
10. The variables used in the second and third sets have been used in Beck et al. (2000) and Levine et al. (2000), and the ones in the fourth and fifth sets in Patillo et al. (2002) and Mankiw et al. (1992), among others. Note that the second and third sets are relatively similar to each other. In addition, both the fourth and fifth sets are alike.
11. These results are not presented due to space considerations, but the tables may be provided upon request from the author.
12. The tables may be provided upon request from the author.
13. The tables may be provided upon request from the author.

REFERENCES

Afonso, A., and Jalles, J. T. (2013). Growth and productivity: The role of government debt. *International Review of Economics & Finance*, 25(C):384–407.

Aghion, P., Bacchetta, P., and Banerjee, A. (2004). A corporate balance-sheet approach to currency crises. *Journal of Economic Theory*, 119(1):6–30.

Arellano, M., and Bond, S. (1991). Some tests of specification for panel data: Monte Carlo evidence and an application to employment equations. *Review of Economic Studies*, 58:277–97.

Arellano, M., and Bover, O. (1995). Another look at the instrumental-variable estimation of error-components model. *Journal of Econometrics*, 68:29–52.

Beck, T., Levine, R., and Loayza, N. (2000). Finance and the sources of growth. *Journal of Financial Economics*, 58:261–300.

Blundell, R., and Bond, S. (1998). Initial conditions and moment restrictions in dynamic panel data models. *Journal of Econometrics*, 87:115–43.

Bond, S. (2002). Dynamic panel data models: A guide to micro data methods and practice. Institute for Fiscal Studies Working Paper No. 09/02.

Calderon, C., and Fuentes, J. R. (2013). Government debt and economic growth. IDB Publications (Working Papers) 4641, Inter-American Development Bank.

Checherita-Westphal, C., and Rother, P. (2012). The impact of high government debt on economic growth and its channels: An empirical investigation for the euro area. *European Economic Review*, 56(7):1392–1405.

Cohen, D. (1991). *Private Lending to Sovereign States: A Theoretical Autopsy*. MIT Press.

Cohen, D. (1997). Growth and external debt: A new perspective on the African and Latin American tragedies. Centre for Economic Policy Research Discussion Paper, No. 1753.

De Vita, G., Trachanas, E., and Luo, Y. (2018). Revisiting the bi-directional causality between debt and growth: Evidence from linear and nonlinear tests. *Journal of International Money and Finance*, 83(C):55–74.

Durlauf, S. N., Johnson, P. A., and Temple, J. R. (2004). Growth econometrics. Vassar College Department of Economics Working Paper Series 61.

Elbadawi, I., Ndulu, B., and Ndung'u, N. (1997). Debt overhang and economic growth in sub-Saharan Africa. IMF Institute.

Hadi, A. S. (1994). A modification of a method for the detection of outliers in multivariate samples. *Journal of the Royal Statistical Society*, 56:393–6.

Heimberger, P. (2022). Do higher public debt levels reduce economic growth? *Journal of Economic Surveys*. https://doi.org/10.1111/joes.12536

International Monetary Fund (2010). A historical public debt database. IMF Working Papers 2010/245.

Jeanne, O. (2000). Foreign currency debt and the global financial architecture. *European Economic Review*, 44(4):719–27.

Korinek, A. (2011). Excessive dollar borrowing in emerging markets: Balance sheet effects and macroeconomic externalities. SSRN working papers.

Levine, R., Loayza, N., and Beck, T. (2000). Financial intermediation and growth: Causality and causes. *Journal of Monetary Economics*, 46:31–77.

Levy-Yeyati, E. (2014). Financial dollarization: Evaluating the consequences. *Economic Policy*, 21(45):62–118.

Mankiw, N. G., Romer, D., and Weil, D. N. (1992). A contribution to the empirics of economic growth. *The Quarterly Journal of Economics*, 107(2):407–37.

Moreno-Brid, J. C. (2003). Capital flows, interest payments and the balance-of-payments constrained growth model: A theoretical and empirical analysis. *Metroeconomica*, 54(2–3):346–65.

Patillo, C., Poirson, H., and Ricci, L. (2002, April). External debt and growth. IMF
Working Paper 02/69.

Qureshi, I., and Liaqat, Z. (2020). The long-term consequences of external debt:
Revisiting the evidence and inspecting the mechanism using panel VARs. *Journal of
Macroeconomics*, 63(C):103–84.

Rocha, M., and Oreiro, J. (2013). Capital accumulation, external indebtedness, and
macroeconomic performance of emerging countries. *Journal of Post Keynesian
Economics*, 35(4):599–620.

Sachs, J. (1989). *The Debt Overhang of Developing Countries*. Basil Blackwell.

Schclarek, A. (2004). Debt and economic growth in developing and industrial countries. Working Papers 2005:34, Lund University, Department of Economics.

Schclarek, A., and Xu, J. (2022). Exchange rate and balance of payment crisis risks
in the global development finance architecture. *Journal of International Financial
Markets, Institutions and Money*, 79:101574.

Smyth, D., and Hsing, Y. (1995). In search of an optimal debt ratio for economic
growth. *Contemporary Economic Policy*, 13:51–9.

Tornell, A., and Velasco, A. (1992). The tragedy of the commons and economic
growth: Why does capital flow from poor to rich countries? *Journal of Political
Economy*, 100(6):1208–31.

Windmeijer, F. (2000). A finite sample correction for the variance of linear two-step
GMM estimators. Institute for Fiscal Studies Working Paper No. 00/19.

Woo, J., and Kumar, M. M. S. (2010). Public debt and growth. IMF Working Papers
2010/174.

APPENDIX 14A: DATA SOURCES AND DEFINITIONS

The data were mainly taken from the World Development Indicators 2004 of the World Bank (WDI). However, we also used data from the International Financial Statistics database of the IMF (IFS), the Penn World Tables 6.1 (PWT), the Barro-Lee database on educational attainment, and the Financial Development and Structure database of the World Bank. All the variables are used in log form, with the exception of the growth rate of GDP. Below is a list of the sources and definitions of the different variables used in this study.

- Total external debt (*dbt*): Debt owed to nonresidents repayable in foreign currency, goods, or services. Total external debt is the sum of public, publicly guaranteed, and private nonguaranteed long-term debt, use of IMF credit, and short-term debt. Short-term debt includes all debt having an original maturity of one year or less and interest in arrears on long-term debt. Source: WDI.
- Government external debt (*pubd*): Public and publicly guaranteed debt comprises long-term external obligations of public debtors, including the national government, political subdivisions (or an agency of either), and autonomous public bodies, and external obligations of private debtors that are guaranteed for repayment by a public entity. Source: WDI.
- Private external debt (*prid*): Private nonguaranteed external debt comprises long-term external obligations of private debtors that are not guaranteed for repayment by a public entity. Source: WDI.
- Interest payment (*int*): Interest payments by the central government to domestic sectors and to nonresidents for the use of borrowed money. Source: WDI.
- Debt service (*dbtser*): Total debt service is the sum of principal repayments and interest actually paid in foreign currency, goods, or services on long-term debt, interest paid on short-term debt, and repayments (repurchases and charges) to the IMF. Source: WDI.
- GDP (*gdp*): Gross domestic product. Source: WDI.
- Exports (*exp*): Exports of goods and services. Source: WDI.
- Revenues (*rev*): Current revenue, excluding grants, for the central government. Source: WDI.
- Real per capita GDP growth rate (*growth*): Annual percentage growth rate of GDP per capita based on constant local currency. Source: WDI.
- Initial income per capita (*linitial*): The logarithm of lagged real (PPP) per capita GDP (constant prices). Source: PWT.
- Average years of schooling (*lschool*): The logarithm of one plus the average years of schooling in the total population over age 25. Source: Barro-Lee database.

- Government size (*lgov*): The logarithm of the ratio of general government final consumption expenditure to GDP. Source: WDI.
- Inflation (*lpi*): The logarithm of one plus the inflation rate, which is calculated using the average annual consumer price index. Source: WDI.
- Openness to trade (*ltrade*): The logarithm of the sum of exports of goods and services and imports of goods and services as a share of GDP. Source: WDI.
- Terms of trade growth (*ltot*): The logarithm of one plus the growth rate of the terms of trade. Source: WDI.
- Financial intermediary development (*lprivo*): The logarithm of the ratio of private credit by deposit money banks and other financial institutions to GDP. Source: Financial Development and Structure database.

ALTERNATIVE THRESHOLD VALUES FOR THE DUMMY VARIABLES

As explained in the section "Consistency Tests," we checked the benchmark case results of Equation 14.2 using alternative threshold values for the total external debt, interest payment and debt service indicators. Specifically, for the total external debt-to-GDP ratio, we estimated the equations with nine alternative threshold values ranging from 20 percent to 100 percent in 10-percent intervals. For the total external debt-to-export ratio, the threshold values ranged from 50 percent to 400 percent in 50-percent intervals, and 500 percent. For the total external debt-to-revenues ratio, the threshold values ranged from 100 percent to 500 percent in 50-percent intervals. For the interest payment-to-GDP ratio, the threshold values ranged from 0.5 percent to 3 percent in 0.5-percent intervals, 4 percent, 5 percent, and 6 percent. For both the interest payment-to-exports ratio and the interest payment-to-revenues ratio, the following threshold values were used: 2 percent, 5 percent, 8 percent, 10 percent, 12 percent, 15 percent, 16 percent, 20 percent, and 25 percent. In the case of the debt service-to-GDP ratio, the threshold values ranged from 2 percent to 10 percent in 1-percent intervals. For the debt service-to-exports ratio, the threshold values ranged from 5 percent to 45 percent in 5-percent intervals. Finally, for the debt service-to-revenue ratio, values ranged from 10 percent to 50 percent in 5-percent intervals.

APPENDIX 14B: TABLES

Table 14B.1   Total external debt-to-GDP: linear effects on GDP growth

	(1)	(2)	(3)	(4)	(5)
linitial	−1.781	−1.489	−1.518	−1.819	−1.424
	(1.031)	(1.040)	(1.027)	(0.999)*	(1.040)
lschool	4.145	3.966	3.747	3.607	2.775
	(0.908)***	(1.043)***	(1.037)***	(0.938)***	(1.044)**
dbtgdp	−1.489	−1.372	−1.573	−1.671	−1.423
	(0.414)***	(0.438)***	(0.404)***	(0.371)***	(0.416)***
lgov		−0.095	−0.348		
		(0.562)	(0.527)		
ltrade		0.588	0.619		0.249
		(0.685)	(0.647)		(0.714)
lpi		−0.625	−0.305		
		(0.527)	(0.454)		
lprivo		0.585			
		(0.378)			
lpop				−0.837	−1.773
				(2.623)	(2.363)
linv				4.544	4.675
				(0.863)***	(1.048)***
ltot					7.575
					(8.413)
lfbal					9.812
					(6.055)
Hansen J test	1.000	1.000	1.000	1.000	1.000
AR(1) test	0.032	0.026	0.005	0.092	0.107
AR(2) test	0.887	0.669	0.201	0.710	0.366
Observations	140	136	134	134	123
No. of countries	20	20	20	20	19

Notes: Estimated using one-step system GMM dynamic panel data estimator with time dummies (Arellano and Bover, 1995; Blundell and Bond, 1998).
Columns (1), (2), (3), (4), and (5) display estimates for the first, second, third, fourth, and fifth independent variable sets, respectively.
The Hansen J test reports the p-values of a test of over-identifying restrictions.
The AR(1) and AR(2) tests report the p-values of the Arellano–Bond test for autocorrelation.
Robust standard errors in parentheses: *significant at 10 percent; **significant at 5 percent; ***significant at 1 percent.
Source: World Bank and other (see text).

Table 14B.2   Total external debt-to-exports: linear effects on GDP growth

	(1)	(2)	(3)	(4)	(5)
linitial	−1.432	−1.680	−1.712	−1.433	−1.655
	(0.923)	(1.027)	(1.021)	(0.894)	(1.010)
lschool	3.404	3.844	3.620	2.326	2.597
	(1.289)**	(0.962)***	(0.967)***	(1.336)*	(0.918)**
dbtexp	−1.139	−1.315	−1.493	−1.107	−1.413
	(0.354)***	(0.426)***	(0.374)***	(0.366)***	(0.283)***
lgov		−0.075	−0.311		
		(0.549)	(0.518)		
ltrade		−0.742	−0.894		−1.170
		(0.781)	(0.736)		(0.663)*
lpi		−0.627	−0.340		
		(0.525)	(0.460)		
lprivo			0.525		
			(0.384)		
lpop				−2.854	−2.039
				(3.124)	(2.295)
linv				4.483	4.885
				(1.049)***	(1.040)***
ltot					7.149
					(8.522)
lfbal					9.931
					(5.843)
Hansen J test	1.000	1.000	1.000	1.000	1.000
AR(1) test	0.039	0.027	0.005	0.104	0.112
AR(2) test	0.794	0.668	0.197	0.747	0.379
Observations	138	136	134	134	123
No. of countries	20	20	20	20	19

Notes: Estimated using one-step system GMM dynamic panel data estimator with time dummies (Arellano and Bover, 1995; Blundell and Bond, 1998).
Columns (1), (2), (3), (4), and (5) display estimates for the first, second, third, fourth, and fifth independent variable sets, respectively.
The Hansen J test reports the p-values of a test of over-identifying restrictions.
The AR(1) and AR(2) tests report the p-values of the Arellano–Bond test for autocorrelation.
Robust standard errors in parentheses: *significant at 10 percent; **significant at 5 percent; ***significant at 1 percent.

Table 14B.3   *Public external debt-to-GDP: linear effects on GDP growth*

	(1)	(2)	(3)	(4)	(5)
linitial	−2.091	−1.772	−1.753	−2.097	−1.645
	(1.106)*	(1.097)	(1.089)	(1.060)*	(1.109)
lschool	4.195	4.000	3.793	3.483	2.622
	(0.871)***	(1.033)***	(1.080)***	(0.842)***	(0.963)**
pubdgdp	−1.456	−1.403	−1.518	−1.550	−1.235
	(0.421)***	(0.476)***	(0.442)***	(0.336)***	(0.343)***
lgov		−0.153	−0.385		
		(0.487)	(0.453)		
ltrade		0.775	0.796		0.199
		(0.735)	(0.701)		(0.705)
lpi		−0.503	−0.285		
		(0.575)	(0.532)		
lprivo		0.417			
		(0.302)			
lpop				−1.473	−1.901
				(2.470)	(2.281)
linv				4.558	4.509
				(0.823)***	(1.024)***
ltot					8.791
					(8.452)
lfbal					9.389
					(5.284)*
Hansen J test	1.000	1.000	1.000	1.000	1.000
AR(1) test	0.038	0.031	0.008	0.094	0.109
AR(2) test	0.767	0.607	0.142	0.765	0.402
Observations	140	136	134	134	123
No. of countries	20	20	20	20	19

Notes: Estimated using one-step system GMM dynamic panel-data estimator with time dummies (Arellano and Bover, 1995; Blundell and Bond, 1998).
Columns (1), (2), (3), (4), and (5) display estimates for the first, second, third, fourth, and fifth independent variable sets, respectively.
The Hansen J test reports the p-values of a test of over-identifying restrictions.
The AR(1) and AR(2) tests report the p-values of the Arellano–Bond test for autocorrelation.
Robust standard errors in parentheses: *significant at 10 percent; **significant at 5 percent; *** significant at 1 percent.

Table 14B.4   *Public external debt-to-exports: linear effects on GDP growth*

	(1)	(2)	(3)	(4)	(5)
linitial	−1.749	−1.963	−1.952	−1.731	−1.851
	(0.972)*	(1.091)*	(1.091)*	(0.938)*	(1.079)
lschool	3.509	3.882	3.690	2.416	2.477
	(1.219)***	(0.960)***	(1.013)***	(1.250)*	(0.878)**
pubdexp	−1.246	−1.352	−1.469	−1.190	−1.236
	(0.352)***	(0.476)**	(0.428)***	(0.318)***	(0.246)***
lgov		−0.125	−0.333		
		(0.490)	(0.459)		
ltrade		−0.597	−0.691		−1.039
		(0.742)	(0.719)		(0.685)
lpi		−0.506	−0.307		
		(0.572)	(0.528)		
lprivo			0.366		
			(0.307)		
lpop				−3.023	−2.122
				(2.966)	(2.289)
linv				4.471	4.694
				(1.013)***	(1.024)***
ltot					8.408
					(8.594)
lfbal					9.439
					(5.151)*
Hansen J test	1.000	1.000	1.000	1.000	1.000
AR(1) test	0.046	0.032	0.008	0.109	0.113
AR(2) test	0.733	0.618	0.147	0.769	0.409
Observations	138	136	134	134	123
No. of countries	20	20	20	20	19

Notes: Estimated using one-step system GMM dynamic panel-data estimator with time dummies (Arellano and Bover, 1995; Blundell and Bond, 1998).
Columns (1), (2), (3), (4), and (5) display estimates for the first, second, third, fourth, and fifth independent variable sets, respectively. The Hansen J test reports the p-values of a test of over-identifying restrictions.
The AR(1) and AR(2) tests report the p-values of the Arellano–Bond test for autocorrelation. Robust standard errors in parentheses: *significant at 10 percent; **significant at 5 percent; ***significant at 1 percent.

Table 14B.5   *Private external debt-to-GDP: linear effects on GDP growth*

	(1)	(2)	(3)	(4)	(5)
linitial	−1.539	−1.546	−1.436	−1.776	−2.377
	(0.710)**	(0.753)*	(0.807)*	(0.653)**	(0.624)***
lschool	1.576	1.979	1.741	−0.030	0.289
	(0.909)*	(1.039)*	(0.980)*	(0.953)	(1.093)
pridgdp	−0.076	−0.057	−0.194	−0.111	−0.022
	(0.300)	(0.310)	(0.261)	(0.281)	(0.338)
lgov		−0.582	−0.757		
		(0.619)	(0.568)		
ltrade		−0.371	−0.371		−0.856
		(0.618)	(0.596)		(0.607)
lpi		−1.141	−0.912		
		(0.571)*	(0.462)*		
lprivo			0.664		
			(0.339)*		
lpop				−7.295	−5.695
				(2.797)**	(3.339)
linv				4.540	3.928
				(0.921)***	(0.767)***
ltot					11.551
					(7.103)
lfbal					16.356
					(6.487)**
Hansen J test	1.000	1.000	1.000	1.000	1.000
AR(1) test	0.022	0.019	0.015	0.131	0.058
AR(2) test	0.585	0.547	0.343	0.993	0.586
Observations	119	117	116	117	110
No. of countries	19	19	19	19	18

Notes: Estimated using one-step system GMM dynamic panel-data estimator with time dummies (Arellano and Bover, 1995; Blundell and Bond, 1998).
Columns (1), (2), (3), (4), and (5) display estimates for the first, second, third, fourth, and fifth independent variable sets, respectively.
The Hansen J test reports the p-values of a test of over-identifying restrictions.
The AR(1) and AR(2) tests report the p-values of the Arellano–Bond test for autocorrelation.
Robust standard errors in parentheses: *significant at 10 percent; **significant at 5 percent; ***significant at 1 percent.

Monetary policy challenges in Latin America

Table 14B.6   *Private external debt-to-exports: linear effects on GDP growth*

	(1)	(2)	(3)	(4)	(5)
linitial	−1.538	−1.555	−1.463	−1.791	−2.379
	(0.709)**	(0.767)*	(0.816)*	(0.658)**	(0.624)***
lschool	1.528	1.978	1.741	−0.123	0.296
	(0.896)	(1.036)*	(0.979)*	(0.910)	(1.078)
pridexp	−0.020	−0.056	−0.189	−0.037	−0.029
	(0.248)	(0.310)	(0.259)	(0.199)	(0.338)
lgov		−0.581	−0.757		
		(0.624)	(0.574)		
ltrade		−0.428	−0.562		−0.885
		(0.772)	(0.716)		(0.813)
lpi		−1.144	−0.925		
		(0.565)*	(0.458)*		
lprivo			0.654		
			(0.344)*		
lpop				−7.495	−5.678
				(2.575)***	(3.307)
linv				4.515	3.934
				(0.940)***	(0.756)***
ltot					11.526
					(7.097)
lfbal					16.337
					(6.417)**
Hansen J test	1.000	1.000	1.000	1.000	1.000
AR(1) test	0.024	0.019	0.015	0.137	0.058
AR(2) test	0.561	0.545	0.337	0.973	0.589
Observations	119	117	116	117	110
No. of countries	19	19	19	19	18

Notes: Estimated using one-step system GMM dynamic panel-data estimator with time dummies (Arellano and Bover, 1995; Blundell and Bond, 1998).
Columns (1), (2), (3), (4), and (5) display estimates for the first, second, third, fourth, and fifth independent variable sets, respectively.
The Hansen J test reports the p-values of a test of over-identifying restrictions.
The AR(1) and AR(2) tests report the p-values of the Arellano–Bond test for autocorrelation.
Robust standard errors in parentheses: *significant at 10 percent; **significant at 5 percent; ***significant at 1 percent.

Table 14B.7   *Total external debt-to-GDP: non-linear effects on GDP*
growth

	(1)	(2)	(3)	(4)	(5)
linitial	−1.860	−1.506	−1.564	−1.840	−1.455
	(1.027)*	(1.022)	(1.023)	(0.988)*	(1.017)
lschool	4.569	4.401	4.165	3.761	3.044
	(1.039)***	(1.215)***	(1.217)***	(0.972)***	(1.094)**
dbtgdp	−2.134	−2.028	−2.147	−1.862	−1.767
	(0.472)***	(0.489)***	(0.539)***	(0.443)***	(0.588)***
dbtgdp3d1060	1.365	1.737	1.522	0.389	0.620
	(0.524)**	(0.978)*	(0.971)	(0.470)	(0.560)
lgov		−0.299	−0.501		
		(0.636)	(0.567)		
ltrade		0.370	0.412		0.262
		(0.704)	(0.684)		(0.715)
lpi		−0.945	−0.593		
		(0.701)	(0.632)		
lprivo		0.580			
		(0.392)			
lpop				−0.672	−1.531
				(2.695)	(2.415)
linv				4.438	4.564
				(0.857)***	(0.997)***
ltot					7.334
					(8.421)
lfbal					9.883
					(5.950)
Hansen J test	1.000	1.000	1.000	1.000	1.000
AR(1) test	0.033	0.018	0.004	0.090	0.106
AR(2) test	0.805	0.465	0.121	0.721	0.378
Observations	140	136	134	134	123
No. of countries	20	20	20	20	19

Notes: Estimated using one-step system GMM dynamic panel-data estimator with time
dummies (Arellano and Bover, 1995; Blundell and Bond, 1998).
Columns (1), (2), (3), (4), and (5) display estimates for the first, second, third, fourth, and fifth
independent variable sets, respectively.
The Hansen J test reports the p-values of a test of over-identifying restrictions.
The AR(1) and AR(2) tests report the p-values of the Arellano–Bond test for autocorrelation.
Robust standard errors in parentheses: *significant at 10 percent; **significant at 5 percent;
***significant at 1 percent.

Table 14B.8 Total external debt-to-exports: non-linear effects on GDP growth

	(1)	(2)	(3)	(4)	(5)
linitial	−1.414	−1.827	−1.857	−1.373	−1.739
	(0.943)	(1.071)	(1.072)*	(0.894)	(0.963)*
lschool	3.362	4.175	3.912	2.057	2.826
	(1.359)**	(1.123)***	(1.109)***	(1.369)	(1.011)**
dbtexp	−1.050	−1.816	−1.908	−0.723	−1.722
	(0.541)*	(0.454)***	(0.479)***	(0.491)	(0.554)***
dbtexp3d2250	−0.225	1.310	1.098	−0.981	0.557
	(0.618)	(0.990)	(0.933)	(0.592)	(0.721)
lgov		−0.134	−0.352		
		(0.586)	(0.530)		
ltrade		−1.081	−1.183		−1.307
		(0.858)	(0.851)		(0.616)**
lpi		−1.029	−0.676		
		(0.797)	(0.692)		
lprivo			0.537		
			(0.395)		
lpop				−3.152	−1.892
				(3.191)	(2.357)
linv				4.767	4.839
				(1.140)***	(0.999)***
ltot					7.200
					(8.643)
lfbal					10.398
					(5.725)*
Hansen J test	1.000	1.000	1.000	1.000	1.000
AR(1) test	0.039	0.017	0.004	0.110	0.111
AR(2) test	0.807	0.469	0.116	0.750	0.378
Observations	138	136	134	134	123
No. of countries	20	20	20	20	19

Notes: Estimated using one-step system GMM dynamic panel-data estimator with time dummies (Arellano and Bover, 1995; Blundell and Bond, 1998).
Columns (1), (2), (3), (4), and (5) display estimates for the first, second, third, fourth, and fifth independent variable sets, respectively.
The Hansen J test reports the p-values of a test of over-identifying restrictions.
The AR(1) and AR(2) tests report the p-values of the Arellano–Bond test for autocorrelation.
Robust standard errors in parentheses: *significant at 10 percent; **significant at 5 percent; ***significant at 1 percent.

Table 14B.9   Interest payments-to-GDP: non-linear effects on GDP growth

	(1)	(2)	(3)	(4)	(5)
linitial	−1.472	−1.420	−1.220	−1.358	−1.370
	(0.725)*	(0.775)*	(0.701)*	(0.771)*	(0.863)
lschool	3.967	4.050	3.871	2.406	1.806
	(1.337)***	(1.175)***	(1.210)***	(1.348)*	(1.293)
intgdp	−0.687	−0.797	−0.855	−0.149	−0.104
	(0.416)	(0.320)**	(0.326)**	(0.475)	(0.371)
intgdp3d4025	1.607	2.699	2.736	−0.033	0.902
	(0.703)**	(1.078)**	(1.117)**	(0.857)	(0.787)
lgov		−0.482	−0.764		
		(0.490)	(0.544)		
ltrade		−0.176	−0.181		−0.183
		(0.669)	(0.682)		(0.698)
lpi		−1.892	−1.751		
		(0.591)***	(0.615)**		
lprivo			0.307		
			(0.431)		
lpop				−7.481	−5.719
				(2.973)**	(2.233)**
linv				5.331	4.383
				(1.348)***	(1.407)***
ltot					8.533
					(11.236)
lfbal					19.736
					(8.558)**
Hansen J test	1.000	1.000	1.000	1.000	1.000
AR(1) test	0.040	0.033	0.014	0.093	0.074
AR(2) test	0.249	0.469	0.841	0.155	0.251
Observations	107	105	103	103	98
No. of countries	20	20	20	20	19

Notes: Estimated using one-step system GMM dynamic panel-data estimator with time dummies (Arellano and Bover, 1995; Blundell and Bond, 1998).
Columns (1), (2), (3), (4), and (5) display estimates for the first, second, third, fourth, and fifth independent variable sets, respectively.
The Hansen J test reports the p-values of a test of over-identifying restrictions.
The AR(1) and AR(2) tests report the p-values of the Arellano–Bond test for autocorrelation.
Robust standard errors in parentheses: *significant at 10 percent; **significant at 5 percent; ***significant at 1 percent.

Index